HOW TO DECIDE

HOW TO DECIDE

Simple Tools for Making
Better Choices

ANNIE DUKE

PORTFOLIO / PENGUIN

PORTFOLIO / PENGUIN

An imprint of Penguin Random House LLC

penguinrandomhouse.com

Image on pg. 70: still from CNN/HLN video "Man Taunts Charging Bison,"
https://www.cnn.com/videos/us/2018/08/03/man-taunts-bison-yellowstone-national-park-hln-vpx.hln.

Most Portfolio books are available at a discount when purchased in quantity for sales promotions or corporate use.
Special editions, which include personalized covers, excerpts, and corporate imprints, can be created when purchased
in large quantities. For more information, please call (212) 572-2232 or e-mail specialmarkets@penguinrandomhouse.com.
Your local bookstore can also assist with discounted bulk purchases using the Penguin Random House corporate
Business-to-Business program. For assistance in locating a participating retailer, e-mail B2B@penguinrandomhouse.com.

Library of Congress Cataloging-in-Publication Data
Names: Duke, Annie, 1965– author.
Title: How to decide : simple tools for making better choices / Annie Duke.
Description: New York : Portfolio, 2020. |
Includes bibliographical references. |
Identifiers: LCCN 2020015471 (print) | LCCN 2020015472 (ebook)
ISBN 9780593418482 (paperback) | ISBN 9780593084618 (ebook)
Subjects: LCSH: Decision making.
Classification: LCC HD30.23 .D85 2020 (print) | LCC HD30.23 (ebook)
DDC 153.8/3—dc23
LC record available at https://lccn.loc.gov/2020015471
LC ebook record available at https://lccn.loc.gov/2020015472

Printed in the United States of America

8th Printing

BOOK DESIGN BY TANYA MAIBORODA

To my father, Richard Lederer, who inspires me every day with his passion for teaching and his love of the written word

Contents

YOUR BEST DECISION, AND YOUR WORST   xiii

INTRODUCTION   xv

**1 Resulting: Outcomes in the Rearview Mirror
    May Appear Larger Than They Are**   1

  1. Job Hopping   1
  2. The Shadow of Resulting   4
  3. Luckbox   9
  4. When Bad Things Happen to Good Decisions (and Vice Versa!):
     Pulling apart outcome quality and decision quality   13
  5. Resulting's *Other* Impact on Learning: Don't wait for decision
     errors to find learning opportunities   16
  6. Reexamining Your Best and Worst Decisions   19
  7. Resulting Wrap-up   21

  Resulting Checklist   22
  A Long Time Ago in a Movie Franchise Far, Far Away   23

2 As the Old Saying Goes, Hindsight Is Not 20/20   25

  1. Job Hopper Redux   25
  2. I Chart: Identifying your own hindsight bias   30

3. What Did You Know? And When Did You Know It?   34

4. You Can Find Hindsight Bias Everywhere You Look   39

5. Hindsight Bias Wrap-up   42

Hindsight Bias Checklist   43

You Don't Know It's a Polling Error Until After the Vote   44

3 **The Decision Multiverse**   **46**

1. A Hairbrained Idea   46

2. The Paradox of Experience   48

3. Decision Forestry: The cognitive chain saw massacre   49

4. Putting Down the Cognitive Chain Saw: Reassembling the tree   52

5. Counterfactuals   59

6. The Decision Multiverse Wrap-up   65

The Decision Multiverse Checklist   66

The Man in the High Castle   67

4 **The Three Ps: Preferences, Payoffs, and Probabilities**   **68**

1. Six Steps to Better Decision-Making: Making your view of the future (crystal) clearer   68

2. Pro Tip: Don't taunt the largest animal in North America   70

3. Payoffs: Step 2—Identify your preference using the payoff for each outcome—to what degree do you like or dislike each outcome, given your values?   72

4. Probability Matters: Step 3—Estimate the likelihood of each outcome unfolding   79

5. The Archer's Mindset: All guesses are educated guesses   80

6. A Soft Landing to Probabilistic Thinking: Using words that express likelihoods   86

7. If You Don't Ask a Question, You Won't Get an Answer   93

8. The Three Ps Wrap-up   96

The Three Ps Checklist   98

Bovine Guessing   99

5 **Taking Dead Aim at the Future: The Power of Precision**   **100**

1. Lost in Translation: Now for the bad news about using terms that express likelihoods   100

2. Precision Matters: More clearly define the bull's-eye by making educated guesses   107

3. At Home on the Range   110
4. Taking Dead Aim Wrap-up   119

Taking Dead Aim Checklist   120
Taxed by Imprecision   121

6 Turning Decisions Outside In   122

1. Relationship Chernobyl   122
2. The Inside View vs. the Outside View   125
3. How to Be the Least Popular Guest at a Wedding   130
4. A Truly Happy Marriage: The union of the inside view
   and the outside view   133
5. Turning Decisions Outside In Wrap-up   144

Turning Decisions Outside In Checklist   146
A Sunnier Disposition?   147

7 Breaking Free from Analysis Paralysis: How to Spend Your Decision-Making Time More Wisely   148

1. The Happiness Test: When the type of thing you're
   deciding about is low impact   152
2. Freerolling: Deciding fast when the downside is slim to none   156
3. A Sheep in Wolf's Clothing: High stakes, close calls, fast decisions   161
4. Quitters Often Win, and Winners Often Quit: Understanding
   the power of "quit-to-itiveness"   167
5. Is This Your Final Answer?: Knowing when your
   decision process is "finished"   175
6. Breaking Free from Analysis Paralysis Wrap-up   177

Breaking Free from Analysis Paralysis Checklist   179
The Terminator Was Freerolling   180
Why "Good Enough" Is Good Enough: Satisficing vs. maximizing   181

8 The Power of Negative Thinking   182

1. Think Positive, but Plan Negative: Identifying our difficulties
   in executing on our goals   184
2. Premortems and Backcasting: Whether you deserve an autopsy
   or a parade, you should know why in advance   189
3. Precommitting to Your Good Intentions: Making a U-turn
   on the "road to hell"   199

4. The Dr. Evil Game: Outthinking the evil genius making sure you fail
(P.S. The evil genius is you)   202

5. The Surprise Party No One Wants: When your reaction to a
bad outcome can make things worse   206

6. Deflecting the Slings and Arrows of Outrageous Fortune:
"If you can't beat 'em . . . mitigate 'em"   210

7. The Power of Negative Thinking Wrap-up   212

The Power of Negative Thinking Checklist   214

Darth Vader, Team Leader: Dark side of the Force incarnate,
or unsung hero for negative thinking?   215

Dr. Evil on Fourth Down   216

**9   Decision Hygiene: If You Want to Know What Someone
Thinks, Stop Infecting Them with What You Think**   **217**

1. "Two Roads Diverged": The beauty of discovering where
somebody else's beliefs differ from your own   222

2. How to Elicit Uninfected Feedback: Quarantining your opinion
to stop the contagion   225

3. How to Quarantine Opinions in a Group Setting   229

4. Spin Doctrine: Checklisting the relevant details and
being accountable to provide them   235

5. Final Thoughts   240

6. Decision Hygiene Wrap-up   241

Decision Hygiene Checklist   243

ACKNOWLEDGMENTS   245

CHAPTER NOTES   249

GENERAL REFERENCES AND SUGGESTED FURTHER READING   257

SELECTED REFERENCES   259

HOW TO DECIDE

Your Best Decision, and Your Worst

What was your best decision of the last year? Go with your gut, the first thing that comes to mind. Describe the decision below.

_____

_____

Now, what was your worst decision of the last year? Again, go with the first thing that comes to mind. Describe the decision below.

_____

_____

Did your best decision end up turning out well? (Circle one.)   YES   NO

Did your worst decision end up turning out poorly? (Circle one.)   YES   NO

If you're like most people, you answered yes to both of those questions—and your description of the decision was probably more a description of *the outcome of the decision* rather than the decision process itself.

I've done this exercise with hundreds of people and it always turns out like this. When I ask for their best decision, they tell me their best outcome. When I ask for their worst decision, they tell me their worst outcome.

We'll come back to this exercise in a bit.

Introduction

YOU MAKE THOUSANDS OF DECISIONS every day—some big, some small. Some clearly of great consequence, like what job to take. And some clearly of little consequence, like what to eat for breakfast.

No matter what type of decision you're facing, it's imperative to develop a decision process that not only improves your decision quality, but also helps sort your decisions so you can identify which ones are bigger and which ones are smaller.

Why is it so important to have a high-quality decision process?

Because there are only two things that determine how your life turns out: luck and the quality of your decisions. You have control over only one of those two things.

Luck, by definition, is out of your control. Where and when you were born, whether your boss comes into work in a bad mood, which admissions officer happens to see your college application—these are all things that are out of your hands.

What you do have some control over, what you can improve, is the quality of your decisions. And when you make better-quality decisions, you increase the chances that good things will happen to you.

I believe this is a pretty noncontroversial thing to say: It's important to improve your decision pro-

> **The only thing you have control over that can influence the way your life turns out is the quality of your decisions.**

cess, because it's the one thing you have control over in determining the quality of your life.

Even though the importance of making quality decisions seems obvious, it's surprising how few people can actually articulate what a good decision process looks like.

This is something that I've been thinking about all my adult life. First, as a PhD student in cognitive science. Then, as a professional poker player, where I had to constantly make rapid, high-stakes decisions with real money on the line, in an environment where luck has an obvious and significant influence on your short-term results. And for the past eighteen years, as a business consultant on decision strategy, helping executives, teams, and employees make better decisions. (Not to mention as a parent, trying to raise four healthy and happy children.)

What I've experienced in all these different contexts is that people are generally quite poor at explaining how one might go about making a high-quality decision.

This difficulty isn't just confined to novice poker players or college students or entry-level employees. Even when I ask C-level executives—who are literally full-time decision-makers—what a high-quality decision process looks like, the answers I get are all over the map: "Ultimately, I trust my gut"; "Ideally, I follow the consensus of a committee"; "I weigh the alternatives by making a pros and cons list."

This is actually not that surprising. Outside of vague directives about encouraging critical-thinking skills, decision-making is not explicitly taught in K–12 education. If you want to *learn* about making great decisions, you're unlikely to run into a class on the subject until college or beyond, and even then only as an elective.

No wonder we don't have a common approach. We don't even have a common language for talking about decision-making.

The consequences of being unable to articulate what makes a decision good can be disastrous. After all, your decision-making is the single most important thing you have control over that will help you achieve your goals.

That is why I wrote this book.

How to Decide is going to offer you a framework for thinking about how to improve your decisions as well as a set of tools for executing on that framework.

So what makes for a good decision tool?

A tool is a device or implement used to carry out a particular function. A hammer is a tool used for driving nails. A screwdriver is a tool used for turning screws. There is an elegant simplicity to performing tasks if you have the right tool for the right job.

- A good tool has a use that can be reliably repeated. In other words, if you use the same tool in the same way, you would expect to get the same results.
- The proper way to use a tool can be taught to another person such that they could reliably use the same tool for the same purpose.
- After you've used a tool, you can look back and examine whether you used it properly or not, and so can others.

That means that some of the things that even CEOs use to make decisions turn out to be pretty poor tools.

Your gut—no matter how much experience or past success you've had—is not really a decision tool.

It's not that using your gut can't get you to a great decision. It could. But you can't know whether that is a case of a broken clock being right twice a day or whether your gut is a fine-tuned decision-maker, because your gut is a black box.

All you can see is the output of your gut. You can't go back and examine with any fidelity how your gut arrived at a decision. You can't peer into your gut to know how it's operating. Your gut is unique to you. You can't "teach" your gut to somebody else, such that they could use your gut to make decisions. You can't be sure that you are using your gut the same way each time.

That means your gut doesn't even qualify as a decision tool.

There are also some things, like a pros and cons list, that are technically tools but may not be the *right* tools. What you'll learn from this book is that a pros and cons list is not a particularly effective decision tool if you are trying to get closer to the *objectively* best decision. It's more like using a hammer meant to drive small nails and expecting it would work equally well for breaking asphalt.

For reasons that are going to become clear, a good decision tool seeks to reduce the role of cognitive bias (such as overconfidence, hindsight bias, or confirmation bias) and a pros and cons list tends to amplify the role of bias.

The ideal decision tool

Any decision is, in essence, a prediction about the future.

When you're making a decision, your objective is to choose the option that gains you the most ground in achieving your goals, taking into account how much you're willing to risk. (Or sometimes, if there aren't any good options, your objective is to choose the option that will cause you to lose the least amount of ground.)

It's rare that a decision can have only one possible result. For most decisions, there are lots of ways the future could unfold. If you're choosing a route to work, whichever route you choose has many possible outcomes: traffic could be light or heavy, you could blow a tire, you might get pulled over for speeding, and so on.

Because there are so many possible futures, making the best decision depends on your ability to accurately imagine what the world might look like if you were to choose any of the options you're considering.

That means the ideal decision tool would be a *crystal ball*.

With a crystal ball, you would have perfect knowledge of the world, perfect knowledge of all available options, and—because you could see the future—you would know for sure how any of those choices might turn out.

There are always fortune-tellers promising an easy way to see the future. But sadly, the only working crystal balls exist in fiction. Even then, like in *The Wizard of Oz*, they are illusions. Building a good decision process with a robust toolbox will help you get as close as possible to what the fortune-teller is promising, but you're doing it for yourself in a way that's going to significantly change the potential for how your life turns out.

> Determining whether a decision is good or bad means examining the quality of the beliefs informing the decision, the available options, and how the future might turn out given any choice you make.

Of course, even the best decision process and the best tools won't show you the future with the clarity and certainty you'd get with a crystal ball. But that doesn't mean that improving your process isn't a goal worth pursuing.

If your decision process becomes better than it is now—*improving* the accuracy of your knowledge and beliefs, *improving* how you compare available options, and *improving* your ability to forecast the futures that might result from those options—that is worth pursuing.

The route to better decision-making: a brief road map of this book

Intuitively, it feels like one of the best ways to improve future decisions should be to learn from how your past decisions have turned out. That's where this book will start, with improving your ability to learn from experience.

In the first three chapters, you'll see some of the ways in which trying to learn from experience can go sideways and lead you to some pretty poor conclusions about how you determine whether a past decision was good or bad. In addition to pointing out the hazards of learning from experience, the book will introduce you to several tools for becoming more efficient at understanding what the past has to teach you.

Why did things turn out the way they did? Any outcome is determined in part by your choice and in part by luck. Figuring out the balance of luck and skill in how things turn out feeds back into your beliefs—beliefs that will inform your future decisions. Without a solid framework for examining your past decisions, the lessons you learn from your experience will be compromised.

Starting in chapter 4, the focus turns to new decisions, offering a framework for what a high-quality decision process looks like and a set of tools for implementing that process. This is where you'll see the virtues of building a crystal-ball equivalent, focusing decision quality on the strength of the educated guesses you make about an uncertain future, including numerous ways to improve the quality of the beliefs and knowledge that are the foundation of your predictions and consequent decisions.

As you can imagine, a well-stocked, versatile toolkit that allows you to execute on a high-quality decision process can take a lot more time and effort than glancing into an imaginary piece of glass that gives you perfect knowledge of the future. Taking that extra time will have a profound and positive effect on your most consequential decisions.

But not all decisions merit bringing the full force of your decision toolkit to bear.

If you're putting together a dresser that comes with a set of screws, you could be tempted to use a hammer to save time if you don't have a screwdriver handy. Sometimes, a hammer will do an okay job and it will be worth the time you save. But other times, you could break the dresser or build a shoddy health hazard.

The problem is that we're just not good at recognizing when sacrificing that quality *isn't* that big a deal. Knowing when the hammer is good enough is a metaskill worth developing.

Chapter 7 introduces you to a set of mental models that will help you think about when to bring a robust decision-making process to bear, and when you have the leeway to apply a skinnier, stripped-down process to speed things up. That doesn't come until later in the book because it's necessary to have a firm grasp on what a fully formed decision process might look like before you can figure out when and how you might take shortcuts.

Knowing when it's okay to save time is part of a good decision process.

The final chapters of the book offer ways to more efficiently identify obstacles that might lie in your path and tools for better leveraging the knowledge and information that other people have. This includes eliciting feedback from others and avoiding the pitfalls of team decision-making, especially groupthink.

How to use this book

You'll see that throughout the book there are exercises, thought experiments, and templates that you can use to reinforce the mental models, frameworks, and decision tools offered in these pages.

You'll get the most out of this book if you grab a pencil and try them out. But the exercises aren't required. You'll still get a lot out of the book if you don't fully interact with all the prompts. Either way, the exercises, tools, definitions, tables, trackers, worksheets, wrap-ups, and checklists are meant to help you as ongoing references. They're meant to be photocopied, reused, shared, and reexamined.

Likewise, you'll get the most out of this book if you read it in the order in which the material is presented. Many ideas build on the ideas that came before them.

Nevertheless, the chapters are sufficiently self-contained that you can parachute into any chapter you find interesting if you want to start there.

"On the shoulders of giants"

This book is a synthesis, translation, and practical application of the ideas of a lot of great thinkers and scientists in psychology, economics, and other disciplines who have devoted their lives to studying decision-making and behavior. Whatever contribution this book makes to improving decision-making, to paraphrase Newton and others, depends on how much I've benefited by standing on the shoulders of giants.

You'll see, scattered throughout the text, chapter notes, and acknowledgments, references to the work of particular scientists and professionals in this space. If a concept interests you, in addition to such sources, you should look at the General References and Suggested Further Reading section for ways to take a deeper dive into subjects I've handled in a lighter way.

1

Resulting

OUTCOMES IN THE REARVIEW MIRROR
MAY APPEAR LARGER THAN THEY ARE

ALL OF THE EXERCISES IN *this book are designed to help you gain insight into the way you process information. For you to get the most out of them, it's important that you go with your first instinct when answering rather than trying to figure out the "right" answer. There are no right or wrong answers—just insight into how you think.*

[1]

Job Hopping

1 Imagine you quit your job to take a position at a new company.

The job turns out great! You love your coworkers, feel fulfilled in your position, and within a year you get a promotion.

Was it a good decision to quit your job and take the new position?
(Circle one.)   YES   NO

2 Imagine you quit your job to take a position at a new company.

The new job turns out to be a disaster. You are miserable at the company and within a year you have been laid off.

Was it a good decision to quit your job and take the new position?
(Circle one.)   *YES*   *NO*

I'M GUESSING YOUR GUT told you that in the first case the decision to quit your job was good and in the second case the decision was bad. Doesn't it feel like if the job works out great it must have been a great decision to quit your old job? And if it doesn't work out, it must have been a bad decision?

The thing is, in neither case did I give you any meaningful information about the process used to arrive at the decision. I gave you only two pieces of information: (1) a bare-bones (and identical) description of what went into the decision and (2) how the decision turned out.

Even though you don't have any detail about the decision process, when I tell you how things turned out, it feels like you *really know* something about whether the decision was good or bad.

And this feeling that the *result* of the decision tells you something significant about the *quality* of the decision process is so powerful that even when the description of the decision is *identical* (you quit your job and take a new position), your view of that decision changes as the quality of the result changes.

You can spot this phenomenon across all sorts of domains.

You buy a stock. It quadruples in price. It feels like a great decision. You buy a stock. It goes to zero. It feels like a terrible decision.

You spend six months trying to land a new client/customer. They become your biggest account. It feels like a great use of your time and a great decision. You spend that same six months trying to land the client and you never close the deal. It feels like a waste of time and a terrible decision.

You buy a house. When you sell in five years you get 50% more than you paid for it. Great decision! You buy a house. When you sell in five years the house is underwater. Terrible decision!

You start doing CrossFit and after the first two months you have lost weight and gained muscle mass. Great decision! But if you dislocate your shoulder within the first two days, it feels like a terrible decision.

In every domain, the outcome tail is wagging the decision dog.

There's a name for this: **_Resulting_**.

When people _result_, they look at whether the result was good or bad to figure out if the decision was good or bad. (Psychologists call this "outcome bias," but I prefer the more intuitive term "resulting.") We take this resulting shortcut because we can't clearly "see" whether the decision was good or bad, especially after the fact, but we can clearly see if the outcome was good or bad.

Resulting is a way to simplify complex assessments of decision quality.

The problem? _Simple isn't always better._

Decision quality and outcome quality are, of course, correlated. But not perfectly, at least not in most decisions we make, and certainly not when we have only one try at the decision. The relationship between the two can take a long time to play out.

In a single instance (I quit my job and it turned out horribly), it's hard to say if a bad outcome (or a good one) was _because_ of the quality of the decision. Sometimes we make good decisions and they turn out well. Sometimes we make good decisions and they turn out poorly.

> **RESULTING**
> **A mental shortcut in which we use the quality of an outcome to figure out the quality of a decision.**

You can run a red light and get through the intersection unscathed. You can go through a green light and get in an accident. This means that working backward from the quality of a single outcome to figure out whether a decision was good or bad is going to lead to some poor conclusions.

Resulting can make you think that running red lights is a good idea.

A necessary part of becoming a better decision-maker is learning from experience. Experience contains the lessons for improving future decisions. Resulting causes you to learn the wrong lessons.

[2]

The Shadow of Resulting

To be fair, in the first exercise, I didn't give you enough information to figure out whether the decision was good or bad on its merits. Maybe your mind just fills in the blanks when there isn't much to go on, like what happens with some visual illusions. That is not to say that resulting leads you to good conclusions under those circumstances. We would all learn better if we didn't autofill those blanks because we happen to know the outcome. But maybe resulting is confined to situations when you don't have much information about the decision.

Does our tendency to result disappear when we aren't operating in an information void?

Let's do another example in which we fill in some of those blanks to find out.

▌ You buy an electric car and you love it. It's an awesome car, manufactured by a tech genius widely hailed as a visionary. Based on your experience with the car, you buy stock in the company.

After two years, the company's stock soars and your investment has increased in value twentyfold.

Rate how you feel about the quality of the decision to invest, on a scale of 0 to 5, where 0 is a terrible decision and 5 is a great decision:

Terrible Decision   0   1   2   3   4   5   *Great Decision*

Write down the reasons for your rating.

_____

_____

_____

_____

_____

2 You buy an electric car and you love it. It's an awesome car, manufactured by a tech genius widely hailed as a visionary. Based on your experience with the car, you buy stock in the company.

After two years, the company is out of business and you have lost your investment.

Rate how you feel about the quality of the decision to invest, on a scale of 0 to 5, where 0 is a terrible decision and 5 is a great decision:

Terrible Decision   0   1   2   3   4   5   Great Decision

Write down the reasons for your rating.

_____

_____

_____

_____

IF YOU'RE LIKE MOST PEOPLE, you interpreted the details about why you bought the stock in a different light depending on whether the outcome was good or bad.

For the good outcome, you most likely interpreted the details of the decision to invest in a more positive light: You had personal experience with the product and that should count for a lot. After all, if you love the car it's likely other people will. Plus, the tech genius is known to be successful, so if he is running the company it is likely to be a good investment.

But when the company turns out to be a dud, the poor outcome can make you see those same details in a different light. Now it is more likely that your reasoning includes how picking a stock based on your personal experience isn't a substitute for real due diligence. Are they making a profit? Can they? What's their debt burden? Will they have access to capital until they achieve profitability? Can they keep up with demand and increase their manufacturing capacity? Maybe you were such a happy consumer because they were losing buckets of money on every sale.

This is, of course, not limited to investment decisions.

You quit your job to join a promising start-up because it offers you equity. It ends up as the next Google. Great decision! You quit your job to join a promising start-up because it offers you equity. It fails after a year. You end up out of work for six months and you run through your savings. Terrible decision!

You pick a college because you want to go to the same school as your high school sweetheart. You graduate with honors, marry your high school sweetheart, and land an amazing job. Picking that school feels like a great decision.

You pick a college because you want to go to the same school as your high school sweetheart. Within six months you have broken up. You decide to change majors and the school does not have a good program in your new major. You hate the town the school is in. And by the end of the first year you have transferred. Picking that school feels like a terrible decision.

In all of these cases, the quality of the result filters how we view the decision, *even when we have identical details about the decision process*, because the quality of the outcome drives how we interpret those details.

This is the power of resulting.

WHEN THE OUTCOME TURNS out poorly, it's easy to focus on the details that suggest the decision process was poor. We think we are seeing the decision quality rationally because *the bad process is obvious.*

But once the outcome is flipped, we discount or reinterpret the information about the decision quality because the outcome drives us to write a story that fits the ending.

The quality of the outcome casts a shadow over our ability to see the quality of the decision.

We want outcome quality to align with decision quality. We want the world to make sense in this way, to be less random than it is. In trying to get this alignment, we lose sight of the fact that for most decisions, there are lots of ways things could turn out.

Experience is supposed to be our best teacher, but sometimes we draw a connection between outcome quality and decision quality that is too tight. Doing so distorts our ability to use those experiences to figure out which decisions were good and which were bad.

> **There are more possible futures than the one that actually happens.**

Resulting makes our crystal ball cloudy.

Now that you know what resulting is, think about a time in your life when you resulted. Use the space below to describe the situation.

_____

_____

_____

IF YOU WANT SOME EXAMPLES, go back to the very first questions I asked you: What were your best and worst decisions of the last year? The point of having you write those down is that most people don't actually think much about their best and worst *decisions*. They usually start by thinking of their best and worst *outcomes* and work backward from there.

That's due to resulting.

[3]

Luckbox

For any single decision, there are different ways the future could unfold—some better, some worse. When you make a decision, the decision makes certain paths possible (even if you don't know where they lead) and others impossible. The decision you make determines *which set of outcomes are possible and how likely each of those outcomes is.* But it doesn't determine which of that set of outcomes will actually happen.

Being a better decision-maker means being a better predictor of the set of possible futures. This book is designed to sharpen your skills, getting you closer to having a crystal ball. But, as fortune-tellers correctly warn us, "The future appears hazy," because the way the future will eventually unfold is always uncertain.

In other words, there's an important factor that influences the way our lives turn out: luck.

Luck is what intervenes between your decision (which has a range of possible outcomes) and the outcome that you actually get.

> **LUCK**
>
> Luck exerts its influence between your decision and which of the possible paths you end up on. It is the element you have no control over that determines which of the possible outcomes you actually observe in the short run.

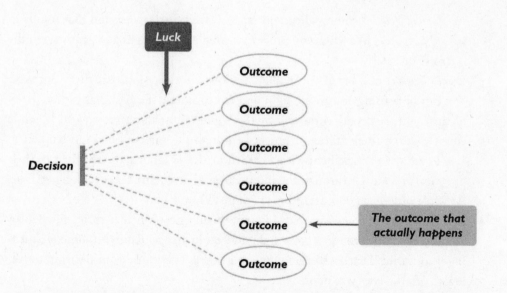

Because any decision determines only the set of possible outcomes (some good, some bad, some in between), this means good outcomes can result from both good and bad decisions, and bad outcomes can result from both good and bad decisions.

We can think about the relationship between decision quality and outcome quality like this:

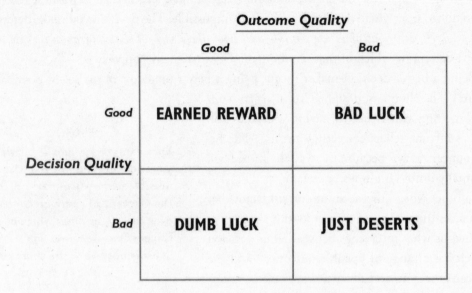

- An *Earned Reward* comes when you make a good-quality decision that results in a good outcome, like when you proceed through a green light and get through the intersection safely.
- *Dumb Luck* comes when you make a poor-quality decision that turns out well. You can be waiting at a traffic light and fail to notice the light has turned green because you are deeply entranced by the world's most important tweet. If, while you are sitting there failing to proceed through the intersection, you happen to avoid getting in an accident with a car whose driver ignores the red light in their direction and barrels through the intersection, that doesn't make looking at Twitter while driving a good decision. That's just Dumb Luck.
- *Bad Luck* comes when you make a good-quality decision that turns out poorly. You can proceed through a green light and get in an accident with someone turning into traffic. That's a bad outcome, but it wasn't because your decision to follow the traffic laws was poor.

- *Just Deserts* means making a poor-quality decision that results in a bad outcome, like running a red light and getting in an accident.

Obviously, there are plenty of examples of all four of these categories in everyone's decision-making history. Sometimes your great decisions turn out great; other times bad luck gets in the way. Sometimes your bad decisions turn out horribly; other times you get lucky.

But resulting can cause you to lose sight of the role of luck in how things turn out.

Once we know what the outcome is, we often treat things as if there were only Earned Rewards or Just Deserts. Bad Luck and Dumb Luck recede into the shadows.

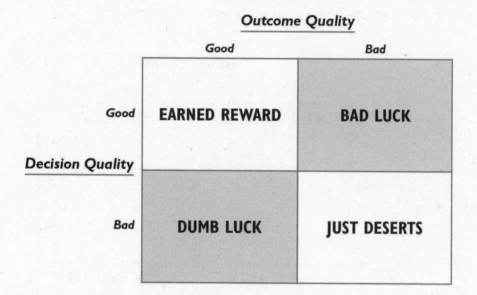

When it comes to learning from experience, those shadows can cause you to learn a lot of bad lessons.

When you make a decision that has only a 10% chance of a bad outcome, you will, by definition, get a bad outcome 10% of the time. And thanks to resulting, that 10% of the time you are in danger of thinking the decision was bad after the fact, even though it had a 90% chance of working out. It was a good decision, but your experience will have taught you not to make decisions like that again in the future.

This is the cost of resulting.

Now let's get you out from under the shadow of resulting by filling in *all* the cells in the matrix with examples from your own life.

First, think of a time in your life when things worked out well and you think your decision-making was also good. Briefly describe the situation in the Earned Reward cell below.

Next, think of a time in your life when things worked out poorly and you think your decision-making was good. Briefly describe the situation in the Bad Luck cell below.

Next, think of a time in your life when things worked out well and you think your decision-making was pretty poor. Briefly describe the situation in the Dumb Luck cell below.

Finally, think of a time in your life when things worked out pretty poorly and you think your decision-making was also pretty poor. Briefly describe the situation in the Just Deserts cell below.

Outcome Quality

	Good	Bad
Good	**EARNED REWARD**	**BAD LUCK**
Bad	**DUMB LUCK**	**JUST DESERTS**

Decision Quality

[4]

When Bad Things Happen to Good Decisions (and Vice Versa!): Pulling apart outcome quality and decision quality

Now let's dig into the pair of decisions you identified in which the quality of the decision did not align with the quality of the eventual outcome, Bad Luck and Dumb Luck.

I What did you identify as your Bad Luck outcome?

_____

Describe some of the reasons you think your decision-making was good despite the bad outcome. Those reasons can include, for example, the probability of that bad outcome (or any set of the outcomes that were undesirable) occurring, the information that went into making the decision, or the quality of the advice you sought.

_____

_____

_____

List at least three reasons why you got the bad outcome despite your decision-making being good. That is, what were some of the things outside your control or things you didn't anticipate in your original decision process?

_____

_____

_____

What are at least three other ways things might have turned out given the decisions you made?

_____

_____

_____

2 What did you identify as your Dumb Luck outcome?

_____

Describe some of the reasons you think your decision-making was poor despite the good outcome.

_____

_____

_____

_____

List at least three reasons why you got the good outcome despite your decision-making being poor. That is, what were some of the things outside of your control or things you didn't anticipate in your original decision process?

_____

_____

_____

_____

What are at least three other ways things might have turned out given the decisions you made?

_____

_____

_____

_____

3 Which was easier to think of an example of, Bad Luck or Dumb Luck? (Circle one.)

Bad Luck   _Dumb Luck_

Why do you think one was more difficult than the other?

_____

_____

IF YOU'RE LIKE MOST PEOPLE, it's easier to blame bad luck for a bad outcome than it is to credit good luck for a good outcome.

When bad things happen, it's comforting that it might not be your fault. Luck lets you off the hook, allowing you to still feel good about your decision-making despite an undesirable result. It gives you an out that helps your self-esteem along, letting you view yourself in a positive light despite things not working out.

On the other hand, taking credit for good outcomes feels good. If you allow for the role of luck in creating your positive result, you forgo the awesome feeling you get from feeling smart and in control. When it comes to good outcomes, luck gets in the way of your self-narrative.

In order to become a better decision-maker, it's imperative to actively explore all four of the ways that decision quality and outcome quality relate to each other.

It's not easy to be willing to give up the credit that comes from feeling like you made good things happen, but it is worth it in the long run. Small changes in how much you notice the luck that you would otherwise overlook will have a big influence on the way your life turns out. Those small changes act like compounding interest that pays big dividends on your future decision-making.

> **Left to our own devices, we will notice some of the bad luck but overlook most of the dumb luck.**

Experience can teach you a lot about how to improve your decision-making, but only if you listen well. Developing the discipline to separate the quality of the result from the quality of the decision can help you to figure out which decisions are worth repeating and which aren't.

[5]

Resulting's **Other** *Impact on Learning: Don't wait for decision errors to find learning opportunities*

When you overfit decision quality to outcome quality, you risk repeating decision errors that, thanks to luck, preceded a good outcome. You may also *avoid* repeating *good* decisions that, because of luck, didn't work out.

Resulting has the biggest effect on learning when outcome and decision quality are misaligned.

Less obviously, but no less importantly, there are lessons to be learned from Earned Rewards that are easily overlooked.

1 Go back to the table you filled out earlier in this section. What did you identify as your Earned Rewards outcome?

_____

Describe some of the reasons you think your decision-making was good. Those reasons might include your assessment of the probability of that bad outcome occurring (or any set of the outcomes that were undesirable), the information that went into making the decision, or the quality of the advice you sought.

_____

_____

_____

_____

Now take some time to think about *what could have been better* about the decision.
   Some questions to consider:

Could you have gotten more or better information before deciding?　　*YES*　　*NO*

Could you have decided more quickly?　　*YES*　　*NO*

Could you have taken more time with the decision?　　*YES*　　*NO*

Was there information you learned after the fact that you could have known beforehand that might have changed your decision?   YES   NO

Were there even better outcomes possible than the outcome you got?   YES   NO

If yes, if you had made a different decision, could you have increased the probability of those better outcomes occurring?   YES   NO

Can you think of any reasons why you would make a different decision if you had to do it over again?   YES   NO

Even if you would likely come to the same decision, can you think of ways you could improve your decision process if you had to do it over again?   YES   NO

2 Use the space below to reflect on any of your "yes" responses.

_____

_____

_____

_____

_____

_____

_____

_____

_____

3 Exploring those cases in which decision quality and outcome quality align is just as important as exploring the cases in which they don't. For Earned Rewards, you may have made a good decision and gotten a good outcome, but you can still find worthwhile lessons examining those decisions.

The same is true for Just Deserts.

Take a moment to go back over this exercise and reflect on how you can apply the same questions to those times when the outcome quality and decision quality were both poor.

EVEN WHEN YOU MAKE a good decision, that doesn't mean that it was the *best* decision. In fact, it rarely is. Striving to improve means being willing to fight the complacency that can come from a good decision leading to a good result.

Learning from experience is what allows you to make better decisions as you go along. Resulting keeps you from sharpening the view into your crystal ball, making you a worse predictor of the future because you skip lessons you could get from the past.

> **Don't assume you can't find worthwhile lessons while taking a victory lap.**

An insidious cost of resulting is that you don't question your assessment when decision quality and outcome quality align. When that happens, especially when things worked out, your decisions are more likely to remain unexamined while you just accept your intuition, which tells you, "Nothing to see here."

[6]

Reexamining Your Best and Worst Decisions

Go back to what you identified at the start of the book as your best and worst decisions.

How do you feel about those answers now? Has your mind changed? Upon reflection, were they actually your best and worst decisions (free of the influence of resulting)? Can you see more clearly how the quality of the outcomes influenced your choice of your best and worst decisions?

Use the space below for reflection.

After reflecting, include other decisions that you might add to the consideration of best/worst.

_____

_____

_____

_____

_____

_____

_____

_____

_____

_____

_____

_____

_____

_____

RESULTING MAKES US LACK compassion for ourselves and others.

When someone has a bad outcome in their life, we judge their decision-making as poor because of resulting. That makes it easy to blame them for the way things turned out. No need to have compassion because the outcome was their fault.

And it's not just other people. We lack self-compassion when we make these connections in our own lives. We beat ourselves up when things don't work out the way we had hoped.

For good outcomes, we're not doing anyone a service by potentially overlooking their mistakes simply because it worked out. We're definitely hurting ourselves, not just in learning, but in assessing our self-worth based on how things turned out rather than on whether we made a good decision under the circumstances.

[7]

Resulting Wrap-up

These exercises were designed to get you thinking about the following concepts:

- **Resulting** is the tendency to look at whether a result was good or bad to figure out whether a decision was good or bad.
- **Outcomes** cast a shadow over the decision process, leading you to overlook or distort information about the process, making your view of decision quality fit with outcome quality.
- In the short-term, for any single decision, there is only a loose relationship between the quality of the decision and the quality of the outcome. The two are correlated, but the relationship can take a long time to play out.
- **Luck** is what intervenes between your decision and the actual outcome. Resulting diminishes your view of the role of luck.
- You can't tell that much about the quality of a decision from a single outcome, because of luck.
- When you make a decision, you can rarely guarantee a good outcome (or a bad one). Instead, the goal is to try to choose the option that will lead to the most favorable *range* **of outcomes**.
- Making better decisions starts with learning from experience. Resulting interferes with that learning, causing you to repeat some low-quality decisions and stop making some high-quality decisions. It also keeps you from examining good-quality/good-outcome decisions (as well as bad-quality/bad-outcome decisions), which still offer valuable lessons for future decisions.
- Resulting reduces compassion when it comes to how we treat others and ourselves.

RESULTING CHECKLIST

☐ How much is the outcome clouding your judgment (or someone's judgment you've observed) about the quality of the decision?

☐ Even if bad decisions preceded a bad outcome, can you identify some good decisions made along the way? Can you identify some ways in which the process of coming to the decision was good?

☐ Even if good decisions preceded a good outcome, can you identify some ways the decision could have been better? Can you identify some ways in which the process of coming to the decision could be improved?

☐ What are the factors outside the control of the decision-maker (who might be you), including the actions of other people?

☐ What are the other ways things could have turned out?

A LONG TIME AGO
IN A MOVIE FRANCHISE FAR, FAR AWAY

Star Wars has been a legendary success. The original film cost $11 million to make, and its total box office has exceeded $775 million. That's just the tip of the iceberg: eleven *additional* financially successful films (for a total worldwide box office, not even taking into account inflation for some numbers that are forty years old, of over $10.3 billion as of early 2020), a gigantic industry of merchandise tie-ins, and theme-park rides. In addition, Disney paid $4 *billion* to buy the rights to the franchise in 2012.

Film studio United Artists had the first opportunity to get in on *Star Wars* and passed. After seeing George Lucas's sci-fi film *THX 1138* at the Cannes Film Festival, UA signed Lucas to a two-picture deal.

The studio passed when Lucas offered them *Star Wars*, after having earlier passed when he offered it *American Graffiti*, which went on to become a huge hit.

Several other studios also rejected *Star Wars*, including Universal (which had cleaned up by distributing *American Graffiti*) and Disney (which paid roughly *four hundred times* what it wouldn't spend in the early 1970s to get in on the franchise thirty-five years later).

The consensus opinion is that United Artists, Universal, and Disney, each in their own way, made a colossal blunder. Syfy Wire, one of numerous websites covering the long-unfolding story of the film franchise, took the typical view, referring to the quality of UA's decisions: "Keep in mind this was the studio that was busy putting out yet another Pink Panther sequel, so they weren't too interested in films that weren't safe or remotely not bad."

The difficulty in getting *Star Wars* made is one of the chief reasons people repeat what the late William Goldman, legendary novelist and screenwriter, famously said about Hollywood: "NOBODY KNOWS ANYTHING."

Those are easy conclusions to make, and practically everyone makes them. There is so much we ignore, however, when we do that. Using the format of the prompt in this exercise, these are ways we can recognize that the conclusion that it was a giant mistake to pass on *Star Wars* was resulting:

Other ways the decision could have turned out: Even without knowing much about the movie business, when a movie is just a concept, as *Star Wars* was when Lucas pitched it, a lot of things could happen. His concept could sound great but look terrible when executed, $10 million later. None of the stars were big names. If Lucas had cast different actors, the movie might have flopped. The mass audience could have decided it wasn't interested in sci-fi films. A recession could have hit just as the movie was being released that kept people from going to the movies.

Information that was overlooked or couldn't have been known: We don't know what the decision looked like when Lucas pitched *Star Wars* to these studios. Twentieth Century Fox, which picked up the film, didn't act like they had a sure-fire franchise. Lucas and Fox executives have said in interviews that the studio didn't understand what Lucas was trying to do. It seemed like a crazy project to them but the studio head told Lucas, "I don't understand this, but I loved *American Graffiti*, and whatever you do is okay with me."

Unreasonable inferences about the decision process driven by the result: What we don't see is any similar decisions these studios made to pass on films that turned out to be great decisions.

Lack of data to draw conclusions about how good the decision was: Until you look at a studio's entire slate of movies and evaluate what they bought and what they turned down, you're reaching a conclusion based on insufficient information.

The point is, it's difficult to reach a conclusion about decision quality from one result. That one result shouldn't count as much as a greater quantity of data (on all the decisions the studio executives made and their overall results) or data of higher quality (on what the decision looked like as it was presented to the studios).

2

As the Old Saying Goes, Hindsight Is Not 20/20

[1]

Job Hopper Redux

You grow up in Florida and go to college in Georgia. Right out of college, you get two job offers, one in Georgia and one in Boston.

The job in Boston is the better career opportunity, but you are very worried about the New England weather. After all, you grew up in the South. You visit Boston in February to see what the winter is like and decide it doesn't seem so bad—not bad enough to give up the better opportunity.

You take the job in Boston.

You're miserable!

A few months into your first winter, you can't take the cold and the gloom. Despite the job being everything you hoped it would be, you quit by the time February rolls around again and move back home.

Circle as many of the things on the next page that you think you might be saying to yourself or that you might hear from other people after you come back home:

A friend says, "I knew you'd hate it there." (Narrator: "They didn't tell you beforehand.")

I knew I should have taken the job in Georgia.

I should have known I couldn't take the winter. It's so obvious I would hate it. I grew up in the South!

I should have seen this coming. The job was never going to be good enough to justify the cold.

A friend says, "I knew you'd be home within a year."

We all have those people in our lives who say "I told you so"—whether they told us so or not.

And most of us are pretty good at beating ourselves up, wondering how we could not have known when it was so obvious it would turn out the way it did.

That's why, if you're like most people, you were probably wondering why there was no "all of the above" option.

2 You grow up in Florida and go to college in Georgia. Right out of college, you get two job offers, one in Georgia and one in Boston.

The job in Boston is the better career opportunity but you are very worried about the New England weather. After all, you grew up in the South. You visit in February to see what the winter is like and decide it doesn't seem so bad—not bad enough to give up the better opportunity.

You take the job in Boston.

You love it!

The winter is no big deal. In fact, you actually like the snow and you even become an avid snowboarder! Plus, the job is everything you hoped it would be.

You end up staying in Boston for the long haul.

How likely is it that you say something like this to yourself: "I can't believe I almost didn't take this job because I was so worried about the weather. I should have known the winter wasn't going to be such a big deal."

Very Unlikely   *0*   *1*   *2*   *3*   *4*   *5*   *Very Likely*

How likely it is that someone in your life says something like, "I told you it would be fine! I knew you'd love it! You should have known the weather doesn't matter that much to happiness, anyway!" (Narrator: "They didn't tell you either of those things beforehand.")

Very Unlikely   *0*   *1*   *2*   *3*   *4*   *5*   *Very Likely*

I'm guessing your gut reaction was that both of these would be pretty likely.

Obviously, the decision about which job to take was the same, no matter how it turned out: You believe the better job is in Boston, but how big a factor will the weather be in your overall happiness?

The catch is you haven't experienced a full New England winter, so you can't know the answer to that question *in advance of experiencing the winter weather for yourself.*

You agonize over the decision to move to Boston. You hate it there. How could you not have known?

You agonize over the decision to move to Boston. You love it there. How could you not have known?

Same decision, opposite outcomes. But either way, love it or hate it, you feel like you should have known it would turn out that way. Either way, you feel like the outcome was inevitable. Either way, your friends are saying, "I knew it!"

It goes without saying that you can't know you'll hate it *and* know you'll love it at the exact same time. But that's how we all feel.

So what gives?

What gives is **hindsight bias**.

When you make a decision, there is stuff you know and stuff you don't know.

One of the things you definitely don't know is which of all the possible outcomes that could happen will be the one that actually happens.

But after the fact, *once you know the thing that actually happened*, you can feel like you should have known it or did know it all along. The actual outcome casts a shadow over your ability to remember what you knew at the time of the decision.

OUTCOME

YOUR KNOWLEDGE AT
THE TIME OF DECISION

Resulting makes you think that you know something about whether a decision was good or bad because you know if the outcome is good or bad.

Hindsight bias adds to the ruckus caused by knowing the outcome, distorting your memory of what you knew at the time of the decision in two ways:

1. You *did* know what was going to happen—swapping out your actual view at the time of the decision with a faulty memory of that view to conform to your postoutcome knowledge.
2. You *should* (or *could*) have known what was going to happen—to the point of predictability or inevitability.

Of course, it's not just you with your own decisions. It's you with other people's decisions and other people with your decisions.

Do you know what's worse than spending your life with the regret of thinking you should have known? Having that regret *plus* having everyone else telling you "I told you so."

> **HINDSIGHT BIAS**
> The tendency to believe an event, after it occurs, was predictable or inevitable. It's also been referred to as "knew-it-all-along" thinking or "creeping determinism."

[2]

I Chart: Identifying your own hindsight bias

You buy some cryptocurrency. Your investment quintuples. You say to your friends, "I told you so. You should have invested, too!"

The cryptocurrency crashes and you lose all the money you invested. You're kicking yourself, saying, "I should have known to sell at the high!"

You're trying to push a sales deal to the limit and the deal breaks. You beat yourself up that you should have known you were pushing too far.

Within a few weeks, the customer comes back to the table, accepting the deal on your terms. You knew it was a good plan all along and you tell anyone who will listen, "I told you so!"

Cues

There aren't any obvious verbal or mental cues that signal resulting. It is not common to hear somebody say out loud, "That decision was terrible because I'm working backward from the awful outcome to determine that the decision was awful."

But there are obvious cues that signal hindsight bias, such as "I can't believe I didn't see that coming," or "I knew it," or "I told you so," or "I should have known it."

Training yourself to listen for those mental and verbal cues is a good way to hone your hindsight bias spotting skills.

Now let's dig into some examples of hindsight bias from your own life.

Here's an actual example that I heard at the grocery store. (Grocery stores, by the way, are amazing laboratories for studying human behavior!)

Man: I heard you talking on the phone. I love your accent. Are you Italian?

Woman: No, I'm Greek.

Man: I knew it!

1 Think of a *Knew It All Along* example, a time when you said to someone or to yourself something like, "I knew that would turn out that way!" Or a time when someone said that to you.

Describe the decision and the outcome.

_____

_____

_____

What did you say to yourself or to the other person? What were the mental and/or verbal cues that hindsight bias was at play?

_____

_____

_____

What did you feel you knew all along or what did the person tell you they knew all along?

_____

_____

_____

Was the information you or the other person thought you knew all along something that revealed itself after the fact, like the way it actually turned out? (Circle one.)   YES   NO

2 Think of a *Should Have Known* example, a time when you said to someone or yourself something like, "I should have known!" or "How could you not have seen that coming?" Or a time when someone said that to you.

Describe the decision and the outcome.

_____

_____

_____

_____

What did you say to yourself or to the other person? What were the mental and/or verbal cues that hindsight bias was at play?

_____

_____

_____

What did you or the other person feel you/they should have known?

_____

_____

_____

Was the information you or the other person thought you/they should have known something that revealed itself after the fact, like the way it actually turned out? (Circle one.)   *YES*   *NO*

THE MOST COMMON THING that people feel like they "knew" is information that reveals itself only after the fact, most particularly, which of the possible outcomes actually happened.

Memory creep is the reconstruction of your memory of what you knew that hindsight bias creates.

> **MEMORY CREEP**
> **When what you know after the fact creeps into your memory of what you knew before the fact.**

And here's the thing: If you misremember the past, you are going to learn useless lessons from your experience.

That can mess you up in two ways:

1. You're not going to remember what you knew at the time of the decision. That makes it hard for you to judge whether a decision was good or bad. To assess the quality of a decision and learn from your experience, you need to evaluate your state of mind honestly and recall what was knowable or not knowable as accurately as possible.
2. Hindsight bias makes you feel like the outcome was much more predictable than it was. This can cause you to repeat some low-quality decisions and to stop making some high-quality decisions.

Hindsight bias can turn a crystal ball into a fun-house mirror.

[3]

What Did You Know? And When Did You Know It?

Our memories aren't time stamped.

When you open a file on a computer, you can see "date created" and "date modified." Our brains, unfortunately, don't work like that.

Left to your own devices, the memory of your knowledge at the time of a decision can get distorted by knowing the outcome. You can help remedy memory creep by taking the time to deliberately reconstruct what was known before a decision and what was revealed only after the fact.

We can visualize this using a Knowledge Tracker, like so:

KNOWLEDGE TRACKER

Stuff you knew before the decision ———→ Decision ———→ Outcome ———→ Stuff you know after the outcome

Stuff you knew before the decision: The sum of your knowledge and beliefs at the time of the decision. For our purposes here, specifically the stuff you brought to bear on making the decision.

Stuff you know after the outcome: This includes all the stuff you knew before the decision and *new stuff that you learned after making the decision.* For our purposes here, we're focusing on new information that revealed itself after the future unfolded however it did.

Using a *Knowledge Tracker* reduces hindsight bias by clarifying what you did and didn't know at the time of the decision. Detailing what you knew and when you knew it helps prevent stuff that revealed itself after the fact from reflexively creeping into the before-the-fact box.

Now let's try using the Knowledge Tracker for the examples of hindsight bias you just identified from your own life. Come up with three key things that informed the decision, describe the decision and the outcome, and then come up with three things that revealed themselves only after the fact.

As an example, here's how you might use the Knowledge Tracker for the decision about taking the job in Boston.

This is what it might look like when you move to Boston and the outcome is that you quit after six months:

KNOWLEDGE TRACKER

Stuff you knew before the decision	Decision	Outcome	Stuff you know after the outcome
1. Average temperature, length of winter, and snowfall in Boston.	→ Take the job in Boston ——	→ Quit after 6 months ——	→ 1. Your experience of months of winter in Boston.
2. Details about the job opportunity.			2. How much you like the job.
3. Your experience from your February visit.			3. That you quit the job after 6 months and move home.

Here's how it might look when you move to Boston and it is a winter wonderland of great outcomes:

KNOWLEDGE TRACKER

Stuff you knew before the decision	Decision	Outcome	Stuff you know after the outcome
1. Average temperature, length of winter, and snowfall in Boston.	→ Take the job in Boston	→ You stay at the job	→ 1. Your experience of months of winter in Boston.
2. Details about the job opportunity.			2. You're a great snowboarder.
3. Your experience from your February visit.			3. That you stay in Boston for the long haul.

Now fill out the Knowledge Tracker for an instance when you exhibited hindsight bias:

KNOWLEDGE TRACKER

Stuff you knew before the decision	Decision	Outcome	Stuff you know after the outcome
1.	→	→	→ 1.
2.			2.
3.			3.

Did tracking your state of knowledge before and after the outcome
help to reduce memory creep?   YES   NO

Did tracking your knowledge help you see that there are things that
you could not have known, even if you feel like you should have
known them?   YES   NO

Use the space below for additional reflection on the experience of using the Knowledge
Tracker.

_____

_____

_____

_____

_____

_____

_____

IT'S HARD TO AVOID that gut feeling that you knew it all along. It's hard to avoid that gut feeling that you should have known. It's unrealistic to assume that you can put a complete stop to that intuitive response.

But the more you identify hindsight bias, especially by being mindful of the verbal and mental cues that accompany it, the better off you will be.

The way you process experiences informs your future decisions. Recognizing the "stuff you knew before the fact" and the "stuff that revealed itself only after the fact" helps prevent hindsight bias from distorting what you learn from your experience. You'll be less likely to make future decisions based on a faulty sense of what you knew or should have known. It will also help you beat up yourself (or others) less.

Tracking your knowledge creates the time stamp that can get lost in the warp of hindsight bias.

HINDSIGHT BIAS VACCINE

As you were using the Knowledge Tracker, it may have occurred to you that it would be a good idea to journal the "stuff you knew before the decision" *while you are in the process of making the decision.*

It can be hard to accurately recall what you knew before the fact once you already know the outcome. Journaling gives you something concrete to refer back to.

Writing down the key facts informing your decision also acts like a vaccine against hindsight bias. Thinking about what you know at the time of the decision in this more deliberative way creates a clearer time stamp, preventing memory creep before it happens.

Later in this book we'll take a deep dive into how to better memorialize decisions.

[4]

You Can Find Hindsight Bias Everywhere You Look

Now that you have a handle on hindsight bias, take a few days to listen for examples of hindsight bias at work or at home, from following the news or sports, or from your boss, friends, or family. *Most importantly*, pay attention to when you catch yourself in the act.

Reflect below on two of the examples you spot.

Example 1:

Briefly describe the example.

_____

_____

_____

Circle the form of hindsight bias involved: *Knew it all along*   *Should have known*

Were there verbal or mental cues?   *YES*   *NO*

If so, what were they?

_____

_____

_____

_____

Complete the Knowledge Tracker for this example.

If the example involves someone else's decision, you obviously can't know for sure what they knew at the time of the decision. But that doesn't mean you shouldn't try to put yourself in their shoes and take your best guess at what was reasonable for them to know. You might even try asking them to fill in the gaps for you.

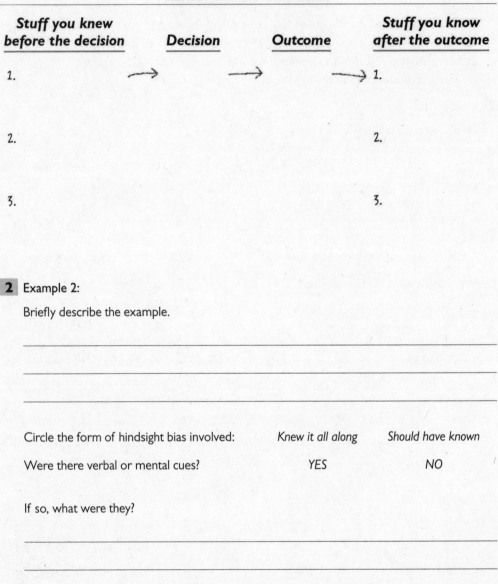

KNOWLEDGE TRACKER

Stuff you knew before the decision	*Decision*	*Outcome*	*Stuff you know after the outcome*
1.	→	→	→ 1.
2.			2.
3.			3.

2 Example 2:

Briefly describe the example.

_____

_____

_____

Circle the form of hindsight bias involved: *Knew it all along*   *Should have known*

Were there verbal or mental cues?   YES   NO

If so, what were they?

_____

_____

Complete the Knowledge Tracker for this example.

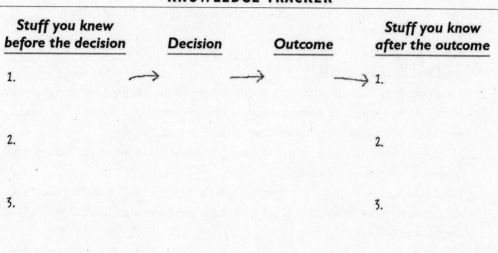

KNOWLEDGE TRACKER

Stuff you knew before the decision	Decision	Outcome	Stuff you know after the outcome
1.	→	→	→ 1.
2.			2.
3.			3.

Hindsight bias and compassion

Hindsight bias, like resulting, makes us lack compassion for ourselves and others. In order to think about what was reasonable for someone to know, we have to have empathy for them. We don't generally take the time to do this, and instead make snap judgments.

We are quick to blame the decision-maker for a bad outcome, neglecting to put ourselves in their shoes at the time of the decision (e.g., "You made us late to the airport with your stupid shortcut. How could you not have known there would be such bad traffic?").

That's true even when we're the decision-maker and we're in *our own shoes*.

This lack of empathy isn't limited to bad outcomes. Hindsight bias makes us unduly punish ourselves and others for being careful or agonizing over a decision that works out well (e.g., "Why did I waste so much time worrying about the weather?").

[5]

Hindsight Bias Wrap-up

These exercises were designed to get you thinking about the following concepts:

- **Hindsight bias** is the tendency to believe that an outcome, after it occurs, was **predictable** or **inevitable**.
- Hindsight bias, like resulting, is a manifestation of the outsized influence of outcomes. In this case, the outcome casts a shadow over your ability to accurately remember what you knew at the time of the decision.
- Hindsight bias distorts the way you process outcomes in two ways: **Should have known** and **Knew it all along**.
- Hindsight bias is frequently connected with a set of verbal or mental cues. (See the exercises in sections (2) and (4) for examples you've identified, as well as the checklist to follow.)
- Once you know how a decision turns out, you can experience **memory creep**, where the stuff that reveals itself after the fact creeps into your memory of what you knew or was knowable before the decision.
- To learn from your choices and their outcomes, you need to strive to be accurate about what you knew at the time of your decision.
- The **Knowledge Tracker** is a tool that can help separate what you knew from what you subsequently learned.
- Hindsight bias leads us to lack compassion for ourselves and others.

HINDSIGHT BIAS CHECKLIST

Identify the bias.

☐ "I should have known it."

☐ "I told you so."

☐ "I knew it all along."

    Use the space below to add to this list of cues, from the exercises in (2) and (4):

_____

_____

_____

_____

_____

_____

Address the bias.

☐ (1) Was there any information that was revealed after the fact?

☐ (2) Was that information *reasonably* knowable at the time of the decision? If you have a journal record of what you knew at the time of the decision, refer back to it.

☐ (3) Was the conclusion about the predictability of the result based on information that was unknowable at the time of the decision?

☐ (4) After addressing the first three questions, reassess how predictable the outcome was.

You Don't Know It's a Polling Error Until After the Vote

On November 8, 2016, Hillary Clinton lost the presidential election to Donald Trump largely because she underperformed in three key states: Michigan, Pennsylvania, and Wisconsin. These states were part of the "blue wall" of traditional Democratic support. She lost the states by tiny margins, adding up to just 80,000 votes out of 14,000,000.

The failure to carry Michigan, Pennsylvania, and Wisconsin turned what would have been a 278–260 electoral victory into Donald Trump's improbable 306–232 win.

The prevailing opinion is that the Clinton campaign lost themselves the election by neglecting those three key states. Just Google "Clinton campaign Michigan Pennsylvania Wisconsin" and you'll see article upon article critiquing her campaign for its terrible strategy:

- HOW THE RUSTBELT PAVED TRUMP'S ROAD TO VICTORY (TheAtlantic.com, November 10, 2016)
- THE CLINTON CAMPAIGN WAS UNDONE BY ITS OWN NEGLECT AND A TOUCH OF ARROGANCE, STAFFERS SAY (HuffPost.com, November 16, 2016)
- REPORT: NEGLECT AND POOR STRATEGY HELPED COST CLINTON THREE CRITICAL STATES (Slate.com, November 17, 2016)

That all seems reasonable, right? Obviously, Clinton's campaign strategy was terrible. She should have campaigned harder in those three states, and because she neglected them, she lost the election.

Here's the problem: Look at the dates of the pieces.

All of these stories are *from after the election.*

I went ten pages deep on Google and couldn't find any critique specifically about Michigan, Pennsylvania, and Wisconsin from before the election. Although there is an abundance of opinion pieces critiquing other aspects of Clinton's campaign strategy, none of them anticipated this particular problem.

In fact, the very few preelection pieces about the candidates' strategy in those states were critiques of Trump for wasting time campaigning in them:

- WHY WAS DONALD TRUMP CAMPAIGNING IN JOHNSTOWN, PENNSYLVANIA? (WashingtonPost.com, October 22, 2016)
- WHY IS DONALD TRUMP IN MICHIGAN AND WISCONSIN? (NewYorker.com, October 31, 2016)

Several states polled as toss-ups before the election, including Florida, North Carolina, and New Hampshire. And that was where Clinton was mainly campaigning.

Meanwhile, the polling averages had her ahead by several points in Pennsylvania, Michigan, and Wisconsin.

In retrospect, it's easy to see that there was likely a polling error in those three states since Trump significantly outperformed the polls in them.

But here's the thing about polling errors: You know there's an error only after the vote is taken.

Polling errors reveal themselves only after the fact, not before.

Making matters worse, there wasn't a national polling error. The national polls tracked the margin by which Clinton won the popular vote pretty accurately. Nor was it a systematic *state* polling error.

How could the Clinton campaign know, before the vote, that there is a problem in exactly those three states (but not others)? It doesn't seem like she could, at least not based on publicly available information.

Yet there is an abundance of "She should have known"s from pundits. There is a lot of "I knew it all along" from them as well, even though a simple Google search reveals that if they did know it all along it was the best-kept secret in politics.

3

The Decision Multiverse

[1]

A Hairbrained Idea

You hate salons and cut your own hair to avoid them.

This gives you the idea to develop an app called Kingdom Comb that matches people who don't want to go to a salon to get their hair done with hairstylists willing to come to the customer.

You want to stake a claim on your piece of the growing gig economy and you're confident that the idea is a winner!

You quit your job and plow your savings into the venture. You also raise a friends-and-family round of start-up capital.

The heavens, it turns out, aren't opening up for Kingdom Comb. Your start-up fails as the app never achieves critical mass. You run through your money (and the money of your friends and family).

You get even further into debt during the six months it takes to find another job, and you feel guilty about the money you lost for those who invested, negatively affecting your relationships with them.

You go back to cutting your own hair.

Going forward, you increasingly doubt your judgment on career and financial decisions.

You take a job as a developer with a small company but go out of your way to keep quiet whenever business discussions involve new ventures or innovation.

Write down at least three other possible outcomes for Kingdom Comb:

1. _____

_____

2. _____

_____

3. _____

_____

We'll come back to this in a moment.

[2]

The Paradox of Experience

Experience is necessary for learning. But we process that experience in a biased way. This means that the very feedback you need to become a better decision-maker can interfere with your ability to learn good lessons from experience.

This creates a paradox.

A lot of experience can be an excellent teacher. A single experience, not so much.

Looking across a large enough set of decisions and outcomes, we can start to tease out the lessons experience might offer us. Looking at just one outcome, we get resulting and hindsight bias.

Therein lies the problem: We process outcomes sequentially, treating each outcome as if it stands alone. We don't sit back and wait to update our beliefs until we have enough data to overcome the uncertain relationship between outcomes and decisions.

Any single outcome doesn't generally tell us too much about whether a decision was good or bad. But we act like it does. We act like one flip of a coin is enough.

That's the paradox.

That individual outcomes play an outsized role provides a clue as to how to resolve the paradox. We need to shrink outcomes down, closer to their appropriate size. A good first step in accomplishing that is to put an individual outcome in the context of all the other outcomes that could have occurred.

> **THE PARADOX OF EXPERIENCE**
>
> **Experience is necessary for learning, but individual experiences often interfere with learning.**

Your timeline, your reality, consists of the decisions you've made and their outcomes. Your experience is constructed only of the things that have actually happened.

If you could glimpse the other timelines that might have materialized if things had turned out differently, you would take a giant first step toward improving your ability to figure out when (and what) to learn from outcomes.

How do you do this? *Explore the decision multiverse.*

[3]

Decision Forestry: The cognitive chain saw massacre

IMAGINE STANDING AT THE base of a tree looking up at all the different branches.

AT THE TIME OF DECISION
Branches = possible outcomes

When you are making a decision, you see the future possibilities like the branches of a tree, each branch representing some way things could unfold.

The thicker the bough, the more likely the outcome. The tinier the twig, the less likely the outcome. Some boughs branch off in multiple ways. These branches-off branches represent things that might occur further in the future, depending on what happens along the way.

That's what the future looks like when it's ahead of you: a tree of possibilities.

A child imagines becoming a firefighter, or a doctor, or a professional tennis player, or an astronaut, or a movie star.

Or you imagine falling in love, or falling out of love, or saving enough for retirement, or falling short, or getting pizza for dinner, or going to the gym, or getting a promotion, or changing careers, or becoming a doctor.

At the time you are deciding, looking ahead to what might happen, you can see so many possibilities. And you can see them in the context of all the other things that might happen.

You glimpse the multiverse before you decide.

WHAT HAPPENS TO THAT tree full of possibilities once the future unfolds and one of those branches that was just a possibility becomes the one branch that actually happens?

Your mind takes a chain saw to the tree, leaving you with only that one branch, the branch representing the outcome you happened to have gotten.

It's as if everyone grew up and we all got the same dream job: chain saw operator.

THE TREE, AFTER THE OUTCOME

I can see it so much more clearly. It must have had a growth spurt.

After you know how things turned out, you hack off all those branches representing possible futures that didn't occur, leaving only one branch. Cognitively, you leave all the other branches forgotten on the ground.

There are many possible futures, but only one past. This makes the past feel inevitable, as even the tiniest of twigs now looks like the thickest of branches because it's the only thing you can see.

The multiverse disappears from view.

The earth had to be round. Dinosaurs had to become extinct. Humans had to evolve as the dominant species on the planet. The Allies had to win World War II. Amazon had to become the dominant online retailer.

You had to be born to your parents at the time and in the place you were born.

[4]

Putting Down the Cognitive Chain Saw: Reassembling the tree

The first step in trying to resolve the paradox of experience is to put the tree back together.

Pick those branches up off the ground and glue them back on the tree so that you can see the outcome in its proper context. In doing this, an improbable outcome will start to look more like the twig that it was than the thick bough it became.

You can get those branches back on the tree by taking the time to sketch out the reasonable set of outcomes, more closely approximating what the tree looked like at the time of the decision instead of how it appears to you after you know how things turned out.

Obviously, it would be unwieldy to sketch pictures of actual trees all over the place. But drawing a simple, abstract version of a tree is a good start to seeing outcomes more clearly, in their proper context.

LET'S SAY YOU WERE trying to better understand what the outcome of the decision to take the job in Boston has to teach you. Here's how you might reconstruct the tree when you quit after six months.

Start by sketching out the decision you made and the outcome that occurred, like so:

Decision

Outcome

Take the job in Boston ————→ You love the job but the winter is so awful that you quit.

If you were to put that tree back together, here is how you might do it:

HOW THE TREE LOOKS AFTER WE PUT THE OTHER POTENTIAL OUTCOMES BACK ON

Decision   **Potential outcomes**

Take the job in Boston

- You love the job and the city. You're a winter fanatic.

- You don't like the weather. But the job is good, so you decide to stick it out.

- You love the job but the winter is so awful that you quit.

- You love Boston but don't like the job. You quit and look for something else in Boston.

- You hate it all: The job, the city, the winter, and you quit. You go back home.

- You later get a better opportunity and quit the job. (This could include other jobs in Boston, in other cities, or going back to school.)

What you are starting to create is the foundation of a *decision tree*, a useful tool for evaluating past decisions and improving the quality of new ones. We will be developing this tool as we go along in this book.

Notice in this example that some of the possible outcomes are better than the one you got and some are worse. This will generally be true as you reconstruct these trees. The outcome that happened to occur will rarely sit at either extreme, best or worst.

Left to your own devices, it might feel like taking the job in Boston was a bad decision. It might feel like you should have known that you couldn't take the weather. But what this tree shows you is that it wasn't inevitable that you'd hate the winter or that you would love the job or that you would leave Boston or that you would stay.

Let's get back to Kingdom Comb.

I Remember, you develop Kingdom Comb to match people who don't want to go to a salon to get their hair done with hairstylists willing to come to them.

Your start-up fails as the app never achieves critical mass. You run through your money (and the money of your friends and family).

(You can go back to the beginning of this chapter to reread the complete scenario if you find that helpful.)

a. Record the decision you made and the outcome you got:

Decision   **Outcome**

b. Using the potential outcomes you identified in the opening exercise, sketch out the tree.

Decision   *Potential outcomes*

Now, here's another scenario:

2 You hate salons and cut your own hair to avoid them.

This gives you the idea to develop an app called Kingdom Comb that matches people who don't want to go to a salon to get their hair done with hairstylists willing to come to them.

You want to stake a claim on your piece of the growing gig economy and you're confident that the idea is a winner!

You quit your job and plow your savings into the venture. You also raise a friends-and-family round of start-up capital.

The heavens, it turns out, are opening up for Kingdom Comb. It shows promise, secures additional funding, and attracts the attention of both ride-sharing companies and haircutting chains. You accept an offer to sell the app, prerevenue, to one of those companies for $20 million.

Your friends and family make a huge return on their investment, as do you.

You are courted by other start-ups and big tech companies. With your pick of jobs, you are off to a great career in tech.

a. Write down the decision and the outcome:

Decision   *Outcome*

b. Sketch out a more complete tree for this scenario, including the other reasonable potential outcomes.

Decision   *Potential outcomes*

3 Did you make the same tree for both scenarios? (Circle one.)   YES   NO

WHETHER THE COMPANY ULTIMATELY fails or ultimately succeeds, the reconstructed tree should look the same.

Maybe Kingdom Comb never gets off the ground.

Maybe its legal bills go through the roof due to class actions from customers getting lopsided haircuts, state fines for unlicensed cosmeticians, and copyright and trademark claims from religious groups *and* salons claiming they own the name.

Maybe it sputters along for years before failing.

Maybe the idea works, but you are quickly outclassed by ventures combining deep pockets, marketing might, and industry acumen, like InstaCuts or FaceClips.

Maybe you grow the business, keep accessing capital, go public, achieve profitability, and eventually buy a national haircutting chain.

Maybe the business is sufficiently viable that you leverage your platform and customer base and keep expanding: other salon services, hair-care products, pet care, prescription delivery, home health care, and elder care.

At the time of the decision, all these possibilities for the future are the same *because the decision is the same.* The decision is what determines the set of possibilities, the paths that are possible. The actual outcome you get, whether the business fails or you find a $20 million exit, has no effect on what was possible at the time you made the decision.

Part of the paradox of experience is that we don't intuitively feel this way. Your gut tells you that the outcome really matters. Your gut tells you that the outcome you got somehow changes the outcomes that were possible.

Taking the time to construct a simple tree helps to put that gut feeling in check.

[5]

Counterfactuals

You can't fully understand what there is to learn from any outcome without understanding the other things that could have happened.

This is the essence of counterfactual thinking.

Exploring counterfactuals helps us to understand *why* things happened or didn't happen.

What if the earth had been flat or square? What if the giant asteroid hadn't killed the dinosaurs? What if humans had become extinct during the last Ice Age?

What if Germany hadn't defeated France in World War II? What if England hadn't allied with the Soviet Union? What if Japan had defeated Germany?

What if you had been born to different parents? Or in a different place? Or in 1600?

How can you possibly understand the effect of your own decision-making on the way your life turns out without exploring the counterfactual at the base of every life: what if I had been born under different circumstances?

Exploring those what-ifs is a reminder that you don't have any control over when or where you were born, things that define the set of possibilities for your life.

The might-have-beens and what-ifs put your experiences in their proper context, helping you to:

> **COUNTERFACTUAL**
> A *what-if*. A possible outcome of a decision that is not the one that actually occurred. An imagined, hypothetical state of the world.

- understand how much luck might have been involved in the outcome;
- compare the outcome you got to the outcomes that might have happened;
- let go of the feeling of inevitability; and
- improve the quality of the lessons you take from the experiences of your life.

I Pick a past terrible outcome from your own life. You can take one you've already used (i.e., worst decision, an instance of resulting, a hindsight-bias example) or a different one. It's particularly good to pick one you've been beating yourself up about.

a. Write down the decision and the outcome:

Decision

Outcome

b. Reconstruct the decision tree.

Decision   *Potential outcomes*

c. Did re-creating the tree change how you feel about your
responsibility for that outcome? (Circle one.)   YES   NO

Reflect on that here.

_____

_____

_____

d. Were there outcomes on that list that were worse than the one
you got? (Circle one.)   YES   NO

2 Pick a past great outcome from your own life. You can take one you're already used (i.e., best decision, an instance of resulting, an instance of Earned Reward, a hindsight-bias example) or a different one. It's particularly good to pick one that you feel you deserve a lot of credit for.

a. Write down the decision and the outcome:

Decision   *Outcome*

b. Reconstruct the decision tree with the other potential outcomes added to the actual outcome.

Decision

Potential outcomes

c. Did re-creating the tree change how you feel about your responsibility for that outcome? (Circle one.)　　　　　　　　YES　　　NO

Reflect on that here.

_____

_____

d. Were there outcomes on that list that were better than the one you got? (Circle one.)　　　　　　　　YES　　　NO

3 Circle which felt better:

　　　Re-creating the Tree　　　　*Re-creating the Tree*　　　　*Felt the Same*
　　　for a Bad Outcome　　　　*for a Great Outcome*

IF YOU'RE LIKE MOST PEOPLE, it felt better to re-create the tree and explore the counterfactuals when the outcome was bad than when the outcome was good.

If Kingdom Comb fails, it feels good to know that the failure isn't all on your shoulders. It feels good to know that there were lots of ways it could have succeeded and maybe worse ways it could have failed.

To some degree, seeing that negative result in the context of the other things that could have occurred, exposing the luck in the way that things turned out, lets you off the hook.

And who doesn't want to be let off the hook when things don't work out?

On the other hand, if creating Kingdom Comb results in a quick $20-million buyout, it doesn't feel so good to know that the success might not be all on your shoulders.

> **There's an asymmetry in our willingness to put outcomes in context: We'd rather do it when we fail than when we succeed.**

It doesn't feel so good to know that there were lots of ways it could have failed and even more stellar ways it could have succeeded.

We all want our successes to stand tall, to take up as much space in our narrative as possible.

Seeing any outcome in the context of the other things that could have occurred can let you off the hook—not just for the bad things that happen but also the good things.

But who wants to be let off the hook for a great result?

You want that.

It might feel good in the moment to accept your success without qualification or examination, but you're going to lose out on so many learning opportunities by doing so. You'll miss seeing the ways the outcome could have been even better. You'll miss exploring whether a different decision might have increased the chances of the outcome you got. Or the better outcomes that were possible. Or the worse outcomes that might have happened.

You'll miss the chance to see when the result you got was lucky.

We have to see outcomes for what they are, no more and no less, and that's true whether what happened was great or terrible. We have to find symmetry in our willingness to explore *all* outcomes.

Once you've banked the great result, no amount of counterfactual thinking can take it away from you. Refusal to understand the outcome in its context, however, can keep you from making better future decisions and ultimately jeopardize your ability to build upon—or hold on to—the fruits of your success.

[6]

The Decision Multiverse Wrap-up

These exercises were designed to get you thinking about the following concepts:

- The **paradox of experience**: Experience is necessary for learning, but individual experiences often interfere with learning. This is partly because of the biases that cause us to overfit outcomes and decision quality.
- Viewing the outcome that occurred in the context of other potential outcomes at the time of the decision can help to resolve this paradox.
- There are many possible futures but only one past. Because of this, the past feels inevitable.
- Re-creating a **simplified version of a decision tree** puts the actual outcome in its proper context.
- Exploring the other possible outcomes is a form of **counterfactual thinking**. A counterfactual is something that relates to an outcome that has not happened but could have happened, or an imagined state of the world.
- Our willingness to examine outcomes is **asymmetrical**. We are more eager to put bad outcomes in context than good ones. Becoming a better decision-maker requires us to try (difficult though it may be) to put those good outcomes in perspective.

THE DECISION MULTIVERSE CHECKLIST

When evaluating whether the outcome provides a lesson about decision quality, create a simplified decision tree, starting with the following:

☐ Identify the decision.

☐ Identify the actual outcome.

☐ Along with the actual outcome, create a tree with other reasonable outcomes that were possible at the time of the decision.

☐ Explore the other possible outcomes to understand better what is to be learned from the actual outcome you got.

The Man in the High Castle

It's 1962. World War II ended just fifteen years ago. Postwar America has changed dramatically since the war. Imperial Japan controls the Greater Japanese States, the former West Coast of the United States, with San Francisco as its capital. The Greater Nazi Reich's sphere includes the former East Coast, with New York City as the capital of the American Reich. The Rocky Mountains form a Neutral Zone between Japan and Germany, the world's two reigning superpowers.

That reality is the setting for Philip K. Dick's 1962 novel, *The Man in the High Castle*, made into a highly successful Amazon Studios television series of the same name in 2015.

The novel and the TV series provide multiple examples of counterfactuals and multiple futures.

The story takes place in a world where the Axis Powers won World War II. This version of the "present" exists because the past diverted from what we consider reality. An assassination attempt on FDR in 1933 (which we know failed) succeeded, altering pre–World War II America and, obviously, its involvement in World War II. That trajectory led to Germany exploiting its technology to develop atomic weapons, bomb Washington, D.C., and force an American surrender in 1947.

The story also includes a possible "alternate reality" in which America won World War II—but not the version we know. There is an underground story circulating, *The Grasshopper Lies Heavy*, about a history in which FDR wasn't assassinated. ("The man in the high castle" is the shadowy figure responsible for writing/filming that account.) FDR's survival changed everything, but not as a default to the world as we know it. Roosevelt retires after two terms. The next president does things differently, so the United States enters and wins the war, but the roles of the United States, Great Britain, and the Soviet Union are much different, as are their relations in a postwar world.

(No spoilers, but the TV version also has a third take on alternate worlds and histories.)

We don't tend to think of the world in such ways, but the story reminds us that our version of the past is not the only way things could have developed, nor is it how things had to turn out.

4

The Three Ps: Preferences, Payoffs, and Probabilities

[I]

Six Steps to Better Decision-Making:
Making your view of the future (crystal) clearer

Up to this point, we've exclusively focused on how we evaluate *past* decisions. The thing about the past is that you can't change it. What you can do is apply what you learn from the past to all the new decisions you have yet to make by developing a repeatable process for better decision-making.

Your greatest challenge as a decision-maker is seeing things that, by their nature, are going to be hazy. For past decisions, you're reconstructing the decision while navigating your way through distortion-inducing biases. For new decisions, you're looking into the future, which is inherently uncertain.

This six-step process will help you improve the quality of both new decisions on your horizon and your assessment of past decisions. It's hard to accurately assess a decision after the fact, in the shadow of an outcome that has already happened. But if you have a good decision process *going forward*, and keep a record of it, you'll be a lot better off.

You won't have to wonder after the fact whether a decision was good or bad, under the haze of resulting and hindsight bias.

Instead, you'll be able to check your work.

And here's the thing: It is not that an outcome is *never* informative. It is that it is informative only when the outcome is *unexpected*, when you didn't anticipate the result in the set of possibilities. It doesn't matter if the result is awesome or the worst. What really matters is whether you didn't foresee it, because your decisions will only be as good as your ability to anticipate how they might turn out.

Unexpectedness is really hard to evaluate in retrospect. But if you do the work in advance, not only will your decisions get better because you will be laser focused on how the future might unfold, but you will also be able to tell when you didn't anticipate the way things might turn out *because you will actually have a record of what you were thinking at the time you made the decision.*

That's the path to supercharging your decision-making skills.

So let's get to building out a great decision process.

SIX STEPS TO BETTER DECISION-MAKING

Step 1—Identify the reasonable set of possible outcomes.

Step 2—Identify your preference using the payoff for each outcome—to what degree do you like or dislike each outcome, given your values?

Step 3—Estimate the likelihood of each outcome unfolding.

Step 4—Assess the relative likelihood of outcomes you like and dislike for the option under consideration.

Step 5—Repeat Steps 1–4 for other options under consideration.

Step 6—Compare the options to one another.

[2]

Pro Tip: Don't taunt the largest animal in North America

Here is a picture of a bison blocking traffic on a road at Yellowstone.

The guy in retreat was sufficiently impatient to get somewhere that he decided it was worth shaving a bit off his travel time to exit his car and try to taunt the largest animal in North America into moving.

Now they're both moving!

Without looking anything up, what's your best guess of the bison's weight (in pounds)?

_____

What are the reasons for your guess?

_____

_____

_____

_____

I'm willing to bet a lot of money that you didn't guess under one hundred pounds or over ten thousand pounds. Later in this chapter, we'll revisit the bison and why I'm confident about that bet.

[3]

Payoffs: Step 2—Identify your preference using the payoff for each outcome—to what degree do you like or dislike each outcome, given your values?

Preference matters

Identifying the set of reasonable outcomes is a huge improvement over having particular outcomes distort your view (the actual outcome for past decisions, or prospective outcomes you especially desire or fear). You want to understand past decisions and improve your assessment of future ones, but it's not sufficient to stop there. To get a fuller grasp of the set of possible outcomes for any decision, you also need to identify your preference for each outcome.

So let's start with explicitly adding information to the trees we have started developing by expressing the desirability of each of the reasonable ways a decision could turn out. The simplest way to do this is to list the potential outcomes on the tree in order of your most preferred to your least preferred.

Here's an example of the tree for the Boston job, reorganized by preference, with the most desirable at the top and the least desirable at the bottom:

Decision	**Potential outcomes**
Take the job in Boston	You love the job and the city. You're a winter fanatic.
	You don't like the weather. But the job is good, so you decide to stick it out.
	You love Boston but don't like the job. You quit and look for something else in Boston.
	You later get a better opportunity and quit the job. (This could include other jobs in Boston, in other cities, or going back to school.)
	You love the job but the winter is so awful that you quit.
	You hate it all: the job, the city, the winter and quit. You go back home.

One person's trash is another person's treasure

Of course, whether and to what degree a result is good or bad will depend on goals and values that are particular to you.

It might seem obvious that if you take a one-week beach vacation, seven straight days of rain would be a bad outcome. That's true if your goal was to sunbathe. But what if your goal was to catch up on the huge stack of books you've been meaning to get to? Then rain every day wouldn't be such a terrible result, even if you were planning to read those books on the beach.

Two people might share the goal of providing for their families. For one person, that could mean financial security. For another, it could mean time spent together as a family. That difference in values would lead them to different career preferences.

The first person would prefer a job that pays more and has more opportunities for advancement, even at the cost of sacrificing time with their family. The second person would take a job that pays less if it offers flexible hours, opportunities to work from home, and evenings and weekends free.

The point is, what you value and what someone else values will be different. And your goals and values will inform your preferences for various outcomes. That means that how much you prefer a particular outcome relative to other possibilities will naturally be different from another person's preference for the same outcome relative to other possibilities.

That doesn't make either of you wrong. It just means that you are different people with particular likes and dislikes.

It also doesn't mean that you can't seek advice from other people. Advice can be an excellent decision tool as long as you are explicit about your goals and values when you are seeking that advice. Otherwise, you run the risk that the person whose advice you are seeking will assume you share their preferences and will answer accordingly.

1 For one of the decision trees you made in "The Decision Multiverse" chapter, reorganize the possible outcomes in order of your preference.

Decision   *Potential outcomes*

2 What goals and values motivated your order of preference?

_____

_____

_____

_____

_____

_____

3 Are any of the outcomes significantly better than the others?

_____

_____

_____

_____

4 Are any of the outcomes significantly worse than the others?

_____

_____

_____

_____

FOR ALMOST ANY DECISION you make, there are some outcomes you hope for and some you don't. By explicitly adding preferences to the tree, you can see at a glance how many of the possible outcomes you like and how many you don't. That's why it's helpful to order the possibilities by preference.

Of course, just because a decision has mostly good or mostly bad outcomes isn't enough to determine whether the decision is, correspondingly, good or bad. You also need to know the magnitude of each outcome—*how good* or *how bad*.

In other words, you need to think about the size of your preference—the degree to which you like or dislike each of the possibilities.

(Payoff) size matters

For almost any set of outcomes, there will be stuff you could gain and stuff you could lose. These gains or losses are called ***payoffs*** and they will drive your preferences because, obviously, you will prefer gains over losses.

If an outcome moves you toward a goal, the payoff is positive. If an outcome moves you away from a goal, the payoff is negative. The magnitude of that move drives how much you prefer or dislike an outcome. The bigger the gain, the bigger the preference for that result. The bigger the loss, the bigger the dislike for that result.

The most straightforward way to understand payoffs is for decisions where the quality of the outcome is measured in money. If you make an investment that earns you money, that's a gain. If you lose money, well, that's a loss.

But payoffs can also be in the currency of anything you value, such as happiness (your own or that of others), time, social currency, self-improvement, self-esteem, goodwill, and health, etc.

If a possible outcome unfolds, will your happiness increase or decrease? Will you gain or lose time? Will your social currency rise or fall? Will you gain or lose self-esteem? Will you make someone important to you happier or less happy?

Anything we value can be the currency of a payoff, positive or negative.

In the set of possible outcomes, some will have payoffs where you gain something you value. These comprise the *upside potential* of a decision. Some will have payoffs where you lose something you value. These make up the *downside potential* of a decision.

Let's say you're deciding whether to invest in a stock. The upside potential is the money you would earn if the stock increases in value. The downside potential is the money you would lose if it goes down in value.

You're deciding whether to go to a cocktail party. The upside is you could have a great time, strengthen friendships, make new friends, or meet people who can help you in your work. You might even meet the love of your life.

The downside is the party could be boring and you could waste the time that you might have spent doing something more fun. You could blow up a friendship after getting into a heated argument about some third-rail political topic. You could ruin your streak of healthy eating after being unable to resist the pizza and birthday cake.

You're running late to work and are deciding whether to drive fifteen miles over the speed limit. The upside potential is that you make it to work on time.

The downside? You still might not make it on time. You could get a speeding ticket (which, in addition to the other costs, would make you even later). Or you could get in an accident you wouldn't otherwise have gotten into if you had been observing the law.

Most decisions have a mix of upside and downside potentials. When figuring out whether a decision is good or bad, you are essentially asking if the upside potential compensates for the *risk* of the downside.

RISK
Your exposure to the downside.

To do that, you need to know the possible outcomes (Step 1) and the potential gains and losses associated with each of them (Step 2). That's why mapping these out is essential to good decision-making. Without examining the size of the payoffs, it is impossible to figure out whether going for the upside is worth risking the downside.

You could have a decision with four possible outcomes that move you toward your goal, and only one possible outcome that causes a loss. But that doesn't mean, on its own, that the decision is worth the risk.

The four upside outcomes might be saving a dollar, minty breath for the next hour, arriving someplace five minutes sooner, or the ability to wear your socks an extra day without washing them. The downside might be that you instantly die.

> **Assessing the quality of a decision involves figuring out whether going for the upside is worth risking the downside.**

That's why size matters.

This is where we begin to more clearly see the limitations of pros and cons lists. The good news about a pros and cons list is that it at least gets you thinking about the upside (the pros) and the downside (the cons), the start of Step 2. The bad news is that a pros and cons list doesn't get you thinking about magnitude, how big a positive any pro is or how big a negative any con is, which is also necessary to Step 2.

Pros and cons lists are flat, as if (payoff) size *doesn't* matter. Because it is merely in list form, a pros and cons list treats the chance of an early arrival as equal to the possibility of getting into a serious traffic accident. Without explicit information about size, about the magnitude of any pro or con, it is unclear how you would compare the positive and negative sides of the list.

If there are ten pros and five cons, does that mean you should go with the decision? It is impossible to say without information about the size of the payoffs, because without that you can't figure out if the upside potential outweighs the downside.

[4]

Probability Matters:
Step 3—Estimate the likelihood of each outcome unfolding

You buy stock in an electric car company. It quadruples in price. You're patting yourself on the back for a great decision. But if the chance that the stock would quadruple was tiny, while the chance that the stock would go down in value was huge, should you be taking so much credit?

You buy stock in an electric car company. It goes to zero. You're beating yourself up for a terrible decision. But what if the likelihood of the stock going to zero was minuscule?

Every time you get in a car, you're risking a big downside: getting in an accident and dying. Of course, you take that risk because the probability is so small that the upside (time saved, increased productivity, etc.) compensates for it. Likewise, even though you could win a fortune in the lottery (against losing only a dollar), the chances of winning are so small that it's not worth risking the dollar.

Other long-shot payoffs may be worthwhile. Investing in a start-up is a high-risk investment. A lot of the time you'll lose your money, because most new businesses fail. The huge upside (if you're good at choosing which ventures to back) can make the risk worthwhile. That is why venture capitalists exist, after all.

Without information about the likelihood of any possibility unfolding, you can break your arm patting yourself on the back because you can't see that a happy result was going to happen only a very small percentage of the time.

Or you can beat yourself up over a bad result because you can't see that the outcome was very unlikely to happen.

Or you can think you just got unlucky getting a bad result that, in reality, was highly probable, so it was not bad luck at all. It was expected.

Or you could make a decision blinded by a highly unlikely but huge potential gain without considering the risk.

Or you could pass on an opportunity because you are afraid of the risk, even though the risk is incredibly small and the upside potential more than compensates for it.

> To figure out whether a decision is good or bad, you need to know not just the things that might reasonably happen and what could be gained or lost, but also the likelihood of each possibility unfolding. That means, to become a better decision-maker, you need to be willing to estimate those probabilities.

The Three Ps: Preferences, Payoffs, and Probabilities   (79)

The Archer's Mindset:
All guesses are educated guesses

If you're like most people, you're uncomfortable estimating the likelihood of something happening in the future. I'm guessing that's in part because, for most decisions, you can't know the exact probability of any given possibility unfolding. Most decisions aren't like a coin flip, where you know for sure the chance of a fair coin landing heads is 50%.

For most decisions, you don't know everything you need to know to come up with an objectively perfect answer about how likely it is that something is going to happen. This can make any answer you give seem completely subjective. *Or, worse, wrong.* And that probably makes you reluctant to guess.

How can you possibly know the likelihood that you'll love Boston or that new job when you've never lived in that city or experienced that particular job?

How can you know the likelihood that you'll like a college you've never attended?

How can you know the likelihood a particular stock is going to go up in the future?

How can you know the likelihood that you'll close a sale with a new customer when they're a *new customer*?

To sum it all up in one phrase, you're probably thinking "I'd just be guessing."

And that brings us back to the bison.

Back to the bison

Whatever you guessed the bison weighs, you almost definitely didn't get the right answer if "right" means the exact weight of that particular bison.

There is a lot you don't know about that bison. You're trying to guess from *a picture*. Even if you were there in person, you probably wouldn't be able to measure the bison to get its exact height, or know its age, or whether it's a male or a female. It's unlikely you'd have a livestock scale handy, assuming that you knew how to coax the bison onto the scale.

When you guess, the gap between perfect knowledge and your knowledge bothers you.

You know there's an objectively correct answer—the bison's actual weight. If you had perfect information, if you were omniscient, you'd know that exact number. But you're not omniscient.

That weighs on you at least as much as if, instead of making a guess, you had to give the bison a piggyback ride. (At least if you had to give the bison a piggyback ride, you wouldn't need to know its weight, because you know it's enough to crush you.)

If there's a right answer out there and you don't know it, guessing feels bad. You know your answer won't be right. And what is the opposite of *right*?

Wrong.

And who wants to be wrong?

> **This way of thinking, that there is only "right" and "wrong" and nothing in between, is one of the biggest obstacles to good decision-making. Because good decision-making requires a willingness to guess.**

"I'd just be guessing"

People deflect making such estimates all the time with "I'd just be guessing." That implies that anything less than perfect knowledge makes your answer random. We get hung up on not having all the information, which causes us to overlook all the things we *do* know.

Although it's true that you don't know the bison's exact weight, that doesn't mean you don't know anything. As a person who lives in the world, you know a lot of stuff.

- You know a lot about the weights of things in general. Appliances weigh more than cardboard boxes. Rocks weigh more than feathers. Very big things almost always weigh more than very small things. Bison weigh more than people.
- You probably have an idea of the average weight of a cat or a dog. Or maybe you even know the average weight of a cow.
- You can see the general size of the bison in relation to surrounding cars and the guy taunting it.
- You know how much you weigh.
- You know the bison weighs more than the guy.
- You have some idea of what cars weigh and that the weight of the car is probably greater than the weight of the bison.

All your knowledge, imperfect as it might be, means that your guess isn't random. Although you don't have *perfect* information, you have a lot more than *no* information about what the bison weighs.

That's why I was willing to bet that you wouldn't guess below one hundred pounds or above ten thousand pounds, because I know you know a lot of stuff.

You almost always know something, and something is better than nothing. You might not get it perfect, but when it comes to decision-making, *you get credit for showing your work.*

If you dismiss making estimates of probability by saying, "I'd only be guessing," then you're letting yourself off the hook of trying to figure out what you know or what you could find out. Once you say "I'd only be guessing," there's no more work to be done. By giving up, you won't even bother to apply the knowledge you do have to the decision.

> **Don't overlook the territory in between right and wrong.**
>
> **Don't overlook the value in being a little less wrong or a little closer to right.**

The knowledge that you can apply to any single estimate might be small, but it will make a difference in the quality of your decisions. Those differences, even if they are modest, will add up over time. Like compounding interest, those small increases in decision quality will pay big dividends in the long run.

Don't toss the stuff you know in the trash can just because you'd "just be guessing."

Accentuate the educated

We have a way to distinguish informed guesses from uninformed ones. We call the informed guesses *educated guesses.*

It's not a matter of whether or not any guess is educated. It's a matter of to what degree.

> **Here's a secret: All guesses are *educated* guesses because there is almost no estimate you could make about which you literally know nothing.**

You can think about your state of knowledge on a continuum from no information to perfect information.

NO INFORMATION →   **PERFECT INFORMATION** →

KNOWLEDGE

No information would mean that you know nothing. Perfect information would mean that you know everything. For most things you are trying to estimate, you won't be at either extreme, having no information or perfect information. Mostly, you will be somewhere in the middle.

Mostly, you're in bison territory.

A little knowledge is not for nothing. Even with the little bit that you know about the weight of the bison, you can narrow the range from zero to infinity pounds to something in the area of 800 to 3,500 pounds. That eliminates a lot of ground. That narrows the field. You might not be certain of the weight, but you've made a lot of progress getting closer to the answer.

If you're thinking about taking a job in Boston, you can't know for certain if you'll like the job, and you can't know for certain if you'll like the city. But you know some things about jobs and some things about cities. What you know counts for something. Just like the bison.

There's a lot of value in making an educated guess. The more willing you are to guess, the more you'll think about and apply what you know. In addition, you'll start thinking about what you can find out that will get you closer to the answer.

> **Whether you're estimating the weight of a bison or the likelihood that Kingdom Comb will succeed, your job as a decision-maker is to figure out two things:**
>
> **(1) What do I already know that will make my guess more educated?**
>
> **(2) What can I find out that will make my guess more educated?**

The Archer's Mindset

Part of becoming a better decision-maker is shifting your mindset about guessing. Instead of being uncomfortable with guessing because you probably won't be "right" (and anything that's not exactly right is "wrong"), think about your guesses the way an archer thinks about a target.

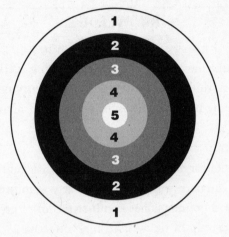

Just like decision-making, archery is not all or nothing, where you get points only for hitting the bull's-eye and everything else is a miss. An archer gets points for hitting the *target* at all.

The value of guessing isn't in whether the guess is "right" or "wrong." Your guesses are like the archer's arrows. If you were omniscient and your guesses were always exactly right, you'd score all bull's-eyes. When you make an educated guess, you're aiming at the *bull's-eye* and, though it's likely you'll miss the exact answer, like the archer you will still score points for getting in the vicinity.

It's okay to acknowledge that you're not usually going to hit the bull's-eye; the important thing is to *take aim*. Aiming for that bull's-eye by making an educated guess gets you closer to a precise hit because it motivates you to assess what you know and what you don't know. It motivates you to learn more.

Recognizing the value in taking aim is the archer's mindset. Recognizing that guesses aren't random, that all guesses are educated guesses, is the archer's mindset. Otherwise, your decision-making will more closely resemble a game of pin the tail on the donkey. You'll be purposely blindfolding yourself to the target.

The reason pin the tail on the donkey has gone out of favor at kids' birthday parties (at least where they use a real pin) is that if you're blindfolded, spinning around, and stabbing a pointy object, you're about as likely to shiv the person cutting the cake as you are to land on the donkey's butt.

Most of us are living our lives with the pin-the-tail-on-the-donkey mindset.

Besides, you're already doing it

Here's another secret: Even when you are trying to pin the tail on the donkey, you are still aiming at a target. You're just doing a terrible job of aiming because you're wearing a blindfold.

That's also true of decision-making. Even if you aren't explicitly thinking about the set of possibilities, your preferences, and the probabilities, you are still making these estimates. Implicit in any decision is the belief that the option you choose has the highest probability of working out better for you than the options you don't choose.

Therefore, whether you acknowledge it or not, making a decision is making a guess about how things might turn out.

If you're shooting arrows, they are going to hit *something*. If you're guessing anyway, you can be like an archer and take careful aim, or be like you're at an old-timey birthday party, poking a pin around with a blindfold on until you draw blood or get lucky. Better to take off the blindfold and aim with your eyes wide open.

> **Your choice is always an estimate of the likelihood of different outcomes unfolding.**

Once you acknowledge that you're guessing anyway, it maximizes your ability to bring to bear on your decisions the things you already know, and it makes you ask what you need to learn to move yourself on the continuum away from no knowledge and closer to perfect knowledge.

[6]

A Soft Landing to Probabilistic Thinking:
Using words that express likelihoods

As a first stab at Step 3, adding probabilities to the decision tree, you can use common terms that express likelihoods.

There are a lot of natural language terms that express the likelihood of something occurring or something being true, like "frequently" and "rarely." Andrew Mauboussin and Michael Mauboussin came up with this pretty comprehensive list of these types of terms for a survey they conducted:

Almost always	More often than not	Serious possibility
Almost certainly	Never	Slam dunk
Always	Not often	Unlikely
Certainly	Often	Usually
Frequently	Possibly	With high probability
Likely	Probably	With low probability
Maybe	Rarely	With moderate probability
Might happen	Real possibility	

Using this list, you can add this information about the chances of an outcome occurring to any decision tree. Remember, all guesses are educated guesses, so don't be afraid to take a stab at how likely any outcome is, even if you don't know for sure. An educated guess is better than no guess at all.

Here is an example of how you might use these terms to express the likelihoods of different outcomes for the Boston job decision:

Decision	Potential outcomes	Likelihood
	You love the job and the city. You're a winter fanatic.	Real possibility
	You don't like the weather. But the job is good, so you decide to stick it out.	Probably
	You love Boston but don't like the job. You quit and look for something else in Boston.	With low probability
Take the job in Boston	You later get a better opportunity and quit the job. (This could include other jobs in Boston, in other cities, or going back to school.)	Unlikely
	You love the job but the winter is so awful that you quit.	Rarely
	You hate it all: The job, the city, the winter, and you quit. You go back home.	With low probability

Both resulting and hindsight bias can lead you to beat yourself up (or beat other people up) after a bad outcome, such as when the choice to move to Boston doesn't work out. By putting the tree back together, including getting your preferences in order and making an estimate of the chances of each outcome occurring, you can see more clearly that the most likely outcomes ranged from extremely good (loving the job, city, and weather) to pretty good. The two really bad outcomes were unlikely to happen.

> Having added this information to the tree, you can now scan the possibilities to see how the upside compares to the downside, whether the possible gains compensate for the risk. In other words, you can now execute Step 4: Assess the relative likelihood of outcomes you like and dislike for the option under consideration.

Of course, if you do this *before* making the decision about whether to move to Boston, that's even better. Mapping out the possibilities and probabilities gives you a better view of the quality of the decision.

This exposes yet another dimension that pros and cons lists lack: information about the likelihood of any of the pros or cons unfolding. Pros and cons lists make it impossible to execute Steps 3 and 4 of the decision process with any fidelity, because both of those steps require you to think about probability.

If you can't execute on the steps that help you evaluate a single option under consideration (Steps 1–4), then you can't execute on Step 6 (comparing options to one another).

A pros and cons list is not really designed as a tool to help you compare choices, but rather as a tool to help you evaluate a single choice. And because a pros and cons list is flat, it is not even particularly useful for that. While it might be better than not using a tool at all (although even that isn't clear), you might as well be using a hammer to pound that screw into the dresser.

That's going to create an unstable structure.

What do you really care about: a general scenario or particular payoffs?

So far, we've been talking about outcomes as general scenarios. But for many decisions, there is a particular aspect of the outcome set—a particular payoff—that you really care about. When that's the case, you can sharpen your focus on what matters to you by narrowing your estimates to those payoffs.

If you're choosing an investment, you likely care specifically about monetary payoffs. In that case, you might focus on the likelihood that, within a certain time frame, your investment quadruples or doubles or gains 50% or loses half its value or goes to zero.

If you're trying to eat healthier, you may be deciding whether you should stop going by the breakroom to reduce your exposure to breakroom donuts. When considering that decision, you can ask yourself, "What's the likelihood, if I go to the breakroom, that I'll eat zero donuts, one donut, two donuts, or all but the crumbs?"

Imagine you are hiring a job candidate and your biggest pain point is employee turnover. Narrowing your focus to the likelihood a prospective hire will still be with the company in six months, a year, or two years allows you to more clearly assess the aspect of the decision most important to you.

Here's what a decision tree focused on employee retention might look like:

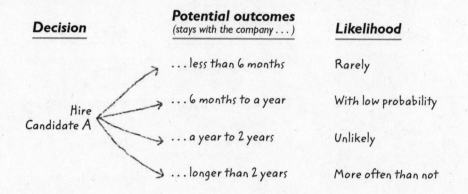

Decision	**Potential outcomes** (stays with the company . . .)	Likelihood
	. . . less than 6 months	Rarely
Hire Candidate A	. . . 6 months to a year	With low probability
	. . . a year to 2 years	Unlikely
	. . . longer than 2 years	More often than not

You can see how narrowing focus in this way, simplifying the set of outcomes by homing in on a particular dimension of the way things might turn out, clarifies Step 4. It also naturally clarifies the assessment of one option against other available options by creating a clear apples-to-apples comparison.

Now you can repeat the process for other candidates (Step 5) and compare each option (Step 6) to figure out which is most likely to address your exploding recruitment costs. You can look at both options and see which has the highest likelihood of getting you the outcome you desire.

In the case below, Candidate A would be the clear choice.

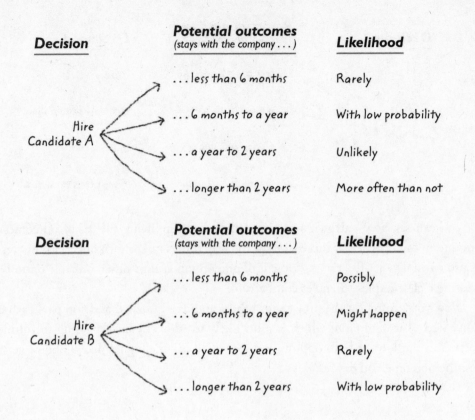

Decision	Potential outcomes (stays with the company . . .)	Likelihood
Hire Candidate A	. . . less than 6 months	Rarely
	. . . 6 months to a year	With low probability
	. . . a year to 2 years	Unlikely
	. . . longer than 2 years	More often than not

Decision	Potential outcomes (stays with the company . . .)	Likelihood
Hire Candidate B	. . . less than 6 months	Possibly
	. . . 6 months to a year	Might happen
	. . . a year to 2 years	Rarely
	. . . longer than 2 years	With low probability

Let's try some of these probability terms on for size.

At your most recent medical checkup, your doctor notices that your blood sugar levels are well above normal (damn you, breakroom donuts!) and advises you to modify your diet and start exercising regularly.

You agree to her dietary recommendations, and even volunteer that you'll eat more vegetables that haven't been deep-fried. You also consider joining a gym called Sweat Sensations to follow her advice about exercising more regularly.

In considering whether to join Sweat Sensations, the payoff you care about is how often you will actually go work out. You are trying to increase your amount of exercise, per doctor's orders, so how often you'll go (assuming you exercise vigorously once there) is the aspect you most care about in evaluating your decision. The more you go to the gym, the more you will exercise, and the bigger the upside to your health. The less you go, the smaller the upside.

Here is a reasonable set of potential outcomes:

- The last time you go to the gym is when you pick up your photo ID. You carry it around for a long time, intending to go, but eventually bury the ID in a desk drawer. In other words, you go zero times a week.

- You start going regularly but taper off until you're going just once a week, drinking a smoothie while sitting, stationary, on the oldest exercise bike in the place.

- You go to the gym three times a week, and it eventually becomes a routine.

- You become workout crazy, hire a trainer, and go five times a week.

1 Drawing from the Mauboussins' set of terms, add a term for the likelihood of each outcome if you decide to join Sweat Sensations. You may be a regular gymgoer or are allergic to gyms, so for this exercise (no pun intended), answer in a way you think an average person considering joining a gym would answer.

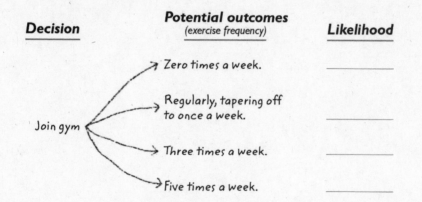

Decision	**Potential outcomes** (exercise frequency)	**Likelihood**
	Zero times a week.	_____
Join gym	Regularly, tapering off to once a week.	_____
	Three times a week.	_____
	Five times a week.	_____

2 What beliefs and knowledge did you bring to bear on making those estimates?

_____

_____

_____

_____

_____

The advantages of using terms that express probabilities

Adding probability estimates to the decision tree will significantly improve the quality of your decisions versus simply identifying the possibilities and your preferences. To make better decisions, you have to consider the likelihood of any outcome occurring, including the ones you prefer and the ones you want to avoid. Without taking this extra step, it is difficult to assess the quality of any option on its own, and even harder to compare options.

If your goal is to exercise three times a week and it looks from your estimates that a gym membership isn't going to cut it, that can spur you to look at other options. Home exercise equipment? Cycling? Making the fifteen flights of stairs to your workplace into your gym? You can compare and determine which option gives you the best likelihood of getting you the desired payoff of improved health.

[7]

If You Don't Ask a Question, You Won't Get an Answer

One of the biggest benefits of the Archer's Mindset, of making yourself take aim, is that it prompts you to ask yourself those two questions we discussed earlier about the value of guessing:

1. What do I already know that will make my guess more educated? (And how can I apply that knowledge?)
2. What can I find out that will make my guess more educated?

Taking aim will make you hungry to answer these questions, moving things from the "stuff you don't know" box to the "stuff you know" box.

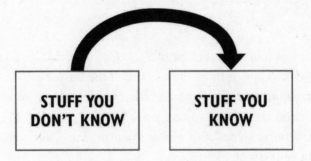

Your beliefs are part of the foundation of every decision you make. Your beliefs inform what options you think are available and the ways that your decision might turn out. Your beliefs inform how likely you think things are to occur or things are to be true. They inform what you think the payoffs are, and even inform your goals and your values.

> **Your chief weapon to improve your decisions is turning some of the "stuff you don't know" into "stuff you know."**

And here's the problem: The previous drawing is not to scale. It should really look more like this:

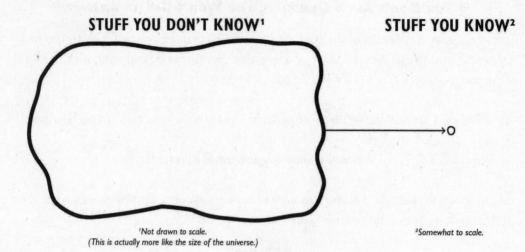

STUFF YOU DON'T KNOW[1]   **STUFF YOU KNOW**[2]

[1]*Not drawn to scale.*
(This is actually more like the size of the universe.)   [2]*Somewhat to scale.*

What you know is more like the size of a speck of dust that could fit on the head of a pin. What you don't know is more like the size of the universe.

It might seem daunting that the speck of what you know is so small. But there's good news, especially if you take a constructive attitude about guessing: Every time you learn something and transform some "stuff you don't know" into "stuff you know," you make the foundation of your decisions stronger.

We have two main problems when it comes to the stuff we know. *First, we just don't know very much.* Learning new stuff strengthens the foundation, making it sturdier.

Second, the stuff we do know is riddled with inaccuracies. A lot of our beliefs are not perfectly true. We can think about these inaccuracies as cracks in the foundation. The only way to fix those cracks and shore up the foundation is to find the inaccuracies in our beliefs. And the only place we are going to find that information is in the universe of stuff we don't know.

That's part of why it's so important to good decision-making to ask yourself about the possibilities, the payoffs, and the probabilities that the future will unfold in various ways. It forces you to assess what you know and seek out what you don't.

And here is even more good news: That little speck can often be enough to get you close to the bull's-eye. You don't need to know as much as you think to make a significant dent in the possible answers. Like when you are estimating the weight of a bison.

That's the beauty of an approach to decision-making that starts with examining what you know, even if you think you need a microscope to do it. A little bit of knowledge can go a long way. And the more you know, the better off you are.

Why this matters

There are two ways uncertainty intervenes in the decision process: imperfect information and luck. Imperfect information intervenes before the decision. Luck intervenes after the decision but before the outcome.

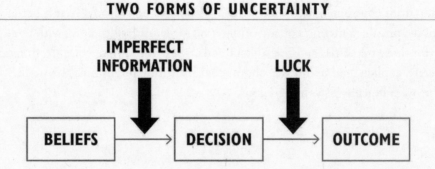

TWO FORMS OF UNCERTAINTY

Luck, by definition, is something you can't do anything about. The expression "You make your own luck" is wishful thinking or a poor understanding of luck. If you have two choices and one will work out 5% of the time and the other will work out 95% of the time, you have control over your choice. If you make the better choice, you'll improve your likelihood of succeeding.

But once you choose, even if you pick the option that will work out 95% of the time, you don't have any control over how that decision will work out on that try. By definition, things *will* turn out poorly 5% of the time and you can't control when that 5% will happen.

Much of the focus of this book has been about doing things to help you choose the better option. But your choices can't *guarantee* great outcomes, because of luck.

In contrast, you have some control over uncertainty in the form of imperfect information. Your beliefs inform your decisions and you have the ability to improve the quality of those beliefs. You can rarely get to perfect information, but you can get closer.

While terms like "usually," "often," and "rarely" are blunt instruments, they are better than nothing, because they get you started at taking aim. Because these are terms you already use every day, you're probably pretty comfortable with them. They will provide an easy transition into thinking probabilistically.

Even if you never get past using these blunt, imprecise instruments for estimating probability, you will still have a tool that can mitigate some of the tremendous damage that biases like resulting and hindsight can wreak on your judgment when it comes to learning from your outcomes. When making new decisions, you'll have a better overall idea of the possible outcomes of any option you are considering, along with your preferences for those outcomes and their likelihoods. This will initiate you into thinking in a deliberate, explicit, and useful way about what the future might hold, naturally improving the overall quality of your decisions.

[8]

The Three Ps Wrap-up

These exercises were designed to get you thinking about the following concepts:

- Incorporating **preferences**, **payoffs**, and **probabilities** into a decision tree is an integral part of a good decision process.
- **Preference** is individual to you, dependent on your **goals and values**.
- **The payoff** is how an outcome affects your progress toward or away from a goal.
- Some possibilities will have payoffs where you gain something you value. These comprise the **upside potential** of a decision.
- Some possibilities will have payoffs where you lose something you value. These comprise the **downside potential** of a decision.
- **Risk** is your exposure to the downside.
- Payoffs can be measured in anything you value (money, time, happiness, health, the happiness or health or wealth of others, social currency, etc.).
- When you're figuring out whether a decision is good or bad, you're comparing the upside to the downside. Does the upside potential compensate for the **risk** of the downside potential?

- **Probabilities** express how likely something is to occur.
- Combining probabilities with preferences and payoffs helps you to better resolve the paradox of experience, allowing you to get out from under the shadow of the particular result that you are dealt.
- Combining probabilities with preferences and payoffs helps you more clearly evaluate and compare options.
- A pros and cons list is flat. It lacks information about both the size of the payoffs and the probability of any pro or con occurring. Because of that, it is a low-quality decision tool for evaluating options and comparing them to one another.
- Most people are reluctant to estimate the likelihood of something happening in the future. ("That's speculative." "I don't know enough." "I'd just be guessing.")
- Even though your information is usually imperfect, you know *something* about most things, enough to make an **educated guess**.
- **The willingness to guess** is essential to improving decisions. If you don't make yourself guess, you'll be less likely to ask "What do I know?" and "What don't I know?"
- You can start **expressing probabilities by using common terms**. That gets you thinking about how often outcomes will occur, presents a view of relative likelihood, and gives you a snapshot of the overall likelihood of the best and worst outcomes.

THE THREE PS CHECKLIST

When evaluating a past decision or making a new decision, refer to the **Six Steps to Better Decision-Making**:

☐ **Step 1—Identify the reasonable set of possible outcomes.** These outcomes can be general scenarios or be focused on particular aspects of the outcomes that you especially care about.

☐ **Step 2—Identify your preference for each outcome—to what degree do you like or dislike each outcome, given your values?** These preferences will be driven by the payoffs associated with each outcome. Gains comprise the upside and losses comprise the downside. Include this information in your decision trees.

☐ **Step 3—Estimate the likelihood of each outcome unfolding.** As a start, use common terms that express probabilities. Don't be afraid to guess.

☐ **Step 4—Assess the relative likelihood of outcomes you like and dislike for the option under consideration.**

☐ **Step 5—Repeat Steps 1–4 for other options under consideration.**

☐ **Step 6—Compare the options to one another.**

Bovine Guessing

In 1906, British scientist Francis Galton watched eight hundred people buy tickets to guess the weight of a fat ox. After the contest, Galton collected the tickets, expecting to prove through this impromptu experiment that a collective guess would be far inferior to asking an expert.

What he found was that while an expert might be closer than most individual guesses, the guesses converged on the actual weight, and the *average* of all those guesses (1,197 pounds, slaughtered and dressed) was within one pound of the ox's actual weight!

In 2015, NPR's *Planet Money Podcast* conducted an online version of this experiment. They posted a picture of one of their correspondents (who weighed 165 pounds) standing next to a cow named Penelope and asked readers to guess the cow's weight. Over seventeen thousand people responded. They didn't come quite as close as the people at Galton's fair, but the average of guesses, 1,287 pounds, was pretty close to Penelope's actual weight of 1,355.

HOW MUCH DOES THIS COW WEIGH?

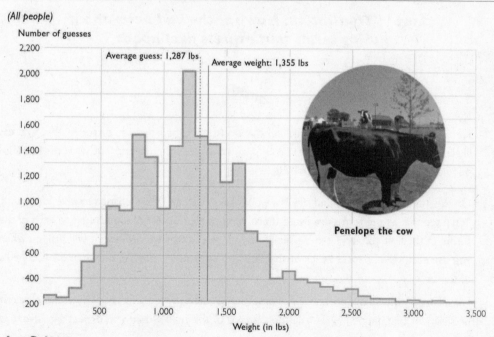

Penelope the cow

Source: The Internet
Credit: Quoctrung Bui/NPR

5

Taking Dead Aim at the Future: The Power of Precision

[1]

Lost in Translation: Now for the bad news about using terms that express likelihoods

Let's get back to Andrew and Michael Mauboussin's exhaustive list of terms that express likelihoods. They compiled that list so they could do a survey to find out what probabilities people have in mind when they use these terms.

On the next page, you will find the Mauboussins' survey and get a chance to take it yourself. You'll see that all the terms are listed there, next to four blank columns. Next to each of the terms, in the first column fill in the likelihood *you intend* that a future event will happen when you use each term. Express each probability as a percentage chance, between 0% and 100% of the time.

For example, what's the probability of an event occurring when you say, "I think there's a *real possibility* of that happening"? What percentage of the time would you expect that event to happen?

Some people aren't comfortable using probabilities expressed as percentages. After all, that's part of why people prefer using these natural language terms. If that applies to you, you may find it easier to ask yourself: "For me to use this term to describe the likelihood of an outcome occurring, how many times out of a hundred do I think that outcome would be the one that happens?"

For example, if you flipped a coin a hundred times, how many times out of a hundred do you think it would land heads—and what term would you use to describe that probability?

If Mike Trout came to the plate a hundred times, how many times out of a hundred would he get a hit—and what term would you use to describe that probability?

If you hit a first serve in tennis a hundred times, how many times out of a hundred do you think the serve would go in—and what term would you use to describe that probability?

If you passed by the breakroom at work a hundred times, how many times out of a hundred do you think you would eat a donut—and what term would you use to describe that probability?

If you started a business based on the Kingdom Comb app a hundred times, how many times out of a hundred do you think you'd be offered a multimillion-dollar buyout at an early stage—and what term would you use to describe that probability?

The number of times out of a hundred that you think an event will happen directly converts to a probability expressed as a percentage. If you think an event will happen 20 times out of a hundred, that converts to a 20% chance. If you think an event will happen 62 times out of a hundred, that converts to 62%. If you think it will occur 99 times out of a hundred, that converts to 99%.

So if you think something that's "super-duper likely" (not one of the terms in the survey) is going to happen 85 times out of 100, that means "super-duper likely" is the equivalent of an 85% chance. In that instance, if you said "I'm super-duper likely to eat a donut if I so much as pass by the breakroom at work," that would convert to 85 times out of 100, or an 85% chance that you'd be diving into those breakroom donuts.

After filling in your answers below, survey three other people.

It's important that no one taking the survey sees the answers from anyone else until they've completed it. Ask them the terms and record their answers, or carefully cover the already-filled-out columns.

	You	Person A	Person B	Person C
Frequently				
Almost certainly				
Often				
Not often				
Slam dunk				
With low probability				
Probably				
Almost always				
Usually				
Maybe				
Real possibility				
Likely				
With moderate probability				
More often than not				
With high probability				
Unlikely				
Certainly				
Always				
Never				
Serious possibility				
Rarely				
Might happen				
Possibly				

2 Compare the four sets of answers. How much agreement was there? (Circle one.)

    A lot   *A moderate amount*   *A little*   *Almost none*

3 Which terms had the biggest spreads between the lowest and highest probability?

_____

_____

4 Did you find the amount of disagreement to be surprising?   *YES*   *NO*

Land of confusion

I'm guessing that you discovered there was a lot of disagreement about what these terms mean. This is also what the Mauboussins found in their 1,700-person survey. The figure on the next page shows the range of probabilities people gave for each term across their sample. (The average response for each term is shown as a line inside the shaded, boxed area.)

You can clearly see the huge variation in what people have in mind when they use these terms.

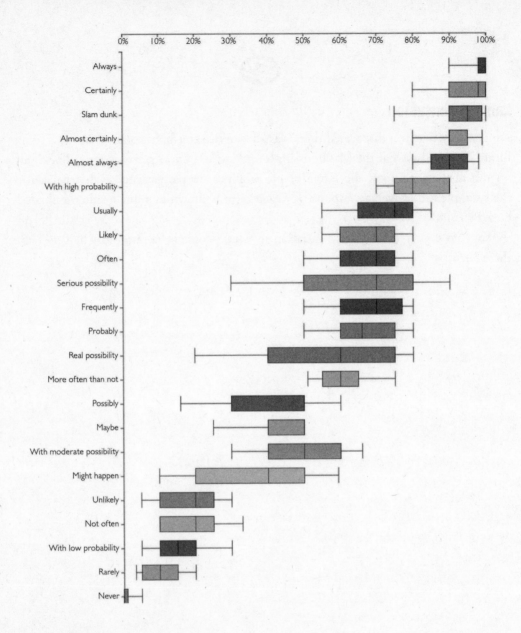

Some of these terms had startlingly wide ranges, which I imagine you experienced in your four-person survey. For instance, "real possibility" had a range of about 20% to 80%. A quarter of the people taking the survey thought the term meant 40% of the time or less. A quarter thought it meant 40% to 60%. A quarter thought it meant 60% to 75%. Finally, a quarter thought it meant over 75% of the time.

People didn't even agree on what the terms *always* and *never* meant!

If you're like most people, you were pretty surprised by these results. Most of us aren't aware of the wide range of what these words mean to different people. We assume that when we use a term, other people use it in the same way we do and mean the same thing we do.

This is especially true when we're using common terms.

This exercise shows that common terms really are blunt instruments to express probabilities. They are inherently ambiguous, reflecting a broad target area. Of course, this is part of why people like to use them. When you use an ambiguous term, you feel like you have a lot more leeway if you're worried about being "wrong." That leeway, however, comes at a steep price: others might interpret those terms differently.

A lot of the stuff you don't know lives in other people's heads

The mushiness of these terms creates a huge problem in executing on the goal of moving some of *the stuff you don't know* into *the stuff you know* category. This makes it harder to fix the cracks in the foundation of your decisions created by the inaccuracies in your beliefs, and makes it harder to strengthen that foundation by broadening your knowledge.

Because a lot of the stuff you don't know lives in other people's heads, getting feedback from other people about the things you believe and the decisions you make will be one of your best tools for extracting knowledge from the world. But when you use these terms in communicating with others, what you intend may be very different from what the other person hears. That's a huge problem, because to get high-fidelity feedback on your decisions and your beliefs, you have to speak the same language as the person who is offering you feedback.

> When you use these blunt terms, you and the other people in the conversation are often speaking different languages without even knowing it.

If you believe something has a 30% chance of happening and you're talking with someone who has reliable information that it has a 70% chance of happening, it is helpful to uncover that disagreement. You need the information that lives in their head to correct your belief. A failure to extract that information is a missed opportunity, and any decision based on your estimate will be lower quality as a result.

If you communicate what you mean with precision, using probabilities expressed as percentages, the disagreement is immediately revealed. If I say something has a

30% chance of happening and you say it has a 70% chance of happening, we know we disagree. There is no ambiguity.

But if instead I say, "This event has a real possibility of happening," the disagreement can remain concealed because you might not know that I think "a real possibility" means a 30% chance and I might not know that you think it means a 70% chance. Because we are speaking different languages, you might just nod in agreement and never offer me the valuable, corrective information in your possession. Because I used ambiguous language, I missed the chance to update and calibrate my belief.

And that's a huge missed opportunity.

Imagine the cumulative effect on the quality of your decision-making of all those missed opportunities over your lifetime.

Precision uncovers disagreement. It uncovers places where your belief is different from someone else's belief. And that's good, because you want to find out when you have something wrong. It gives you the chance to get it right.

Think about it like this: Saying "2 + 2 is a small number" will help you get better at math, but it won't help you become an expert. "A small number" is technically correct, but it is much more helpful for your teacher to find out if you think the answer is 5, or 2, or 4, which are all small numbers. It's true that the less precise answer makes it harder to be wrong, but you want to find out when you have the wrong answer if you are going to get better at math.

This imprecision also makes it harder for you to hold yourself accountable. The broader you allow the target area to be, the less likely you are to search for information that will help get you to a more precise answer. The leeway lets you off the hook not just with other people but also with yourself.

That's why precision matters.

There are lots of real-world examples of how the imprecision of terms for probability created disconnects with high-stakes consequences. Philip Tetlock offered this one in his 2015 book *Superforecasting: The Art and Science of Prediction.* When President Kennedy approved the CIA plan to overthrow Fidel Castro (known as the Bay of Pigs invasion), he asked his military advisers for their opinions about whether the attempt would succeed. The Joint Chiefs of Staff told Kennedy the CIA's plan had a "fair chance" of success (which the writer of the assessment considered to be 25%). Because Kennedy thought "fair chance" meant something much higher, he approved it. The plan was a failure, which looked clumsy and amateurish, and embarrassed the United States at a key moment in the Cold War.

[2]

Precision Matters: More clearly define the bull's-eye by making educated guesses

Of course, it's not that the use of words is worthless. Expressing likelihoods using these terms is a good place to start training yourself to think probabilistically. Working with these terms gets you thinking about the likelihood of an event occurring. It gets you to think about the likelihood of outcomes you prefer versus outcomes you don't like. It gives you a way to compare options. Most important, it starts the process of you asking yourself, "What do I know, and what more can I know?"

That's all good stuff.

But once you start this process, you'll want to move beyond using these terms because of the very thing that makes them so attractive: *the wiggle room they offer that makes it harder to be wrong.*

It may be scary to open yourself up to the precision and accountability of making a specific estimate, but it's well worth it to try. As any archer will tell you, the more you train your sights on that bull's-eye, the more likely you are to hit it (and the more likely you are to get closer and score more points). Yes, you're aiming at the target when you use those terms, but you're not really aiming at the *bull's-eye.*

Graduating from expressing likelihoods as natural language terms to expressing them as percentages is part of taking off that pin-the-tail-on-the-donkey blindfold.

Now for the good news: You already have a list that converts these terms for expressing probabilities into percentages.

What list?

The list you just created out of your answers to the Mauboussins' survey. If you're estimating the likelihood of a particular outcome occurring and one of those terms comes to mind, you can refer back to the list and instead of using that term you can use the probability expressed as a percentage that you mean when you use that term.

Let's do this conversion for the hiring decision from chapter 4. Recall that for this decision the most important aspect of the outcome was how long the candidate would remain with the company. Using the average responses to the Mauboussins' survey, this is what those same two trees would look like, substituting percentages for the natural language terms (the terms from the original trees are included just for reference):

Decision	Potential outcomes (stays with the company . . .)	Likelihood (terms)	Likelihood (%)
	. . . less than 6 months	Rarely	10%
	. . . 6 months to a year	With low probability	15%
Hire Candidate A	. . . a year to 2 years	Unlikely	20%
	. . . longer than 2 years	More often than not	55%

Decision	Potential outcomes (stays with the company . . .)	Likelihood (terms)	Likelihood (%)
	. . . less than 6 months	Possibly	35%
	. . . 6 months to a year	Might happen	40%
Hire Candidate B	. . . a year to 2 years	Rarely	10%
	. . . longer than 2 years	With low probability	15%

You can see how converting terms to percentages clarifies the estimates. This precision particularly helps with Step 6, comparing the options to each other. Expressing likelihoods in this way makes the answer clear: Based on these estimates, Candidate A is more likely to stay with the company longer.

1 Make a similar conversion from natural language terms to probabilities expressed as percentages for the estimates you used in the earlier decision tree about joining Sweat Sensations.

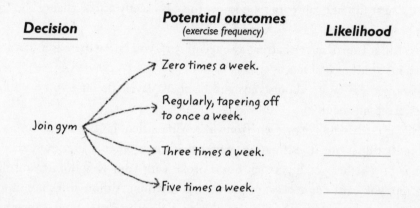

Decision	Potential outcomes (exercise frequency)	Likelihood
	Zero times a week.	_____
Join gym	Regularly, tapering off to once a week.	_____
	Three times a week.	_____
	Five times a week.	_____

2 Did the probabilities add up to a sum over 100%? *Because these outcomes are exclusive of one another,* you should adjust the probabilities to make sure they don't. The total of the potential likelihoods doesn't have to total to *exactly* 100% because the set of possible outcomes is not exhaustive—*you're focusing on reasonable outcomes and not attempting to account for every possibility.*

Sure, there's a minute chance of an asteroid hitting Boston, or you winning the lottery and not having to work ever again, or you joining an underground political movement and becoming mayor of New Boston after Massachusetts secedes from the United States. But those types of outcomes don't really fit into the "reasonable" category, so it's not generally useful to include them in your decision-making process.

Because the list of possibilities shouldn't be exhaustive, the probabilities can total less than 100%. But by the same token, the probabilities of outcomes that are exclusive of one another also can't add up to more than 100%.

[3]

At Home on the Range

When you have perfect (or near-perfect) information, you can know the exact probability. You know precisely where the bull's-eye is and that you'll hit it.

On the next flip of a fair coin, you know there is exactly a 50% chance the coin will land on heads.

Given Mike Trout's career batting average of .305, you know there is a 30.5% chance he'll get a hit at his next at bat.

You know these things about coins and baseball players because you have so much information about them.

But life is rarely coinlike or even Trout-like. More often, it's bisonlike.

For most things you're estimating, whether it's how often you'll exercise at Sweat Sensations or whether you'll get rich or go broke with your Kingdom Comb haircut-sharing app, you can't come close to perfect information. Although it's useful to make your estimates as precise as possible, it's also crucial to be clear about—to others and yourself—how much "educated" there is in your "educated guess."

You want to be explicit about how uncertain your belief is.

A convenient way to express where you are on the continuum from no information and perfect information is to offer, *along with* your exact (bull's-eye) estimate, a range around that estimate. That range communicates the size of your target area by giving the lowest reasonable value you think the answer could be (***the lower bound***) and the highest reasonable value you think it could be (***the upper bound***).

If I were to do this for the bison's weight, my bull's-eye estimate would be 1,800 pounds. My *lower bound* would be 1,100 pounds. My *upper bound* would be 3,500 pounds. That range is wide because my knowledge of that particular bison's weight—or the weight of bison in general—isn't great. Even so, that range eliminates a lot of possibilities because I do know a lot about the weights of things in general.

If you're estimating your commute time on any given day and you live in a small town with little traffic congestion, construction, or weather issues, your estimates of your slowest and fastest commute times won't be very far apart.

If your small town is Snowmass Village, Colorado, however, seasonal traffic and winter weather can turn a quick, scenic drive into a crowded stop-and-go adventure on treacherous, icy mountain roads. That means the difference between your upper and lower bound in estimating your commute time will be narrower in the summer, when weather is easier to predict and there are fewer tourists, than in the winter, when there is more uncertainty about the driving conditions.

If your daily commute involves highway driving in Los Angeles, your range will be a lot wider. A drive in LA that takes fifteen minutes with no traffic can take hours if traffic is heavy, so the distance between your upper and lower bound would reflect that.

Having a wide range is not a bad thing. Rather, it is a way to reflect as accurately as possible how much *educated* there is in your educated guess. A wider range that is true to what you do and don't know is more helpful than a narrower range that oversells your certainty.

A wide range sends a signal, to others and yourself, about how much uncertainty you have. That should activate your decision-making superpower, which is to find out information that might help you narrow that range.

Signaling your uncertainty improves the chances you'll get exposed to new information (especially information that disagrees with you) in two important ways:

> The range around your bull's-eye estimate defines the size of your target area and serves a key purpose: it signals, to yourself and others, how uncertain you are of your guess. It reveals where you sit on the continuum between *no knowledge* and *perfect knowledge*.
>
> The further you are from perfect information, the larger the target you're defining. The closer you are to having perfect information, the smaller the target you're defining. On the rare occasions when you have perfect information and no uncertainty, your target will be all bull's-eye.

1. When you express a false sense of certainty—which you can do, albeit unintentionally, if you share only your bull's-eye estimate—others are much less likely to shore up the cracks in the foundation of your decisions by offering you *corrective information* about your beliefs. This can happen either because they think *they're* wrong and don't want to embarrass themselves by sharing what they think, or they may think you're wrong and they're worried about embarrassing you. *This is particularly problematic if you're in a leadership role.*

2. Offering a range around your estimate implies a question to the listener: *Can you help me with this?* When you create an upper and lower bound, you express that you're sitting somewhere between no knowledge and perfect knowledge. Letting the listener know that you're unsure makes them more likely to share helpful information and perspectives *because you have asked them for help.*

When you express probabilities as percentages and offer a reasonable range around those probability estimates, you maximize your exposure to the universe of *stuff you don't know*. That increases the chance that you uncover corrective information that will help you repair inaccuracies in your beliefs and improve the quality of your decisions.

The Shock Test

In setting these ranges, your goal is to think about the lowest and highest *reasonable* values for whatever you are estimating. But what does *reasonable* mean?

What reasonable *does not* mean is creating a range that is *guaranteed* to include the correct answer within the upper and lower bound. That range simply wouldn't be informative.

What's the weight of the bison? I could guarantee my range would include the actual answer if I said "Zero to infinity pounds."

What's the probability of Mike Trout getting a hit on his next at bat? "Zero to one hundred percent." Another guaranteed winner.

My range for what 2 + 2 equals? I wouldn't mess around by narrowing it down to "a small number." I'd guarantee that I captured the actual answer by saying, "Negative infinity to positive infinity."

Yay, three for three correct, right?

Not so much, because those ranges don't accurately reflect both the stuff I know *and* the stuff I don't know. I mean, I obviously know that 2 + 2 does not equal infinity.

You almost always know *something* and the range you set should reflect that. A range that ensures the objectively true answer always falls within the upper and lower bound oversells a lack of knowledge. Likewise, an overly narrow range oversells what you *do* know.

You're aiming for the sweet spot between too wide and too narrow, a range that accurately reflects the things you know balanced against the things you don't know.

That is what *reasonable* means.

> **The goal is to set the narrowest range you can, where you would still be *pretty shocked* if the bull's-eye wasn't in the range.**

Wharton professor Abraham Wyner suggests that a good way to get to a reasonable upper and lower bound is to ask yourself, *"Would I be pretty shocked if the answer fell outside this range?"* If you use that as your standard, your range will naturally reflect how much *educated* there is in your educated guess.

"Pretty shocked" strikes a good balance between being overly exact (when you're actually pretty uncertain) and having a range that's so comfortably wide that the answer never falls outside the boundaries.

1 Practice taking the shock test.

For each of the ten items below and on the next page, give your best bull's-eye estimate (your best educated guess if you were forced to guess an exact value) and set a range around that exact estimate representing the lowest and highest possible values you think the correct answer could be.

Remember, the goal is to set the narrowest range where you would be pretty shocked if the correct answer did not fall within that range.

One way to think about being "pretty shocked" is to shoot for capturing the correct answer within your upper and lower bound for nine out of the ten items. Notice that I did not say you are shooting for *at least nine* correct answers in your range. That would mean that getting all ten right would be part of the goal, which would encourage you to set ranges that are overly broad. It means that for each answer you are shooting for a 90% chance of capturing the correct answer.

Shooting for nine out of ten is a good rule of thumb for getting to that sweet spot between too broad and too narrow.

It's important to also remember that, to the extent you're at a different place on the continuum between no knowledge and perfect knowledge for different subjects, the distance between your upper and lower bound should reflect that. For example, if you don't know much about Meryl Streep but you know a great deal about Prince, you would likely have a broader range for item B below than for item C.

	Bull's-eye Estimate	Lower Bound	Upper Bound
a. The current population of the town in which you were born			
b. Meryl Streep's number of Academy Award nominations			
c. Prince's age at his death			
d. The first year Nobel Prizes were awarded			
e. The number of teams in the National Football League			

	Bull's-eye Estimate	Lower Bound	Upper Bound
f. The probability that a person in the U.S. lives in a city with a population above 1 million			
g. The number of people who voted for Abraham Lincoln in the 1860 presidential election			
h. The height of the tip of the Statue of Liberty			
i. The number of Billboard No. 1 singles by the Beatles			
j. The probability that the cause of death of an average adult in the United States will be heart disease			

Turn to page 121 for the answers.

2 How many of your ranges (out of the ten) included the correct answer? _____

3 Do you feel like you did a pretty good job of applying the shock test?   YES   NO

4 If yes, why?

_____

_____

If no, why not?

_____

_____

5 Which answer did you feel most certain of?

_____

Why?

_____

_____

Did the range you set reflect that?   YES   NO

Did that range include the actual answer?   YES   NO

6 Which answer did you feel least certain of?

_____

Why?

_____

_____

Did the range you set reflect that?   YES   NO

Did that range include the actual answer?   YES   NO

IF YOU'RE LIKE MOST PEOPLE, you were probably surprised by how many of your ranges didn't include the correct answer. If you missed the correct answer with just one or two of your responses, kudos to you. Most people who take this kind of test don't score more than 50%.

What this shows is that we're generally overselling our knowledge rather than underselling it. We're usually much more certain of our guesses than the accuracy of our beliefs warrant.

Hopefully, this exercise and the shock test have shown you a better approach to these kinds of estimates. It works to your benefit to assume that you may not know as much as you think you do, that your beliefs may not be as accurate as you think they are, and that you may need more help from others than you think you do.

> Similar to how you tried out how others interpret probability terms in section I, try this exercise with three friends and see how well they do on the test. You'll see that people are pretty bad at passing the shock test.

Approach the quality of the stuff you think you know with more skepticism. That skepticism will make you more willing to question your own beliefs and more eager to seek out what other people know. And that will improve the quality of your decisions.

1 Take one of the decision trees you've already developed in this book and give your bull's-eye estimate for the likelihood of each of the potential outcomes and include a lower and upper bound around each bull's-eye estimate.

Decision	Potential outcomes	Likelihood	Lower bound	Upper bound

2 For the outcomes that had the widest ranges, what information could you seek out that would help you narrow down those ranges?

_____

_____

_____

_____

3 For the outcomes that had the narrowest ranges, what information could you seek out that would help you figure out if the range reflected overconfidence on your part?

_____

_____

_____

_____

4 Pick one of the outcomes. Imagine that you somehow discovered that the actual likelihood of that outcome occurring wasn't contained in your range. What do you think the reason(s) for that would be?

_____

_____

_____

_____

THE TENDENCY TOWARD OVERCONFIDENCE vexes decision-making.

In general, we don't question our own beliefs enough. We have too much confidence in what we think we know and we don't have a realistic view of what we don't know. Whether it's about the things we believe to be true, our opinions, or how we think the future might unfold, we could all use a healthy dose of skepticism.

Making it a habit to ask yourself, "If I were wrong, why would that be?" helps get you to approach your own beliefs with more skepticism, disciplining your naturally overly optimistic view of what you know and getting you more focused on what you don't know.

Asking yourself why you might be wrong will also increase the accuracy of the things you believe, the opinions you hold, and how you think the future might unfold. That's because when you ask yourself what information you could discover that would make you change your mind, _you can actually go find out some of that stuff._ And in asking and answering the question, you are just more likely to go look for it.

Even when the information that would change your mind isn't readily available, it might be available in the future. Doing the advance work of thinking about the things that might change your mind increases the chances that you'll both be on the lookout for that corrective information in the future _and that you'll be open-minded to it when you come across it._

1 For each of the reasons you gave in your answer to question 4 in the exercise above, ask yourself if you could go find out that information right now. If so, go find it.

2 Did going through the process of asking yourself why you might be wrong cause you to re-calibrate any of your beliefs? Reflect on that here.

_____

_____

_____

_____

[4]

Taking Dead Aim Wrap-up

These exercises were designed to get you to think about the following concepts:

- Natural language terms that express likelihoods, like "very likely" and "unlikely," are useful but blunt instruments.
- The drive to improve on your initial estimates is **what motivates you to check your information and learn more**. If you hide behind the safety of a general term, there's no reason to improve on it or calibrate.
- Terms that express likelihoods mean very different things to different people.
- Using **ambiguous terms** can lead to confusion and miscommunication with people you want to engage for help.
- Being more precise, by **expressing probabilities as percentages**, makes it more likely you'll uncover information that can correct inaccuracies in your beliefs and broaden your knowledge.
- You can use your answers to the Mauboussins' survey to help you convert natural language terms to exact probabilities.
- In addition to making **precise (bull's-eye) estimates**, offer a range around that estimate to express your uncertainty. Do this by including a **lower and upper bound** that communicate the size of your target.
- The **size of the range** signals what you know and what you don't know. The larger the range, the less information or the lower the quality of the information informing your estimate, and the more you need to learn.
- Communicating the size of the range also signals to others that you need their knowledge and perspective to narrow the range.
- Use the **shock test** to determine if your upper and lower bounds are reasonable: Would you be really shocked if the correct answer was outside that boundary? Your goal should be to have approximately 90% of your estimates capture the objectively true value.
- Develop a habit of asking yourself, "What information could I find out that would tell me that my estimate or my belief is wrong?"

TAKING DEAD AIM CHECKLIST

Improve your estimates by taking dead aim in the following ways:

☐ Take the Mauboussins' survey on the meaning of common terms for probability.

☐ If you are uncomfortable making specific estimates, use the term that comes to mind and convert it to a specific bull's-eye estimate by referring to your answers from the survey.

☐ In addition, make a target estimate, comprising a range of the reasonable upper and lower bounds.

☐ Test the reasonableness of your upper and lower bounds with the shock test.

☐ Ask yourself, "What information could I discover that would make me change my mind?"

☐ If the information is available, go find it.

☐ If it isn't, keep an eye out for it in the future.

Taxed by Imprecision

Members of some communities have recognized the problems caused by using inexact terms. As a result, they have agreed that in their professional communications certain terms have exact meanings that they agree upon. For example, when attorneys provide tax opinions, an opinion that a tax position "will be" sustained means a likelihood of 90–95%. Written tax advice that says a position "should be" sustained means 70–75% probability. "More likely than not" means above 50%. "Substantial authority" for an opinion means 34–40%. "Realistic possibility" means 33%. "Reasonable basis" means 20–30%.

Tax opinions frequently involve high stakes for the client as well as the attorney. Such opinions can be the basis for a taxpayer taking an uncertain position. Clients need to know how much risk they are taking if their position is not upheld. It can also affect whether the taxpayer is also responsible for additional penalties if ultimately ruled incorrect. For the attorney issuing the opinion, there is a risk of malpractice for misleading the client.

We should strive to do the same thing. Predicting outcomes is uncertain in the same way as an attorney's written opinion on the allowability of a deduction in a complex financial transaction. Like tax attorneys, we should recognize the uncertainty, make sure anyone else involved recognizes it, and meet it head-on by being as precise as possible.

ANSWERS:

a. You'll have to look that up yourself!

b. Ms. Streep has been nominated for twenty-one Academy Awards.

c. Prince Rogers Nelson was fifty-seven at the time of his death on April 21, 2016.

d. The first Nobel Prizes were awarded in 1901.

e. The NFL has thirty-two teams.

f. There is approximately an 8% chance that a person in the United States lives in a city with over 1 million people.

g. 1,865,908 people voted for Abraham Lincoln in 1860.

h. The Statue of Liberty is 305 feet high.

i. The Beatles topped the Billboard chart with twenty songs.

j. One in four American adults dies of heart disease, so 25%.

6

Turning Decisions Outside In

[1]

Relationship Chernobyl

You have a close, long-time friend who considers you their go-to for recounting their relationship woes. Whether they're meeting people through online dating, singles groups, or random meetups, everyone they date seems to be a weirdo or a jerk. You've lost track of the hours you've spent listening to your friend bemoaning their bad luck.

On the rare occasion when your friend declares, "Miracle of miracles, I found the last normal person on earth," the relationship inevitably meets a prolonged, messy end. "They turned out to be one of the worst ever. They were just good at concealing it, like a chameleon."

The next time you get together with them, they tell you their latest relationship tale.

"Do you remember Jordan, who got deployed to the Middle East and thought it would be better if we broke up? Get this: It was a lie. Yesterday, I saw Jordan buying socks at Target."

"I've given up on dating," they tell you for the umpteenth time. "I'm going to start looking for an exorcist instead, because I must be cursed."

Circle any of the items below that you are likely to be thinking to yourself during this conversation (but not necessarily saying out loud).

"Seems to me you might be picking jerks."

"Your luck is bound to turn around. I know you're going to meet the right person."

"Is there something about the way you behave in relationships that might bring out the jerkiness in your partners?"

"Wow, you have the worst luck in relationships!"

"Is it possible you're getting something out of all this drama?"

"Is there something about you that attracts people who turn out to be jerks?"

I Circle any of the items below that you are likely to say out loud to your friend.

"Seems to me you might be picking jerks."

"Your luck is bound to turn around. I know you're going to meet the right person."

"Is there something about the way you behave in relationships that might bring out the jerkiness in your partners?"

"Wow, you have the worst luck in relationships!"

"Is it possible you're getting something out of all this drama?"

"Is there something about you that attracts people who turn out to be jerks?"

2 If the items you circled that you would say out loud to your friend are different from the items you would think to yourself, why do you think that is?

_____

_____

_____

_____

3 In general, are you better at solving other people's problems than you are at solving your own?　　　　YES　·　NO

If you answered yes, why do you think that is?

_____

_____

_____

_____

IF YOU'RE LIKE MOST PEOPLE, you were probably thinking that it's not just bad luck that your friend has dated a string of jerks. Most people realize that if someone has a pattern in the people they date (or the jobs they take or how they get along with their friends or are always running into traffic that makes them late to work, etc.), that pattern is probably not just bad luck or a weird coincidence or an actual curse.

You can see what your friend seems unable to see, that there is likely something about your friend's approach to dating that is causing this string of jerks to show up. If your friend could just realize this, they might be able to do something about it.

As an outside observer, you can see this clearly when you are in the "friend" position. But your vision becomes muddied when you are on the inside and it's your problem. What you can see so clearly in others is hard to see in yourself. That's why almost everybody feels like they are better at solving other people's problems than their own.

Your perspective isn't so good when you are at the center of it.

(As for whether you'd _tell_ your friend they weren't necessarily 100% blameless victims of bad luck, we will return to that near the end of the chapter.)

[2]

The Inside View vs. the Outside View

What is hopefully (crystal ball) clear by now is that your beliefs create a *bottleneck* to good decision-making. It doesn't matter how good the quality of your decision process is if the input into that process is junk.

That input is your beliefs, and there is a lot of junk in there.

The shock test showed that we are pretty bad at figuring out what we don't know. We're pretty bad at figuring out when our beliefs are inaccurate. We have too much confidence in what we think we know.

One reason for these weaknesses is that it's very hard for us to see the world from outside our own perspective.

It's like you have a KICK ME sign on your back when it comes to identifying inaccuracies in what you know and believe. You can't see the sign because your eyes can see only what's in front of you. No matter how fast you spin around, you just can't see yourself from the back. Someone keeps kicking you, it's getting irritating, and you can't figure out why, even though you can clearly see the KICK ME signs on everybody else.

Inside view

We all naturally see the world through the lens of our own specific circumstances, from inside of our own beliefs and the experiences that are particular to each of us. It's hard for anyone to get outside of their own head to understand how someone else would view their situation.

How could it be otherwise? You've only had the experiences that you have had. You've only been exposed to the information that you have been exposed to. You've only lived the life that you have lived.

You're *not* somebody else. You're you.

You are trapped in the ***inside view*** and that makes it hard to see your own beliefs, opinions, and experiences objectively. It makes it hard to see that KICK ME sign on your back.

Resulting is a good example of an inside view problem. The outcomes *that you happen to observe* cast a shadow over your ability to see those outcomes in the context of all the things that objectively could have happened. This affects the quality of the lessons you learn. If you experienced a different outcome, you would learn a different lesson. If you experienced a different outcome, you would assess the quality of the decision that preceded the outcome differently.

> **INSIDE VIEW**
> The view of the world from inside of your own perspective, your own experiences, and your own beliefs.

The luck in the way the future happens to unfold *for you* plays an outsized role. It matters little how objectively likely or unlikely an outcome is. What matters most is that you happen to have experienced it.

Here are some other commonly known cognitive biases that are also, in part, inside view problems:

- *Confirmation bias*—Our tendency to notice, interpret, and seek out information that confirms or strengthens our existing beliefs.

- *Disconfirmation bias*—Confirmation bias's sibling. Our tendency to apply a higher, more critical standard to information that contradicts our beliefs than to information that confirms them.
- *Overconfidence*—Overestimating our skills, intellect, or talent, interfering with our ability to make decisions depending on such estimates.
- *Availability bias*—The tendency to overestimate the frequency of events that are easy to recall because they are vivid or because we've experienced them a lot.
- *Recency bias*—Believing that recent events are more likely to occur than they actually are.
- *Illusion of control*—Overestimating our ability to control events. In other words, to underestimate the influence of luck.

You can see how all these biases are products, in part, of the inside view.

Confirmation bias means that you notice and seek out information that conforms to what *you already believe*.

Disconfirmation bias means that you apply a higher standard when evaluating information that contradicts *your beliefs*. You ask "*Could* this be true?" of information that agrees with what you already believe, but ask "*Must* this be true?" of information that disagrees with you.

Availability bias means that events that are easy *for you* to recall distort your estimates of their likelihood.

The other biases, similarly, are ways you give your own experiences and beliefs disproportionate weight.

Outside view

We naturally make decisions from inside our own perspective. Often, however, the world looks very different from the outside. We've all experienced this when we're with someone who is struggling with their distorted perspective and unable to recognize it. It's like the friend who can't recognize their own part in their disastrous dating history and thinks the best solution to their latest relationship problem is to look for an exorcist.

You know you can see their situation accurately, while they are clueless. You can see *their* KICK ME sign.

I'm betting that lots of examples come to mind of interactions you've had with someone who's trapped in the inside view. If those examples flow so easily, it stands to reason that you're doing it too.

Part of why it's easier to see other people more objectively than you can see yourself is that you are motivated to protect your beliefs when it comes to reasoning about your own situation. Your beliefs form the fabric of your identity. Discovering that you're wrong about something, questioning your beliefs, or admitting that some bad outcome was because of a bad decision you made and not just bad luck—these all have the potential to tear that fabric.

We are all motivated to keep that fabric intact. When it comes to your own reasoning, your beliefs end up in the driver's seat steering you toward a narrative that protects your identity and self-narrative. (I'm not the jerk! They are!)

You aren't motivated in the same way when reasoning about other people's problems because you aren't endowed with other people's beliefs the way you are endowed with your own.

What you've probably figured out by now is that the remedy for the inside view is to open yourself up as much as possible to other people's perspectives and what's true of the world in general, independent of your own experiences, because that's where the corrective information lives.

> **OUTSIDE VIEW**
> What is true of the world, independent of your own perspective. The way that others would view the situation you're in.

That's the *outside view*.

Your intuition serves at the pleasure of the inside view. Your gut does too. Intuition and gut are infected by what you *want* to be true.

The outside view is the antidote for that infection.

The value of getting other people's perspectives is not just that they know facts that you don't know that might be helpful to you. It is not just that they might be able to correct inaccuracies in the facts you think you know. *It is that even if they had the exact same facts as you, they might view those facts differently.* They might come to a very different conclusion given the exact same information.

Just like when you and your friend have the same facts about their dating history, but you see their situation in a different light.

Allowing those perspectives to collide, by embracing ways in which other people see things differently, will get you closer to what is objectively true. And the closer you can get to what is objectively true, the less junk you will input into your decision process.

You'll be more likely to spot that KICK ME sign from the outside view.

When we approach a decision, we have already started to form an opinion about what the right option is. Usually we don't even know we have already formed an opinion, but that opinion can, nonetheless, end up in the driver's seat, directing our decision process.

This exposes the biggest issue with a pros and cons list: Like your intuition and gut, it also serves at the pleasure of the inside view, getting you to the decision you want to make rather than the decision that is objectively better.

Want to reject an option? You'll focus on the con side of the list, expanding that side of the comparision. Want to move forward with an option? You'll focus and expand on the pro side of the list as the cons hide in the shadows.

A pros and cons list is generated entirely from your perspective, absent the outside view, easily infected by reasoning in a way that is motivated to support a conclusion you want to get to. In fact, if you wanted to create a decision tool to *amplify* bias, it would look like a pros and cons list.

[3]

How to Be the Least Popular Guest at a Wedding

Here is a good way to think about the inside view and the outside view:

You're at a wedding, waiting your turn in the receiving line for your first interaction with the altar-fresh, newly married couple.

By the time it's your turn, you feel the newlyweds have already received their quota of tears of joy, kisses, over-the-top well wishes, and inspirational and/or sage and/or biblical advice. Instead of giving them more of that, you cut to the chase and ask, "What do you guys think the chances are your marriage will end in divorce?"

(To be clear, I'm absolutely not suggesting that you try this. But it makes for a vivid, if somewhat cynical, thought experiment.)

One would assume that most couples would answer somewhere around a 0% chance. "We're special. We're getting married for all the right reasons. This is true love. Our love will endure forever."

That's the inside view.

At about this time, somebody bumps into you from behind. It's the father of the bride, who has overheard your question and is not at all amused. He asks you to leave.

To kill time, you crash another wedding reception going on at the same hotel and accidentally step into the receiving line.

Stuck for small talk, you vow not to repeat the same mistake you just made. You compliment the couple on the wonderful reception by saying, "I ducked my head into the reception down the hall and it wasn't nearly as nice. By the way, what do you think the chances are that *that couple* ends up divorced?"

Most likely, their answer will be somewhere between 40% and 50%, because that's what's true of couples in general. They're certainly not going to say of the strangers in the adjacent ballroom, "They're special. They must be getting married for all the right reasons. Their true love will endure forever."

That's the outside view.

1 Describe a past situation in which a friend or family member or someone in a work situation was caught in the inside view.

_____

_____

_____

_____

2 Did you let them know?   YES   NO

3 Why or why not?

_____

_____

_____

4 Describe a past situation in which you feel like _you_ got caught in the inside view.

_____

_____

_____

_____

5 In what ways did being caught in the inside view negatively affect your decision-making?

_____

_____

_____

_____

_____

6 Take some time over the next few days to listen for people being trapped in the inside view. Note some examples and your overall impression based on spending some time listening for the prevalence and influence of the inside view.

_____

_____

_____

_____

_____

_____

_____

_____

_____

_____

_____

[4]

A Truly Happy Marriage:
The union of the inside view and the outside view

- More than 90% of professors rate themselves as better-than-average teachers.
- About 90% of Americans rate their driving ability as better than average.
- Only 1% of students think their social skills are below average.

Obviously, it's impossible for over 90% of the population to be better than average at something. Yet even though we know that half the population must be, by definition, below average (the outside view), we seem to rarely think that we could be part of that half (the inside view).

This phenomenon is called the better-than-average effect.

Here's the problem: If you don't have a clear view of your skill level, you can make some pretty bad decisions. Like texting while driving because you think you are a better than average multitasker.

Of course, you are certainly better than average at many things. You can't, however, be better than average at *everything*.

The issue is that it's very hard, because you're living inside your own experience without access to a poll of the whole population, for you to know which things you're better than average at and which you aren't.

That's where getting to the outside view would be very helpful.

If you had a crystal ball that would give you perfect knowledge of the world, you would know exactly where you sit relative to the population distribution for any particular skill. You would know, for instance, that you were in the 75th percentile in driving skills or the 50th percentile in social skills or the 25th percentile in teaching skills.

Accuracy lives in the intersection of the outside view and the inside view.

We tend to rely on the inside view, our own experience and perspective, for those judgments. "I haven't gotten in an accident in twenty years, so I'm sure I'm a better-than-average driver." Or, "My friends seem to like me and we get along well, so I must be above average in social skills." Or, "My students seem to like me and I really enjoy teaching, so I must be at the top in teaching ability."

The outside view disciplines the distortions that live in the inside view. That's why it's important to start with the outside view and anchor there, considering things like what's true of the world in general or the way someone else would view your situation.

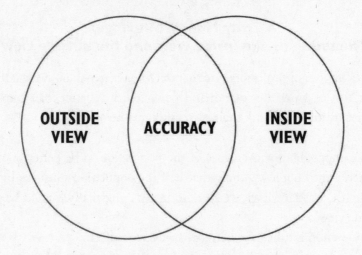

A successful marriage between the outside view and the inside view, like any union, takes work. Because your beliefs form the fabric of your identity and much of the way you think about the world is motivated by the desire to keep that fabric intact, it's very hard to incorporate the outside view—especially when that view threatens to tear a hole in the fabric.

That's part of why nearly 50% of marriages will end in divorce but only 5% of couples have prenuptial agreements.

What's true of marriages in general is hard to incorporate into your decision-making because it conflicts with what you want to be true, that your love is better than average. It is uncomfortable to think about the possibility of failure, but it's worth it to live in that discomfort because you will be better prepared if things don't turn out according to your ideal.

Marrying the outside and inside view gives you a clearer view of yourself, how you ended up where you are, and what the future might hold for you. That will improve the quality of what you learn from the past and the quality of the decisions you make going forward.

Being smart makes it worse

Here's the good news: Now you know about how the inside view can lead your decision-making astray. Here's more good news: I'm guessing that if you picked up this book, you're smart.

Now for the bad news: Being smart doesn't make you less susceptible to the inside view. If anything, it makes it worse. It straps your beliefs into the driver's seat more firmly.

Research across a variety of settings has shown that being smart makes you better at *motivated reasoning*, the tendency to reason about information to confirm your prior beliefs and arrive at the conclusion you desire. And just to be clear, in this case "better" is not a good thing.

- If you're interpreting data on a politically charged subject such as gun control, everyone is more likely to interpret data that contradicts their prior beliefs as actually supporting their view. But, counterintuitively, being better at accurately interpreting data in general (about nonpolarizing topics) doesn't protect you from misreading data to fit your prior beliefs about a political topic. In fact, it makes it more likely that you'll do that.
- When it comes to our own biases, we all have a blind spot. We can't see when our reasoning is biased in the same way we can see it in others. That's part of the inside view. Being smart doesn't protect you from your blind spot. It makes it worse.
- If you're trying to solve logic problems about subjects involving your political beliefs, everyone is likely to come to a conclusion consistent with their beliefs when the correct answer disagrees with those beliefs. But if you have prior experience or training in logic, you're more likely to make this error.

If you think about it, this makes a lot of sense. Smart people often think more highly of their beliefs and opinions. They are less likely to think the stuff they know needs correcting. They have more confidence in what their intuition or gut tells them. *After all, they're really smart.* Why wouldn't they have more confidence in those things? When you're smart, you're naturally less skeptical about the things you believe to be true.

Smart people are also better at constructing convincing arguments that support their views and reinforce the things they believe to be true. Smart people are better at spinning narratives that convince other people that they are right, not in the service of misleading those people but in the service of keeping the fabric of their own identity from tearing.

The combination of motivated reasoning, the propensity to mislead yourself, and an overconfidence in intuition makes smart people less likely to seek feedback. When they do seek feedback, their ability to spin a persuasive narrative makes other people less likely to challenge them.

That means that the smarter you are, the more vigilant you have to be about getting to the outside view.

> **The person you're most likely to mislead is yourself. And you don't know you're doing it, because you're living in the inside view.**

Base rates: An easy way to get the outside view

One way to get to the outside view is to make it a habit, as part of your decision process, to ask yourself what is true of the world in general, independent of anyone's point of view.

A helpful way to get an idea of what's true of the world in general is to find out if there is information available about the likelihood of different outcomes in situations similar to yours.

That information is called a ***base rate***.

There are plenty of places to get surveys, studies, and statistics on aspects of relationships, health, investing, business, education, employment, and consumerism that would likely be relevant to any type of decision you might be making. In fact, we've already referenced a bunch of base rates in this book. Here are just a few of them:

- The divorce rate in America is between 40% and 50% for first marriages.
- The likelihood that the cause of death for an American adult will be heart disease is 25%.
- Eight percent of the American population lives in a city with a population over 1 million.

Here are a few other examples of base rates:

- The likelihood a high school graduate will attend college without taking any time off is 63.1%.
- Sixty percent of new restaurants fail within the first year.

A base rate gives you a place to start when you are trying to estimate the likelihood of any outcome (or the upside and downside potential). It is not that your estimate should always be identical to the base rate. As should be clear by now, the particulars of your situation, the inside view, do matter. But if you're thinking of starting a restaurant and you estimate the probability of success at 90%, knowing that only 40% of new restaurants make it past the first year is going to help discipline your overconfidence.

Whatever your forecast of the future is, it needs to be in the orbit of the base rate. A base rate gives you a center of gravity.

> **BASE RATE**
> How likely something is to happen in situations similar to the one you're considering.

1 Go back to the estimates you made about the Sweat Sensations gym membership decision in chapter 4. Now take a few minutes to look up the following base rates and write your answers here:

What percentage of people who join a gym quit within the first half year? _____%

What percentage of gym memberships go completely unused? _____%

What percentage of gym members go to the gym once a week or less? _____%

If there was anything else you found in a few minutes of online searching relevant to the likelihood that joining a gym will lead to someone exercising regularly, note that here.

_____

_____

_____

2 Looking back at the tree with this base-rate information in mind, does that information change any of your estimates? If so, briefly explain why.

_____

_____

_____

HERE ARE SOME EXAMPLES of available information on base rates related to gym membership:

Zachary Crockett of TheHustle.co in January 2019 cited a survey from the Statistic Brain Research Institute that found that 82% of gym members go once a week or less. Of those 82% of members going to the gym once a week or less, 77% of those memberships went completely unused.

Eighty percent of gym members who join in January—prime New Year's resolution folks—quit within five months (according to CouponCabin). Half of all new gym members quit going within six months, according to the global trade association of the fitness industry, the International Health, Racquet & Sportsclub Association (IHRSA).

As you're thinking about your doctor's orders and imagining that there's a 90% chance that you'll go to the gym three times a week, these statistics suggest strongly that you should adjust your prediction. No matter how much motivation you think you have, it would be rare that the likelihood you'll stick with it would be that far off the base rate.

Educating yourself about what is true of most people in your situation will give you a glimpse into the outside view that will improve your ability to compare options (such as buying in-home equipment, joining a gym, or doing something else).

When you learn that you're planning on doing something that the base rates tell you is difficult, a realistic view of what the future might have in store for you will encourage you to identify the obstacles that stand in the way for most people. That advance warning gives you the opportunity to develop ways of avoiding or surmounting those obstacles so you can increase your chances of success.

Another way to the outside view: Actively find out what other people know

To paraphrase Tennessee Williams's character Blanche DuBois, we all have to depend on the kindness of strangers. When it comes to the outside view, there's no shortage of strangers to help us, but they're confused about what being kind means.

Have you ever had this happen to you?

Someone points out to you that you have a sizable piece of spinach caught in your teeth. When they bring it to your attention, they start off by apologizing for saying anything. It's clear they're embarrassed and reluctant to tell you because they think you're going to be embarrassed by the news.

As you thank them and remove the spinach, you take a mental inventory. "When did I eat that spinach?" You realize it was long enough ago that a bunch of people must have noticed the spinach and not said anything.

You're miffed that someone didn't tell you sooner. It's generally not that those people are trying to be unkind, gleefully letting you suffer the embarrassment of an afternoon spinach-smile. It is that *they are trying to be kind* by sparing you the embarrassment of being told you have spinach in your teeth.

It's embarrassing when someone tells you that you have something stuck in your teeth. It's more embarrassing when that stuff stays stuck in your teeth because no one told you. By "being kind" and keeping what they see from you, they inadvertently deny you the chance to get the spinach out of your teeth.

It's the same with decision-making.

That's why, in the first exercise, most people answer that the things they are thinking to themselves are different from the things they would say out loud to their friend who always has a bad dating story to share.

You are trying not to hurt your friend's feelings. You are trying to be kind. But in doing so, you're denying them valuable input that could improve the quality of their future dating decisions. In being kind to your friend in the now, you are being unkind to the versions of your friend in the future who will have to make new dating decisions.

When you look at it that way, you realize that withholding your perspective is the greater harm to your friend. Likewise, the greater harm to you is to shield yourself from disagreement because it feels bad in the moment. That might avoid a temporary tear in the fabric of your identity, but uncovering that disagreement has the power to improve all your future decisions, strengthening the fabric in the long run.

> **Be thankful when people disagree with you in good faith because they are being kind when they do.**

Just asking for advice or feedback isn't enough to ensure that you get the outside view, because people are mostly reluctant to disagree for fear of being unkind, for fear of embarrassing you by challenging your beliefs, or for fear of offering a perspective that might cast you in an unflattering light. Worse, we all like to hear the inside view repeated back to us and we seek out people we suspect view the world the same way we do.

That's why we naturally end up in echo chambers. The inside view feels especially good when it's sold as the outside view, in the guise of someone supposedly offering an objective perspective that merely confirms what you believe. But that only serves to amplify the inside view, strengthening your view of the world because it feels certified by others.

A lot of the strategies in this book have been geared toward avoiding the echo of your own beliefs, maximizing the chances you uncover corrective information and unique perspectives. The more you can interact with the world in a way that invites people around you to give you the outside view, the more accurate your model of the world will become.

Seek out the outside view with an open mind. You'll be more likely to find out about the KICK ME sign on your back, the spinach in your teeth, and all the things you're having trouble seeing from your perspective. That will help you clear out the junk, which will improve your decisions.

1 Think about a problem that you've been grappling with. (Maybe it's a problem that motivated you to pick up this book.)

It could be retrospective, like why none of your relationships have worked out or why you keep having friction with your coworkers. Or it could be prospective, like where you should apply to college, the best way to meet the love of your life, if you should change careers, or which approach you should take to solve a particular sales problem.

Now take the time to do some PERSPECTIVE TRACKING.

Below are two columns. Use the space in the OUTSIDE VIEW column to describe your situation as best as you can entirely from the outside view. Use the INSIDE VIEW column to describe the situation from the inside view.

Notice that in the Perspective Tracking tool, you start with the outside view and *then* go to the inside view. Starting with the outside view gives you the best opportunity to anchor to what's true of the world in general or how other people might view your situation instead of too strongly anchoring to your own perspective.

Here are two tactics you might try in getting to the outside view:

(1) Ask yourself, if a coworker or friend or family member were to have this problem, how would you view their problem? How might your perspective differ from theirs? What advice might you give them? What kind of solutions would you offer?

(2) Ask yourself if there are any relevant base rates or information you could find about what's true of people in your situation in general.

PERSPECTIVE TRACKER

OUTSIDE VIEW

INSIDE VIEW

2 Use the space below to marry the two narratives. Describe what you think is an accurate intersection of the two views.

_____

_____

_____

_____

_____

_____

_____

_____

_____

_____

3 Did this exercise change the way you view your situation?   YES   NO

If yes, why?

_____

_____

_____

_____

JUST AS KNOWLEDGE TRACKING gets you thinking about what you know and don't know, motivates you to go find out more, and creates a record of your beliefs at the time of your decision that creates accountability and prevents memory creep, *Perspective Tracking* has many of the same benefits.

Incorporating a habit of Perspective Tracking into your decision process helps scooch your beliefs out of the driver's seat. It helps you view your gut feelings with more skepticism. Perspective Tracking forces you to consider the outside view. And to consider the outside view, you must seek it out: both how other people might view the decision and what is true of the world in general.

Whether you're trying to estimate the chance a decision will work out favorably or unfavorably, or thinking about the possible outcomes of a choice or the potential payoffs, taking the time to explore the outside view and, separately, the inside view, will get you to a place of more accuracy.

Making a habit of journaling the outside view and the inside view will help you get better feedback about how you thought about your decision. As the future unfolds, which inevitably changes your perspective, you will have a record of how you viewed the situation at the time, creating a higher quality feedback loop and adding a layer of accountability to your process.

Perspective Tracking: another tool for addressing the paradox of experience

Whether you missed out on a promotion or failed to meet your sales goals or dated a string of jerks, Perspective Tracking will help you more accurately answer why that happened. And an accurate answer will improve the decisions you make to address the situation going forward.

When it comes to the bad stuff, the inside view tends to lead you to blame luck rather than your own decision-making. After all, luck is the easiest escape hatch for keeping your self-narrative intact. But identifying luck as the primary culprit for your situation won't help you much in addressing the situation.

If luck is the culprit, your decision-making is off the hook. If luck is the culprit, the outcome was out of your control. It means there is nothing to be learned except that the world is full of jerks and you are just unlucky that you keep running into them.

When it comes to the bad stuff, the outside view tends to see the skill more clearly, the ways in which your decision-making led you to where you are. You can't change luck. You can only change your decisions. The outside view gets you to focus on what you can change.

It's the good stuff, too

When it comes to the good stuff, you flip the script.

Whether you landed that dream job or overshot your sales goals or just met the love of your life, the inside view tends to lead you to credit your own decision-making and downplay luck's role. While that certainly helps your self-narrative along, it can lead you to think the success you had is more reliably repeatable than it actually is.

If you want to decrease the chances of continued success, living in the inside view—overselling the skill and underselling the luck in the way things turn out—is a good strategy for doing that. The outside view puts the luck more in focus. That's why Perspective Tracking is so imperative when it comes to success.

Don't trade the future for the now

When it comes to success or failure, it can be painful to explore the outside view, especially when the inside view feels so good. But it is worth the discomfort. You can choose to swat away the skill in your bad outcomes and the luck in your good ones to keep the fabric of your identity intact in the moment. Or you can choose to embrace the outside view and strengthen that fabric so that the input into the decisions you make in the future contains less junk.

That's the trade you should take.

[5]

Turning Decisions Outside In Wrap-up

These exercises were designed to get you thinking about the following concepts:

- The **inside view** is the view of the world through your own perspective, your own beliefs, and your own experiences.
- Many common cognitive biases are, in part, the product of the inside view.
- Pros and cons lists amplify the inside view.
- The **outside view** is the way that others would see your situation, or what's true of the world in general, independent of your own perspective.
- It's important to explore the outside view even if you think you've got your facts straight, because it's possible other people could look at the same facts and come to different conclusions.
- The outside view acts to discipline the biases and inaccuracies that live in the inside view, which is why you want to anchor first to the outside view.
- Accuracy lives at the intersection between the inside view and the outside view. The things that are particular to your situation matter, but those particulars should be married with the things that are true of the world in general.
- When it comes to reasoning about the world, your beliefs are in the driver's seat.
- **Motivated reasoning** is the tendency to process information to get a conclusion we want rather than to discover what is true.
- Smart people aren't immune to motivated reasoning and the inside view. In fact, being smart can make it worse because smart people have more confidence in the truth of their beliefs and can spin better narratives to sway other people (and themselves) toward their point of view.
- A good way to get to the outside view is to look for any **base rates** that might apply to your situation.
- Another way to get to the outside view is to seek out other people's perspectives and feedback. It's important, however, that they feel comfortable expressing disagreement or a perspective that might cast you in an unflattering light. Otherwise, they're only amplifying the inside view, strengthening your belief in your

accuracy because it feels certified by others. You should be eager to hear people disagree with you and motivate them to do so.

- **Perspective Tracking** is a good decision habit to develop. Intentionally considering your situation entirely from the outside view and then entirely from the inside view can get you to a more accurate view that incorporates both.

TURNING DECISIONS OUTSIDE IN CHECKLIST

- [ ] Describe your situation entirely from the outside view. The outside view should include (a) applicable base rates and (b) perspectives provided by other people.

- [ ] Describe your situation entirely from the inside view.

- [ ] Find the intersection of the outside view and the inside view to land on a more accurate narrative.

A Sunnier Disposition?

Most people believe that living in a place with nice weather makes them happier. But when Nobel Laureate Daniel Kahneman and colleague David Schkade tested this belief, they found that an area's weather has little effect on people's happiness. In one study, they measured the happiness of nearly two thousand students at Ohio State, the University of Michigan, UCLA, and the University of California, Irvine. Most of the midwesterners and Californians *expected* that Californians would be happier, but what they actually found is that there was little difference in happiness between the students attending schools in the Midwest (where the weather is objectively not as good) and students attending the California schools.

This is a good example of the benefit of allowing the inside view and the outside view to collide. We think we know something about how the weather will affect us and we're pretty confident about it. But once we find out what's true of the world in a scientific way, we learn that our gut instinct (even though it involves how we think *we* will react to something) is actually quite inaccurate. We can only discover that inaccuracy by getting to the outside view.

When you're thinking about weather (as you were in the Boston job example and as millions of students and adults do when contemplating relocating to a warmer climate), you may think that moving from the warmth of the South or the West to a Northeast winter would be a no-go for you. You may believe that weather has a big effect on people's happiness and that it's certainly going to happen to you if you move somewhere cold.

If you take a moment to get to the outside view, it may get you to a more realistic view of how much weather might affect your happiness. Just because on average weather doesn't have a big effect on happiness, that doesn't mean that it won't have an effect on your happiness. It does, however, mean that you shouldn't necessarily rely on a presumption you believe about weather's effect on happiness, even if that's a widespread presumption.

7

Breaking Free from Analysis Paralysis

HOW TO SPEND YOUR DECISION-MAKING TIME MORE WISELY

Estimate how much time you spend, in minutes per week, deciding each of the following:

	Minutes per week:
1. What to eat:	
2. What to watch on Netflix:	
3. What to wear:	

HERE'S HOW LONG THE average person spends per week on these decisions:

- *What do you want to eat?*—150 minutes a week.
- *What do you want to watch on Netflix?*—50 minutes a week.
- *What do you want to wear?*—90 to 115 minutes a week.

This means that if you're like most people, you're spending a lot of time in analysis paralysis.

The time the average person spends deciding what to eat, watch, and wear adds up to *250 to 275 hours per year.* That's a lot of time spent on decisions that intuitively feel like they are inconsequential.

It may seem that spending an extra minute of your time here and there on these routine decisions isn't that big a deal, but that's because it's a death by a thousand cuts. These tiny expenditures mount up over time until you have spent seven workweeks a year deciding what to eat, watch, and wear.

Time is a limited resource that you need to spend wisely. The time you take to decide is time that you could be spending doing other things, like actually talking to the person sitting with you in the restaurant. The ability to figure out when you can decide faster (and when you need to slow down) is a crucial decision skill to develop.

The cost of going too fast

But here's where it gets tricky: The cost of deciding too slow is that you can't use that extra time to do other things, including making other decisions that might have a lot of potential upside. But going too fast also has a cost. The faster you decide, the more you sacrifice accuracy.

The challenge for any decision-maker is that you want to accomplish two things at once: You don't want to waste too much time and you don't want to sacrifice too much accuracy. Like Goldilocks, you're looking for a balance that is "just right." Given the stats on picking what to eat, watch, and wear, for most people getting to "just right" will mean speeding up.

> **THE TIME-ACCURACY TRADE-OFF**
> Increasing accuracy costs time. Saving time costs accuracy.

How on earth can this framework speed you up?

You probably agree that, yes, it would be nice to speed up a lot of your decisions. But at this point you may also be wondering how on earth the framework in this book is going to help with that. Having worked on creating decision trees, forecasting probabilities, identifying counterfactuals, and so forth, you might be thinking, "I'll be lucky if I make one decision every three days."

It might be counterintuitive, but the decision-making framework offered in this book will actually help you go faster, and here's why:

The key to achieving the right time-accuracy balance is figuring out what the penalty is for making a lower-quality decision than you would have if you had taken more time. How much leeway is there to sacrifice accuracy for speed?

The smaller the penalty, the faster you can go. The bigger the penalty, the more time you should take on a decision. The smaller *the impact* of a poor outcome, the faster you can go. The bigger the impact, the more time you should take.

The six-step decision process gets you to imagine the possibilities, consider the pay-offs associated with those possibilities, and estimate how likely each possibility is to occur. That's why this framework helps you manage the time-accuracy trade-off, because it means you are thinking in terms of upside and downside potential.

And that means you are thinking about impact.

Imagining how the future will unfold given any decision you're considering will make it easier for you to identify when the costs of not getting it "just right" are small.

For most decisions, this framework will help you speed up, even for decisions that are much more consequential than what to have for dinner. Using the decision tools offered in this book will slow you down when you're using your gut or some other low-quality shortcut to make decisions that deserve more careful consideration—and that's when you *should* be taking more time.

An added benefit of saving time: Poking at the world!

A recurring theme of this book has been that you should be laser focused on looking for ways to extract information from the world, transforming some of the universe of stuff you don't know into stuff you do know. The information you gather is not just about learning new facts, or figuring out how things work, or refining your estimates of how things might turn out.

It's also about figuring out your own preferences, your own likes and dislikes.

The more you know your own preferences, the better your decision-making will be. One of the best ways to figure out your likes and dislikes is to try stuff. The faster you make decisions, the more stuff you can try. That means more opportunities to experiment and poke at the world. That means more opportunities for you to learn new stuff, including new stuff about yourself.

So let's get to figuring out how to speed up.

[1]

The Happiness Test:
When the type of thing you're deciding about is low impact

We're eating together in a restaurant and you're agonizing over what to order. You finally figure out what you want, you put in your order, and the waiter brings you your food. Maybe your food is great. Maybe it's just okay. Maybe it's not very good. Maybe it's even so bad you push your plate away in disgust.

1 I run into you *a year* later and ask, "How's your year been?" You might tell me it's been a great year, or an awful year, or something in between. Regardless of whether your year has been good or bad, imagine I then ask, "Remember that meal we had together a year ago? How much of an effect did the food you ate that night have on your happiness over the past year?"

Give your answer below, on a scale of 0 to 5, where 0 is "no effect" on your happiness over the course of the year and 5 is a "massive effect" on your happiness.

No effect at all   0   1   2   3   4   5   *Massive effect*

2 Now let's say I run into you *a month* after the meal and ask the same question. On a scale of 0 to 5, how much of an effect did the food you ate that night have on your happiness over the course of that month?

No effect at all   0   1   2   3   4   5   *Massive effect*

3 Now let's say I run into you *a week* after the meal and ask the same question. On a scale of 0 to 5, how much of an effect did the food you ate that night have on your happiness over the course of the week?

No effect at all   0   1   2   3   4   5   *Massive effect*

IF YOU'RE LIKE MOST PEOPLE, you answered that the food you ate at that one meal didn't affect your happiness much, if at all, a year later. If you're like most people, that's also true if I asked you after a month, or even a week. Regardless of whether your food is good or bad, it is unlikely to have any significant effect on your happiness in the long run. The same is also true if you watch the beginning of a bad movie on Netflix or wear pants that turn out to be uncomfortable.

What this tells you is that choosing what to eat, watch, or wear are types of decisions that are low impact.

The *Happiness Test* is one way to figure out if you're deciding about something that's low impact.

There are whole categories of decisions where, whatever option you choose (the chicken or the fish, the gray suit or the blue one, *Austin Powers* or *The Princess Bride*), the outcome won't have much of an effect on your happiness in the long run (or the short run, for that matter).

If the category of thing you're deciding about passes the Happiness Test, that tells you that you can speed up because there isn't much of a penalty for getting it less "right." Broadly defined, happiness is a good proxy for understanding the impact of a decision on achieving your long-term goals. When you find out that the potential gains or losses (as measured in happiness) are small, that means the decision is low impact and you can go fast.

> **THE HAPPINESS TEST**
> Ask yourself if the outcome of your decision, good or bad, will likely have a significant effect on your happiness in a year. If the answer is no, the decision passes the test, which means you can speed up.
>
> Repeat for a month and a week.
>
> The shorter the time period for which your answer is "no, it won't much affect my happiness," the more you can trade off accuracy in favor of saving time.

The time you gain is time you can spend on a more impactful decision or time you can spend making a low-risk experimental choice to poke at the world.

Faster than fast: when options repeat

You're stuck between choosing to order the chicken or the fish. You decide on the fish and it is bone dry and tasteless. You think to yourself, "I should have ordered the chicken!"

You're deciding between two outfits to wear to a party, one really dressy and one more casual. You decide on the dressier choice, and when you show up, everyone else is dressed down. You immediately regret not choosing the other option.

Even though many decisions won't have a significant impact on your *long-term* happiness, there is still a *short-term* cost of a bad result: *regret*.

Regret (or fear of regret) can make you indecisive about nearly any choice.

Pretty much everyone feels regret in the immediate wake of a bad outcome. Anticipating that feeling can induce analysis paralysis because you naturally think that taking more time will make it less likely you'll get a bad outcome, so less likely you'll feel the accompanying pain of regret.

Rather than thinking about the long-term impact (which is what really matters), you get trapped in the short term, so afraid of regret that you can't decide. Fear of regret costs time.

Repeating options help defray the cost of regret.

Options repeat for decisions where you will get another crack at the same choice, which is especially useful if the choice comes up again quickly. You might really dislike the dish you order in a restaurant, but you will get another chance to pick something to eat in just a few hours. And that helps take the sting out of any short-term regret.

Choosing college classes is a repeating option.

Choosing who to go on a first date with is a repeating option.

Choosing driving routes is a repeating option.

Choosing a movie to see is a repeating option.

When a decision passes the Happiness Test, you can go fast. When an option repeats, you can go even faster, because getting another shot at the decision helps reduce what little cost there is of a bad outcome, as measured in regret, from a low-impact decision.

Decisions that repeat also provide opportunities for choosing things you are less certain about, like a food you've never tried or a new TV show, because you don't get penalized as heavily for taking those gambles. At little cost, you get information in return about your likes and dislikes, and you might find some surprises in there.

> ### REPEATING OPTIONS
> When the same type of decision comes up over and over again, you get repeated chances to choose options, including options you may have rejected in the past.

Whatever you learn will inform all your future decisions. That means that when you do face a high-impact decision, it will be better informed than if you hadn't done all that low-risk poking at the world.

1 Identify a type of decision you're currently struggling with and/or have struggled with in the past that you now realize is low impact because it passes the Happiness Test.

_____

_____

_____

_____

Do you think you could speed up that decision? How?

_____

_____

_____

_____

2 Identify up to five more decisions that you've agonized over in the past that pass the Happiness Test. At least one of those should also be an option that quickly repeats.

_____

_____

_____

_____

[2]

Freerolling: Deciding fast when the downside is slim to none

The Legend of Trivia Man

You're walking down the street. Some guy walks up to you and says, "I'm going to ask you a trivia question. If you get it right, I'm going to give you ten bucks."

You're suspicious. "What if I lose? Will I owe you ten bucks?"

"Nope! I just really love trivia and it delights me to reward people with money when they get my trivia questions correct."

You figure you have nothing to lose, so you say, "Go ahead."

"What state's capital has the smallest population?"

You guess "Vermont." He claps with delight and hands you a ten-dollar bill for getting the answer right.

"For another ten dollars, what's the name of the city?"

Ugh. You're not sure, so you say the name of the only city you know in Vermont. "Burlington!"

Sadly, he shakes his head. "Pity. It's Montpelier."

As promised, you owe him nothing for the wrong answer. You never see him again, but you're ten dollars richer.

That's a *freeroll*.

Have you ever been in a situation where you have a friend who is agonizing over whether to ask someone out on a date and you say, "Just ask them out. This could be the love of your life. The worst that can happen is they'll say no!" If so, you understand freerolling, even if you've never heard the term before.

The concept of a freeroll is a useful mental model for spotting opportunities you can decide to seize quickly. The key feature of a freeroll is *limited downside*,

> **FREEROLL**
>
> **A situation where there is an asymmetry between the upside and downside because the potential losses are insignificant.**

meaning there isn't much to lose (but there might be a lot to gain). The usual penalty for speeding up—the possbility of a greater likelihood of a worse outcome—doesn't apply when you are in freeroll territory.

You can identify decisions with limited downside by asking yourself one or both of the following questions:

1. What's the worst that can happen?
2. If the outcome doesn't go my way, am I worse off than I was before I made the decision?

If the worst that can happen isn't that bad, or you will be no worse off than you were before if the outcome doesn't go your way, the decision fits into the freeroll category. That means you can speed up because the penalty for sacrificing accuracy is limited.

Obviously, there is always some cost to making any decision, even if it is just the time it takes to answer Trivia Man's questions. Applying the concept of a freeroll isn't so much about looking for situations with zero downside potential, but rather about looking for an asymmetry between the upside and downside potential of a decision.

> The bigger the asymmetry between the upside and downside, the more you have to gain when potential losses are limited, and the bigger the freeroll.

Actually, there *is* such a thing as a free lunch

You may think that freerolls are too good to be realistically available. But once you're on the lookout for them, you'll find that freerolls are more abundant than you think.

You're applying to colleges. Your dream college is a huge reach because you have a very low percentage chance of getting accepted. Should you still apply? Assuming the cost of applying isn't significant, you're not really worse off if you don't get in, but if you do get in, you are going to your dream school.

You're looking for a house to buy. As always seems to be the case, your realtor shows you the ideal house, but the asking price is 20% above the maximum you've set. Do you make an offer? If you make an offer within your price range and the seller rejects it, you're no worse off. But if they accept, you get your dream house at a steal.

Once you identify a freeroll, you don't need to think too hard about *whether* to seize the opportunity, but you still want to take time with the execution of the decision. Go fast deciding *whether* to apply to a college that is a big stretch, but take time making sure the application is high quality. Go fast deciding *whether* to offer on your dream house, but take time making sure the offer is sound.

> The faster you engage, the less likely it is that the opportunity goes away. The faster you decide to seize the opportunity, the faster you get the chance at realizing the one-sided, upside potential of the decision.

All that time you save is time you can use to make other decisions that might bear fruit, including seizing other freeroll opportunities. Yet, just like your friend who agonizes over whether to ask someone out on a date, people can agonize about these types of decisions, often passing on these opportunities. Why don't more people see (and seize) freerolls?

One likely reason is that freerolls generally *don't* pass the Happiness Test. Each of these examples has the potential for a much more meaningful upside than Trivia Man giving you ten or twenty bucks. Where you go to college and what home you buy are high-impact decisions. People can get caught up in analysis paralysis about these types of decisions because of that potential impact.

In this way, the impact of the decision overshadows the limited downside, making it hard to see that you are in a freeroll situation.

What gets missed is that, for freerolls, the potential big impact on your happiness is *one-sided in your favor.*

In addition to impact obscuring the freeroll, the fear of failure or rejection can also be paralyzing, especially when there is a high probability that things won't go your way. Receiving the rejection letter from your dream school hurts in the moment. No one wants to hear a realtor say, "The buyer thought your offer was a joke."

When you pass on such opportunities or let those small, temporary negatives slow you down, you're magnifying the moment of rejection and ignoring the asymmetry working in your favor. You're saving yourself from those short-lived feelings if the opportunity doesn't pan out, but you're costing yourself the chance for a meaningful, long-term boost to your well-being.

1 Identify a decision you're currently considering and/or have considered in the past that qualifies as a freeroll—a decision where there is mostly upside and limited downside—on which you've taken a long time deciding.

_____

_____

Do you think you could speed up that decision? How?

_____

_____

_____

_____

2 Identify some additional past decisions that qualify as freerolls.

_____

_____

_____

_____

Warning: A free donut is not a freeroll

When considering whether a decision has limited downside potential, it's crucial to think about the cumulative effects of making the same decision repeatedly, rather than focusing on just the onetime, short-run potential harm.

If you've resolved to eat healthier and someone at work brings in donuts on their birthday, it's easy to look at that donut as a freeroll. After all, your well-being won't hinge on eating a single baked good. The enjoyment you get from that sweet treat likely outweighs the nominal cost to your health of just one donut.

But if you make that decision repeatedly, it's a different story. If you did the same thing yesterday with a slice of pizza, and the same thing with a giant movie-theater popcorn the night before (because you were having a great time on a date), and the same thing last week with a cheesecake (because you were miserable over a breakup) . . . Well, you can see the potential for multiple "onetime" insignificant costs that add up to something meaningful.

It's the same with buying a lottery ticket. Losing the few dollars on a Powerball ticket won't much affect your long-term happiness. And if you win the jackpot, it will be life changing. That might trick you into thinking the lottery is a freeroll. But the lottery is such a losing financial proposition that, in the long run, the potential losses far outweigh the potential gains. Once you think about playing multiple tickets every single week, you can see that the lottery is a big loser, not a freeroll at all.

When asking yourself "What's the worst that could happen?" make sure you follow up by examining the effects of making the same type of decision repeatedly. That's how you recognize that a free donut is not a freeroll.

[3]

A Sheep in Wolf's Clothing:
High stakes, close calls, fast decisions

You have a week of vacation time next year and you've decided to take a big trip. You've already narrowed it down to two destinations, Paris or Rome. (If you have a pair of favorite or bucket-list destinations, ones you've never been to before, substitute those in this thought experiment.)

1 How difficult would it be, on a scale of 0 to 5, once you've narrowed your decision to Paris or Rome (or two other destinations you consider highly desirable), to choose between them?

Not difficult at all   0   1   2   3   4   5   *Extremely difficult*

2 I run into you in a *year* after your vacation and ask, "How's your year been?" Maybe you tell me it's been a great year, or an awful year, or something in between. After you tell me, I ask, "On a scale of 0 to 5, how big an effect did that vacation have on your happiness over the year?"

No effect at all   0   1   2   3   4   5   *Massive effect*

3 I run into you in a *month* after your vacation and ask, "How's your month been? On a scale of 0 to 5, how big an effect did that vacation have on your happiness over the month?"

No effect at all   0   1   2   3   4   5   *Massive effect*

4 I run into you in a *week* after your vacation. "On a scale of 0 to 5, how big an effect did that vacation have on your happiness during the week immediately following it?"

No effect at all   0   1   2   3   4   5   *Massive effect*

IF YOU'RE LIKE MOST PEOPLE, you agonize over this type of decision.

After all, deciding between Paris and Rome doesn't pass the Happiness Test. Taking a vacation like this will certainly affect your happiness in a week, a month, and even over the course of a year. Unless you're a jet-setter constantly traveling between exotic destinations, it's not a repeating option; it might be a once-in-a-lifetime choice. And there is a high cost if it doesn't work out. Whether you choose Paris or Rome, it is an expensive trip.

We all face lots of high-impact decisions like the European vacation choice.

You might get accepted to two colleges at the top of your list or find two amazing homes on your house hunt or get two different dream-job offers. Then you agonize over which option to choose, trying to distinguish the small differences between two or more great choices. You find yourself endlessly researching each option, coming up with additional criteria, asking for more and more people's opinions, wavering back and forth trying to figure out which is the "right" choice.

So, here's a weird little thought experiment: What if, instead of choosing between Paris and Rome, you were choosing between a vacation in Paris and a vacation at a trout cannery? Would you have trouble or experience any anxiety making that choice?

I'm assuming the answer is no.

That tells you that the *closeness of the options* is what's slowing you down. You'd have no trouble choosing between options as far apart in their potential payoffs as a week in Paris versus a week spent among discarded fish parts.

And that's a clue as to why you can and should speed up these types of decisions.

When a decision is hard, that means it's easy

The very thing that slows you down—having multiple options that are very close in quality—is actually a signal that you can go fast, because this tells you that whichever option you choose, you can't possibly be that wrong, since both options have similar upside and downside potential.

Instead of thinking about the similarity between options in terms of their *overall potential payoffs*, both the positives and the negatives, we mostly get focused on anxiety about the downside. What if the option you choose works out badly?

A rogue cabdriver could charge you a fortune and drop you off in the middle of nowhere. You might slip and break your leg on the day of the first snowfall after you move to the Northeast. You might pick the dream house with a next-door neighbor who turns out to be a maniac.

This asymmetric focus on the downside is a way in which resulting rears its ugly head, slowing you down. Yes, there is a lot to gain. But there is also a lot to lose. Never mind that the chances of a bad outcome are nearly identical whichever option you pick. When your vacation sucks, you feel like you chose poorly. So you agonize, taking extra time, trying to avoid making a big mistake.

From that vantage point, the decision looks like a *wolf*, a dangerous, high-impact beast of nonrepeating options and lots of potential downside. Close calls might feel like the wolf is at your door. But this type of decision is really a *sheep in wolf's clothing*.

If you look at the decision through the frame of the *relative quality of the options as compared to each other*, your vantage point changes. Instead of taking tons of time trying to tease out the small differences between the choices, reframe the decision by asking yourself, *"Whichever option I choose, how wrong can I be?"*

That question allows you to think prospectively, understanding that what matters for decision quality is the potential of each of the options, not which of many possible outcomes happens to be the one that unfolds. That question allows you to see that you have two similarly great options to choose from, so whichever option you go with, it's unlikely you're making that big a mistake.

In this way, these kinds of choices are actually **hidden freerolls**. Because the choices you have are so close, you're freerolling on whichever option you choose. You can't be that wrong either way.

This unlocks a powerful decision-making principle: *When a decision is hard, that means it's easy.*

> ### WHEN A DECISION IS HARD, THAT MEANS IT'S EASY
> When you're weighing two options that are close, then the decision is actually easy, because whichever one you choose you can't be that wrong since the difference between the two is so small.

Tilting at windmills

When you agonize over close options, you're usually wasting time tilting at windmills. You're spending time at the margins, hoping, at best, to resolve tiny separations in potential payoffs, trying to parse out indistinguishable differences.

You can't *know*, absent actually going to Paris or Rome, which you will like better. Even if you have been to those places before, you can't *know* which you will like better this time. No matter who you ask for their opinion or how many reviews you read on a travel advisory website, those people are not you. They are different people with different preferences, so their advice can only go so far. They can't *know* which you will like better.

You can't bend time and space to find out, before you take a job in Boston, how the job and the city will work out. You can't know which of two similar houses you'll enjoy more over the next ten years, or which of two colleges of similar quality you'll like more over the next four.

Because we all live in the space between no information and perfect information, it's not realistic to think that you will be able to discern which option is better.

You're chasing an illusory certainty by taking all that extra time.

Even if, given enough time, you could be certain which option is best, it's still not a great use of that limited resource anyway. Let's say, hypothetically, that an amazing European vacation has the potential, on average, to increase your happiness over the course of a year by 5%. And let's say that, if you had perfect information, you could know that a Parisian vacation has the potential to increase your happiness by 4.9%, while Rome might increase your happiness by 5.1%.

That would mean that you're spending all that time to try to resolve a .2% difference between the two options. That's time you could be spending on other decisions or doing other things that will have much more than a tiny fraction of a percent of potential impact on your happiness or your ability to reach your long-term goals.

Breaking through the deadlock: The Only-Option Test

Barry Schwartz points out in his book, *The Paradox of Choice*, that this kind of sheep-in-wolf's-clothing decision is more likely to come up the more options you have to choose from. The greater the number of available options, the greater the likelihood that more than one of those options will look pretty good to you. The more options that look pretty good to you, the more time you spend in analysis paralysis.

That's the paradox: more choice, more anxiety.

Remember, if the only choices are between Paris and a trout cannery, no one has a problem. But what if the choices are Paris or Rome or Amsterdam or Santorini or Machu Picchu? You get the picture.

A useful tool you can use to break the grid-lock is the *Only-Option Test*.

If this were the only thing I could order on the menu . . .

If this were the only show I could watch on Netflix tonight . . .

> ### THE ONLY-OPTION TEST
> **For any options you're considering, ask yourself, "If this were the only option I had, would I be happy with it?"**

If this were the only place I could go for vacation . . .

If this were the only college I got accepted to . . .

If this were the only house I could buy . . .

If this were the only job I got offered . . .

The Only-Option Test clears away the debris cluttering your decision. If you'd be happy if Paris were your only option, and you'd be happy if Rome were your only option, that reveals that if you just flip a coin, you'll be happy whichever way the coin lands.

I For the next week, practice applying the Only-Option Test whenever you're at a restaurant. Look through the menu and figure out which items you'd be happy with if they were your only option. After sorting the menu in this way, decide among the options that pass the Only-Option Test by flipping a coin. Use the space below to reflect on how that feels.

_____

_____

_____

_____

_____

_____

_____

The Menu Strategy

This strategy for choosing what to order from a menu can be broadly applied to decision-making in general. For any decision, spend your time sorting the world into stuff you like and stuff you don't like.

After that, go fast.

The big gains that you get from your decision-making time are in the *sorting*: figuring out, given *your* values and *your* goals, what makes an option "good." Sorting options is the heavy lifting of decision-making and that's the place you will get the most value out of slowing down.

> **THE MENU STRATEGY**
>
> **Spend your time on the initial sorting. Save your time on the picking.**

Once you've done the sorting and you've got one or more good options, there's not a big penalty for speeding up. If your options are very close, you can usually just flip a coin and move on. Extra time spent choosing among options that meet your criteria won't generally gain you much in accuracy over picking by chance.

That's why identifying low-impact decisions, especially ones that repeat, is so important. Those types of low-risk decisions give you the opportunity to experiment. Experimentation gets the world to tell you what works and what doesn't work and helps you figure out your preferences, your likes and dislikes.

And all that experimentation will make you better informed, paying off in more accurate sorting.

[4]

Quitters Often Win, and Winners Often Quit:
Understanding the power of "quit-to-itiveness"

You go to the local movie theater and see a movie showing on screen 1 at 7:00 p.m. That means you can't see what's on screens 2 through 18 at the same time.

You spend four years getting your college degree. That's time you can't spend giving your band your undivided attention.

You read the official biography of Winston Churchill (eight volumes, 8,562 pages, which took two generations of biographers twenty-six years to write). You can't spend that time reading thirty-five other books or completing two semesters of law school.

Any choice that you make has associated *opportunity cost*. When you choose an option, you're also *rejecting* other options, along with the upside potential of those things you chose not to do. The greater the gains associated with the options you don't pick, the higher the opportunity cost. The higher the opportunity cost, the greater the penalty for going fast.

When you choose something from a menu and you don't like how it tastes, you immediately become aware of the opportunity cost. You could have ordered a different dish, which might have been great, and maybe if you had taken more time

> **OPPORTUNITY COST**
> When you pick an option, you lose the potential gains associated with the options you don't pick.

deciding, you wouldn't have gotten your order "wrong." That's also true when you don't like the movie you picked, or the job you took, or the house you bought.

Opportunity cost and impact

Opportunity cost is part of what determines the impact of a decision, so opportunity cost *should* be a factor in how you manage the time-accuracy trade-off. The bigger the gains associated with the options you don't pick, the more you give up by not picking those options. That means a bigger penalty for sacrificing accuracy in favor of speed. The smaller the opportunity cost, the less you give up, the faster you can go.

This is part of what the Happiness Test gets at. If the category of thing you're deciding about is low impact, any of your available options will have low opportunity costs associated with them. There just won't be much to gain (or lose) from any of your options.

Repeating options defray opportunity cost. When a decision repeats, you can go back and choose an option you didn't pick before. That means you quickly get a chance at participating in the upside potential of any of the options you passed on in short order. You aren't permanently passing on the gains associated with the things you didn't do.

There's another way to defray opportunity cost: quitting.

Stick-to-itiveness vs. Quit-to-itiveness

"Quitters never win, and winners never quit." That's the ubiquitous message from business pioneers like Thomas Edison and Ted Turner; from sports figures like Vince Lombardi and Mia Hamm; from authors like Dale Carnegie and Napoleon Hill; and from entertainers like James Cordon to Lil Wayne.

It seems to be accepted wisdom that *stick-to-itiveness* creates success. Stick-to-itiveness has value, but so does **quit-to-itiveness**.

Quitting doesn't deserve its nearly universal negative reputation. Quitting is a powerful tool for defraying opportunity cost and gathering intel, intel that will allow you to make higher-quality decisions about the things you decide to stick to.

Whenever you choose to invest your limited resources in an option, you're doing so with limited information. As your choice plays out, new information will reveal itself. And sometimes that information will tell you that the option you chose isn't the best option for advancing you toward your goals.

As you learn more, it could be that you figure out that a decision you thought was great actually has much more downside potential than you realized and so has a higher probability to cause you to lose ground rather than gain it. Or it could be that you are gaining ground with the option you chose, but you would gain *even more ground* if you made a different choice.

That's a good time to consider quitting.

Poker players understand this, as does everybody who has heard Kenny Rogers sing "You gotta know when to fold 'em." If you put your resources toward a choice that you no longer feel has the best chance of working out and you have the option to change course, that's a good time to cut your losses and "fold 'em."

Of course, there are costs to quitting: loss of money, goodwill, reputation, social capital, time, etc.

Quitting a relationship after the first date costs a lot less than quitting a relationship after getting married.

The cost of moving out of a rental house you don't like is lower than selling and moving out of a house that you own.

The cost of changing your mind after moving to a different neighborhood is much less than changing your mind after moving to another country.

Part of a good decision process includes asking yourself, *"If I pick this option, what's the cost of quitting?"* The lower the cost of changing course in the future, the faster you can make your decision, since the option to quit lowers the impact by reducing opportunity cost.

You can take less time deciding who to ask on a first date than deciding who to marry. You can take less time deciding which house to rent than deciding which one to buy. You can take less time deciding whether to move to a different neighborhood than deciding whether to move to another country.

> **QUIT-TO-ITIVENESS**
> The lower the cost to quit, the faster you can go, because it's easier to unwind the decision and choose a different option, including options you may have rejected in the past.

Being quit-to-itive is not intuitive

Because of the way the human mind works, we tend to view decisions as permanent and final, particularly if they are high impact. We don't think much in advance about the option to quit. But once you look at decisions through the frame of quit-to-itiveness, you'll find that for many decisions you thought (or simply assumed) you couldn't unwind, the cost isn't prohibitively high.

When people are choosing colleges, for example, they agonize partly because they think they're making a decision that's permanent for the next four years of their life. But the outside view reveals that 37% of college students transfer to a new school and nearly half of those transfer multiple times.

Once you realize that transferring is an option, you can shift your frame from not even considering the option to quit to asking what it would cost to do so. Will your credits transfer? What's the cost of leaving your friends? How hard will it be to make new ones? What is the cost to move? Will you be able to get into a better college?

No matter what your answers are, I'd bet the cost of quitting is lower than you thought—because you likely weren't even thinking about it before.

Being quit-to-itive improves decision quality.

Two-way-door decisions: Deciding fast *and* learning more

Decisions where the cost to quit is manageable also give you an opportunity to gather information through innovation and experimentation. Amazon founder Jeff Bezos and Virgin Group founder Richard Branson include the concept of a *"two-way-door" decision* in their decision process. A two-way-door decision is, simply put, a decision where the cost to quit is low.

When you figure out that you've got a two-way-door decision, you can make choices you're less certain about, giving yourself more low-risk opportunities to expose yourself to the universe of stuff you don't know. The information you gather in the process will help you implement the menu strategy, improving your accuracy in sorting options into ones you like and ones you don't.

Try stuff you can quit. Figure out what you like and what you don't like. Figure out what works and what doesn't work.

If you want to know if you'd like playing the piano, sign up for some lessons. If you don't like it, quit. You don't have to play the piano for the rest of your life. Sign up for improv classes or learn how to cook with a salt block.

Of course, you're going to want to stick to some things. It's hard to succeed at anything if you don't have grit and stick-to-itiveness. But being "quitty" allows you to make better choices about when to be gritty.

Decision stacking

Once you have the mental model of quit-to-itiveness, seeing the world through the lens of the cost to quit, this reveals an effective strategy for improving the quality of your decisions: *decision stacking*.

You will face lots of high-impact, one-way-door decisions that carry a high cost to unwind (like buying a house, or moving to another country, or changing professions). When you know that you have such a decision on the horizon, consider whether there are lower-impact, easier-to-quit decisions that you can stack in front of the high-impact choice to help inform your one-way-door decision.

Dating is a natural application of decision stacking. If you go out on a lot of dates, you learn more about your likes and dislikes before deciding about a committed relationship. Likewise, if you're thinking about buying a house in a particular neighborhood, you can rent a house in that neighborhood first.

> ### DECISION STACKING
> **Finding ways to make low-impact, easy-to-quit decisions in advance of a high-impact, harder-to-quit decision.**

Deciding fast and learning by choosing options in parallel

Ivan Boesky was a Wall Street trader who became a symbol of success—and excess—in the 1980s before pleading guilty to insider trading, paying a $100-million fine, and going to prison. As an iconic symbol of that era, he became the subject of numerous larger-than-life stories: he slept three hours a night; he never sat down at work; he gave the original "greed is good" speech during a business-school commencement address; he was the model for Gordon Gekko in *Wall Street*. Legend had it that when Boesky dined at the famous New York City restaurant Tavern on the Green, he would order every item on the menu and take one bite of each.

Although the story is certainly apocryphal, it does illustrate a useful decision-making principle: When you are weighing which option to choose, sometimes you can pick more than one of them at the same time.

Choosing options in parallel obviously lowers opportunity cost because you get to participate in the upside potential of multiple options at once. Finding ways to exercise options in parallel also lowers your exposure to the downside.

You might not be Ivan-Boesky rich, but at a restaurant you may be able to convince your dining companion to share items, allowing you to order multiple appetizers or entrées.

If you want to watch multiple sporting events at the same time, you can set up multiple monitors—or go to a sports bar.

If you're choosing between two marketing campaigns, you might be able to figure out a way to try both in test markets and see which works better.

You could plan a vacation where you visit Paris *and* Rome.

When you can do more than one thing at a time, you get many more opportunities to poke at the world, getting the input from multiple experiences.

Exercising options in parallel also lowers your exposure to the downside. Even for decisions that have only a 10% chance of going awry, that means that 10% of the time you'll get a bad outcome. But if you can do a bunch of things at the same time that each have a 10% chance of going awry, the chances that *all of them* don't work out becomes vanishingly small. That naturally lowers the penalty for going fast.

Doing things in parallel does come at a cost. Ordering everything on the menu obviously costs more than ordering one item. When you do more than one thing at a time, there is a cost in the quality of your execution. Your attention is flexible, but it's not unlimited. You want to balance what you're gaining by doing multiple things at once with what you're losing in money, time, and other resources—and in the quality of your execution of multiple options.

If you've ever seen a TV show using the two-dates-to-the-prom trope, you know that merely because you *can* do more than one thing at a time doesn't mean you *should*.

Think about a high-impact decision that you've been struggling with. Alternatively, think about a high-impact decision that you struggled with in the past. Evaluate that decision using the mental model of quit-to-itiveness.

I   Briefly describe the decision and your main options.

_____

_____

_____

_____

_____

_____

_____

2 What are/were the costs, after choosing an option, of quitting and making a different choice?

_____

_____

_____

_____

3 Is/was this potentially a two-way-door decision with a manageable cost to quit?   YES   NO

4 If yes, what is/was the cost to quit?

_____

_____

_____

_____

5 If no, what are some ways you could decision stack, putting lower-cost decisions in front of the one-way-door decision, giving you an opportunity to gather information for the later decision?

_____

_____

_____

_____

6 For this decision, describe ways in which you could exercise options in parallel, if possible.

_____

_____

_____

_____

_____

Here is a simple flow chart that captures the ideas offered in this chapter about how to manage the time-accuracy trade-off:

HOW FAST CAN I GO?

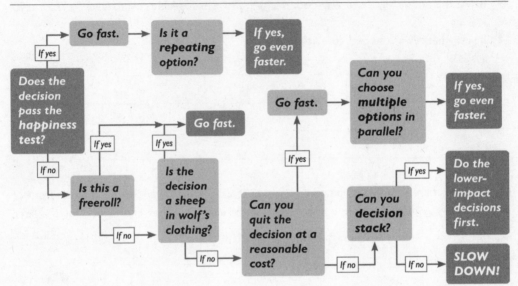

[5]

Is This Your Final Answer?:
Knowing when your decision process is "finished"

In the late 1950s and early '60s, there was a popular sitcom about a "typical" suburban family, *Leave It to Beaver*. "Beaver" was the nickname of the youngest of the two sons and episodes frequently involved him getting into minor mischief. For example, in one episode, Beaver insists that he can go by himself to get his hair cut. He loses the haircut money and asks his older brother, Wally, to bail him out by cutting his hair.

Wally wields the scissors, hair accumulates on the floor, and Beaver asks, "Are you finished?"

When the viewer sees Beaver for the first time, huge clumps of his hair are missing. Wally says, *"Well, I don't know if I'm finished but I think I better stop."*

You're in a similar position when it comes to wrapping up your decision-making. When should you stop analyzing and just decide?

If your goal is to get to certainty about your choice, you'll never be *finished*. Chasing certainty causes analysis paralysis. The point of this chapter is to help you to figure out how to get to a decision more quickly by letting go of certainty as your goal.

Once you settle on a choice that's good enough—regardless of how long you've taken, whether you've flipped a coin or conducted a lengthy decision process, or whether your options are indistinguishable or you have a clear favorite—part of a good decision process includes asking yourself a final question:

"Is there information that I could find out that would change my mind?"

You flipped a coin and it comes up "Paris." Is there information you could find out that would make you switch your choice to Rome?

You go through a meticulous hiring process and decide on Candidate A. Is there information you could find out that would switch your choice to a different candidate or cause you to continue your search?

Pretty much every decision is made with incomplete information. This final question gets you to imagine what information would be helpful if you were omniscient, if you had a crystal ball.

If you could attain a state of perfect knowledge, is there something that would cause you to change your mind? If the answer is yes, ask yourself if that information is available, absent omniscience or psychic powers.

A lot of the time, the answer is going to be no. If you're struggling with whether to spend a week in Paris or Rome, the information you would need to clarify that decision would be foreknowledge of how each vacation would turn out. As a mere mortal, without a time machine, that kind of information—and, consequently, getting that kind of certainty—is unavailable.

If the answer is "No, there isn't any information that I could find out," go ahead and decide. You're done. It's time to stop.

If the answer is yes and you *can* find out that information, ask the follow-up question of whether you can afford to get it.

Information, even if it's available, can be too expensive for a variety of reasons: time, money, social capital.

If you are considering moving to Boston to take a new job, you *could* find out if you could manage northeastern winters, but that would mean living in Boston for a winter before deciding. Aside from the cost of doing the test run in Boston, the job opportunity would have evaporated by the time you figure out if the winters are bearable. That makes getting the information too expensive.

If you're hiring someone, you can always reinterview the candidates or hire a search firm or conduct more interviews with the person you are considering. But that doesn't mean you *should* do all those things. That's time the job would remain unfilled. You would also have to take the time or pay the money to do those additional things. You could also lose your preferred candidate (or any other candidates you've interviewed that pass the Only-Option Test) if you significantly prolong the process.

If you think decisive information is available and believe that it's worth it and you can afford it, then go find it.

But if the answer is no, just go ahead and decide.

Here's a simple chart to help you navigate, once you have settled on an option, the final step in a good decision process.

FINAL STEP FOR ANY DECISION

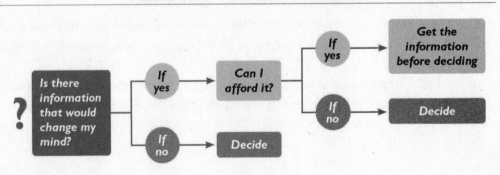

How to Decide

[6]

Breaking Free from Analysis Paralysis Wrap-up

These exercises were designed to get you thinking about the following concepts:

- We spend an enormous amount of time on routine, inconsequential decisions. The average person spends 250–275 hours per year deciding what to eat, watch, and wear. That's the equivalent of the time they spend at work in six or seven weeks.

- There is a **time-accuracy trade-off**: Increasing accuracy costs time. Saving time costs accuracy.

- The key to balancing the trade-off between time and accuracy is figuring out **the penalty for not getting the decision exactly right**.

- Getting an initial understanding of **the impact** of your decision (through the framework of evaluating possibilities, payoffs, and probabilities) will identify situations in which the penalty is small or nonexistent, giving you leeway to sacrifice accuracy in favor of deciding faster.

- Recognizing when decisions are low impact also maximizes opportunities to **poke at the world**, which increases your knowledge and helps you learn more about your preferences, improving the quality of all future decisions.

- You can identify low-impact decisions with the **Happiness Test**, asking yourself if how your decision turns out will likely have an effect on your happiness in a week, a month, or a year. If the type of thing you are deciding about passes the Happiness Test, you can go fast.

- If a decision passes the Happiness Test and the **options repeat**, you can go even faster.

- A **freeroll** is a situation in which there is limited downside. Save time deciding whether to seize a freeroll; take time in deciding how to execute it.

- When you have multiple options that are close in potential payoffs, these are **sheep in wolf's clothing** decisions. Close calls for high-impact decisions tend to induce analysis paralysis, but the indecision is, in itself, a signal that you can go fast.

- To determine if a decision is a sheep in wolf's clothing, use the **Only-Option Test**, asking yourself for each option, "If this were the only option I had, would I be happy with it?" If your answer is yes for more than one option, you could flip a coin since you can't be that wrong whichever option you pick.

- Allocate your decision time using the **menu strategy. Spend time sorting**, determining which options you like. Once you have options you like, **save time picking**.

- When you pick an option, you're passing on the potential gains associated with the options you don't pick. This is the **opportunity cost**. The higher the opportunity cost, the higher the penalty for making choices that are less certain.

- You can defray opportunity cost and decide faster by being **quit-to-itive**, looking at decisions through the framework of whether you can change your mind, quit your choice, and choose something else at a reasonable cost.

- Decisions with a low cost to quit, known as **two-way-door decisions**, also provide you with low-cost opportunities to make experimental decisions to gather information and learn about your values and preferences for future decisions.

- When you're facing a decision with a high or prohibitive cost of changing your mind, try **decision stacking**, making two-way-door decisions ahead of the one-way-door decision.

- You can also defray opportunity cost if you can exercise multiple options **in parallel**.

- Because you can rarely approach perfect information or be certain of the outcome of your decision, you will make most decisions while still uncertain. To figure out when additional time is no longer likely to increase accuracy in a worthwhile way, ask yourself, "Is there additional information (available at a reasonable cost) that would establish a clearly preferred option or, if there is already a clearly preferred option, cause you to change your preferred option?" If yes, go find it. If no, decide and move on.

BREAKING FREE FROM
ANALYSIS PARALYSIS CHECKLIST

To determine whether you can decide faster, ask yourself the following questions:

☐ Does the type of thing you're deciding about pass the Happiness Test? If yes, go fast.

☐ Does it pass the Happiness Test *with* repeating options? If yes, go even faster.

☐ Are you freerolling? If yes, go fast in seizing the opportunity but take time in the execution.

☐ Is your decision a sheep in wolf's clothing, with multiple options that pass the Only-Option Test? If yes, go fast, even flipping a coin to make your choice.

☐ Can you quit your choice and pick a different option at a reasonable cost? If yes, go fast. If no, can you decision stack?

☐ Can you exercise multiple options in parallel? If yes, go fast.

☐ Is there additional information (available at a reasonable cost) that would establish a clearly preferred option or, if there is already a clearly preferred option, change your preference? If yes, go find it. If no, decide.

The Terminator Was Freerolling

The Terminator, conceived and directed by James Cameron, tells the story about a dismal future in which the rise of a self-aware computer network, Skynet, tries to wipe out humanity. A resistance movement, led by survivor John Connor, fights Skynet and its army of machines.

The action focuses on Sarah Connor, a waitress in Los Angeles in 1984. She doesn't know it at the time, but she will someday give birth to John Connor. In 2029, Skynet sends a robot killer, T-800 Model 101 (The Terminator) back to 1984 to kill Sarah Connor to stop her son from being born. The resistance also sends someone back in time—Kyle Reese, a soldier whose mission is to protect Sarah Connor from the Terminator.

The Terminator's return to 1984 Los Angeles could have had two outcomes: It could kill Sarah Connor, preventing Skynet's nemesis from being born; or it could fail, in which case Skynet would still take over the world, start a nuclear war, and wipe out most of humanity. In other words, even if the Terminator were to fail, Skynet would be no worse off than before. It would still have to deal with the Connor-led resistance, but it was already dealing with that. The worst possible outcome (from Skynet's perspective when it sent the Terminator back in 2029) was the status quo.

But if the Terminator were to succeed in killing Sarah Connor? Skynet would be in much better shape in the future.

Skynet and the Terminator were freerolling.

Why "Good Enough" Is Good Enough: Satisficing vs. maximizing

Because we're capable of spending a lot of time being indecisive (on both low-impact and high-impact decisions), the strategies in this chapter are designed to help you figure out when additional time spent on a decision isn't worth it. You want to know when a decision is "good enough," particularly because you don't want to chase the illusory ideal of a "perfect" decision in conditions in which you're operating with imperfect information.

Trying to get as close to 100% certainty as possible in a decision is known as *maximizing*. Most people have a tendency to be maximizers, spending a lot of time chasing certainty about their choice.

> **MAXIMIZING**
> Decision-making motivated by trying to make the optimal decision; not deciding before examining every option; trying to make the perfect choice.

Of course, you can rarely approach perfect information. If you're wasting your time on illusory or infinitesimal gains in precision, you're losing the chance to spend that time where the return is greater, or on better sorting, or on making more experimental choices that provide low-cost information for later decisions. That's why many of the strategies laid out in this chapter are designed to steer you toward a more realistic approach to decisions known as *satisficing* (a term made from the combination of "satisfy" and "suffice").

The framework of this book should get you more comfortable with satisficing, choosing options that are good enough, living in the space between "right" and "wrong."

> **SATISFICING**
> Decision-making motivated by choosing the first satisfactory option available.

8

The Power of Negative Thinking

Take a moment and think about some beliefs you held ten or more years ago that you would have defended vehemently at that time, but that now, looking back, you realize weren't so solid.

1 List up to five of those beliefs.

1._____

_____

2._____

_____

3._____

_____

4._____

_____

5. _____

_____

2 Now take a moment to think about beliefs you hold today that you would defend vehemently. Of those, list up to five beliefs that you think are good candidates for, in ten or twenty years, looking back and realizing weren't so solid.

1. _____

_____

2. _____

_____

3. _____

_____

4. _____

_____

5. _____

_____

3 Which did you find easier: identifying beliefs that you held in the distant past that you now don't consider so solid, or identifying beliefs you hold today that are candidates for doubting in ten years? (Circle one.)

Beliefs from ten years ago   *Current beliefs, in ten years*

If you're like most people, when it came to strong beliefs you held long ago that you have since reconsidered, you were probably looking for more space to write because you could easily think of many examples. Likewise, you probably struggled to come up with many—or, maybe even, *any*—current beliefs to nominate for future revision or reversal.

We'll come back to this later in this chapter.

[I]

Think Positive, but Plan Negative:
Identifying our difficulties in executing on our goals

You make a New Year's resolution that you're not going to stay out late on worknights. By the second week of January, you find yourself out at midnight on a Wednesday, celebrating a close friend's birthday.

You're not alone in quickly breaking your New Year's resolution. Within a week, 23% of New Year's resolutions are abandoned. And 92% of people *never* achieve their goal.

When it comes to reaching our goals, we have an execution problem.

It's one thing to decide that you're going to eat healthier. It's another thing entirely to stick to your pledge when facing down someone's birthday cake.

It's one thing to resolve to go to the gym every day before work. It's another thing entirely to hop out of bed when you're facing down the snooze button.

It's one thing to decide that you're not going to panic when the stock market goes down. It's another thing entirely to stay the course when you're facing down a 5% drop in the market.

There is a big gap between what we know we should do to achieve our goals and the decisions we actually make. Carl Richards, a financial planner, calls this the *behavior gap*, a term he popularized in his 2012 book of the same name.

The behavior gap is about execution. The good news is there are decision tools that can help you narrow the gap. **Negative thinking** is one of the most effective of those tools.

All this and thought magnets too: The power of positive thinking

There is an enormous and popular body of literature in the genre of positive thinking, starting with books such as Napoleon Hill's *Think and Grow Rich*, and, of course, Norman Vincent Peale's *The Power of Positive Thinking*. Peale's work was so popular that his close friends and enthusiasts included Presidents Eisenhower and Nixon. He even officiated at Donald Trump's first wedding.

The premise of this literature is that positive thinking and positive visualization increase the chances you'll succeed. The obverse (sometimes implied and sometimes explicit) is that negative thinking will decrease the chances you'll succeed, or even create failure.

The ultimate (albeit extreme) expression of positive thinking is the book *The Secret*. The book's website says it spent 190 weeks on *The New York Times* bestseller list and has 20 million copies in print. *The Secret* is the power of positive thinking on steroids. The book not only explicitly asserts that there is a causal relationship between positive or negative thoughts and success or failure, it offers the causal mechanism: magnetism.

According to *The Secret*, your brain waves have a magnetic quality that makes positive thoughts attract positive things and negative thoughts attract negative things. Imagine a diamond ring in just the right way and your significant other will give you one. Imagine a traffic jam on your way to work and you'll find yourself bumper to bumper the next morning.

(Pro tip: That's super-wacky. Your thoughts can't magnetically attract things to you.)

Even if the particular causal mechanism that *The Secret* posits is bizarre, the claim of a causal relationship between thoughts and outcomes is uncontroversial in this literature. Pretty much anyone who reads in this genre walks away reasonably inferring that positive thoughts cause positive outcomes and negative thoughts cause negative ones.

Don't confuse the destination with the route

A good portion of the positive thinking literature asks you to set a positive destination and imagine yourself traveling along the route, succeeding at every point. What's implied is that if you imagine how you might fail along the way, that failure will materialize. This conflates destination planning and route planning. There is a big difference between thinking "I am going to fail," and imagining "*If* I were to fail, what are the ways in which that could happen?"

It's important not to confuse the two.

Imagining how you might fail doesn't make failure materialize. In fact, there's a lot of value in picturing the obstacles that might slow you down or get you lost, preventing you from reaching your destination.

You can think about this value as the difference between using an old-fashioned paper map and using a navigation app such as Waze. The paper map allows you to see your destination and the different routes that could lead you there. But all those routes appear as clear roads. A paper map can't show you road closures, heavy traffic, accidents, or speed traps. It can't show you the obstacles that might impede your progress. But Waze can.

That's why people rarely use paper maps anymore.

When it comes to navigation, negative thinking gets you to your destination more reliably.

Waze for decision-making: Mental contrasting

There is a robust body of research on ***mental contrasting*** that demonstrates the power of negative thinking. Mental contrasting is the process of imagining the obstacles that might lie along the route to your destination.

It's like using Waze for decision-making.

Gabriele Oettingen, a professor of psychology at New York University, has conducted over two decades of research showing that anticipating the ways things might go wrong on the path to achieving your goals helps you more successfully reach your destination. For example, among people in a program trying to lose at least fifty pounds, those who imagined the ways in which they might fail lost twenty-six pounds more on average than those who engaged in positive visualization alone. She found that mental contrasting provided a similar boost across a variety of domains, including getting better grades, finishing school projects on time, finding a job, recovering from surgery, or even following through with asking a crush out on a date.

> **MENTAL CONTRASTING**
> Imagining what you want to accomplish and confronting the obstacles that might stand in the way of accomplishing it.

Just like when you're using Waze instead of an old-fashioned map, you want to see where your decision-making might go wrong and bad luck might intervene. Then you won't be surprised when those things happen *and* you'll have a plan to manage your reaction when they do.

That's the power of negative thinking.

Despite the obvious advantages of mental contrasting, it's not a surprise that the power of negative thinking hasn't captured the zeitgeist quite like the power of positive thinking has.

Imagining success affirms your sense of competence and ability to achieve your goals. It also feels much like experiencing success—awesome.

Positive visualization gives you a taste of the emotional high you get from actually succeeding. On the flip side, imagining failure is emotionally similar to actually failing. We are understandably *attracted* to a self-help genre that encourages us to feel good and avoid feeling bad.

But the mental contrasting research tells us that the temporary discomfort from imagining failure is worth it, because embracing that discomfort makes it *more likely that you'll actually experience success.*

Mental pain leads to real-world gains.

Mental time travel: You can see more from the summit than the base

You can improve the process of mental contrasting by combining it with *mental time travel*.

Put simply, mental time travel is the ability to imagine yourself at some time in the past or future. Human beings naturally time travel all the time. You daydream about when you were a child or you imagine what the world will be like in ten or twenty years, or even beyond your lifetime. (Estate planning is an exercise in mental time travel.)

You can turn this organic thing you do, imagining yourself in the past or future, into a productive decision tool called *prospective hindsight*.

Prospective hindsight enhances mental contrasting because looking back from your destination is a more effective way to plan the best route than looking ahead at where you are trying to go.

PROSPECTIVE HINDSIGHT
Imagining yourself at some time in the future, having succeeded or failed at a goal, and *looking back* at how you arrived at that destination.

If you want to climb a mountain to the summit, you have to start at the base. What's directly in front of you takes up most of your visual field and blocks a clear view of the possible routes to the summit and the obstacles you're likely to encounter along the way. Once you reach the summit, you can look back to where you started and see the entire landscape, including the fallen trees or impassable boulders that were invisible from the base. You can clearly see the alternate routes that might have been safer or more efficient than the one you traversed.

That's why it's helpful to get guidance from someone who has already been at the summit before you start your climb.

When it comes to decision-making, current conditions also play an outsized role in how we think because we have a tendency to assume that those conditions will persist. The sense that the way things are now is the way they will always be is known as *status quo bias*.

Of course, nearly everything changes over time. This includes your emotional state, how much money you make, or the political climate. Paradigms shift, challenges change, market conditions evolve, and technology provides additional solutions as well as creating new problems.

STATUS QUO BIAS
Our tendency to believe that the way things are today will remain the same in the future.

When you look forward from the present, status quo bias distorts your view.

But if you plan from an imagined point in the future and look back toward the present, you can improve your ability to see beyond what's immediately in front of you—not just the obstacles farther along the route but how conditions might change.

The Happiness Test is an example of how mental time travel gives you a clearer perspective. The trip to the future that you take when you apply the Happiness Test reminds you that something that feels significant in the present, like picking the wrong movie or the wrong entrée, will fade from view once time has passed.

Another advantage of mental time travel: Getting to the outside view

Remember at the beginning of this chapter when you compared your beliefs of ten years ago to the beliefs you hold today? Recall that, in general, people have a much easier time coming up with things they used to believe but no longer do than things they believe now that are good candidates for change in the future.

This reveals an added advantage of mental time travel: It allows you to get to the outside view, seeing yourself more as another person might see you.

We are all motivated to protect *our own* identity. We are all motivated to keep our beliefs intact. This makes it hard to see yourself objectively. You don't have that same motivation to protect the identity and beliefs of *other people*.

Looking at a past version of yourself is a little more like seeing a different person, like when you're listening to your friend complain about all the jerks they've dated. You see the situation in a more objective and detached way. That's why it's easy to come up with a list of beliefs that a long-ago version of you held that present you realizes aren't so solid.

Prospective hindsight allows you to imagine your future self looking back at your present self. You can think about the goals and decisions of "that person" more clearly from that vantage point than when you're caught in the gravitational pull of the present moment.

[2]

Premortems and Backcasting: Whether you deserve an autopsy or a parade, you should know why in advance

Premortems: An autopsy *before* the patient dies

If you've ever watched a police or medical drama, you're familiar with the *postmortem*, the medical examination of a corpse to determine the cause of death. Businesses commonly conduct postmortems in order to identify the reasons for a bad outcome. The goal is to learn from past mistakes.

Because postmortems happen after the fact, by definition, their benefits are limited to lessons for the future. And we know the quality of those lessons will be imperfect because of biases like resulting.

More fundamentally, a postmortem is limited because *the patient is already dead—* you can't bring the corpse back to life. Likewise, the business has already experienced the failure.

In part for that reason, the psychologist Gary Klein advises using a decision tool he calls a *premortem*. In effect, a premortem allows you to do the same examination of the causes of death *while the patient is still alive*. In a premortem, you imagine that you made a specific decision that worked out poorly or that you failed to reach a goal. From the vantage point of having already experienced the future failure, you look back to the present and identify the reasons why that might have happened.

> **PREMORTEM**
> Imagining yourself at some time in the future, having failed to achieve a goal, and *looking back* at how you arrived at that destination.

Your goal is to go to the gym every morning for the next six months. Imagine that it's six months from now and you went to the gym only three times. Why did that happen?

You have a problem being late on deadlines and you resolve that you'll get your next assignment done on time. Imagine that it's the day after the project is due and you didn't finish the assignment. Why did that happen?

You've done a job search and decided on hiring a particular candidate. Before making the offer, imagine it's a year from now and they've quit. Why did that happen?

How to conduct a premortem, and what you can learn

This is how you can implement a premortem as part of your decision process (adapted from Gary Klein):

> ### STEPS FOR A PREMORTEM
>
> (1) Identify the goal you're trying to achieve or a specific decision you're considering.
> (2) Figure out a reasonable time period for achieving the goal or for the decision to play out.
> (3) Imagine it's the day after that period of time and you didn't achieve the goal, or the decision worked out poorly. Looking back from that imagined point in the future, list up to five reasons why you failed due to your own decisions and actions or those of your team.
> (4) List up to five reasons why you failed due to things outside your control.
> (5) If you're doing this as a team exercise, have each member do steps (3) and (4) independently, prior to a group discussion of reasons.

Broadly speaking, there are two categories of stuff that can interfere with achieving a goal:

- *Stuff within your control*—your own decisions and actions or, as is often the case in a business setting, the decision and actions of your team
- *Stuff outside of your control*—in addition to luck, the decisions and actions of people you have no influence over

An effective premortem should produce reasons for failure within each category.

You need to get to work on time tomorrow for an early meeting. Imagine you're late and miss part of the meeting. Why did that happen?

Reasons having to do with your own decision-making: You overslept because you hit the snooze button too many times. You forgot to set your alarm. You left too thin a margin for traffic. You were texting and driving and got into an accident.

Reasons outside of your control: The power went out and your phone died so your alarm didn't go off. There was a sudden blizzard. Even though there are normally clear roads, there was an accident on the road on your way to work. Someone else was texting while driving and hit your car.

You devote yourself to your start-up, Kingdom Comb. Imagine it's a year from now and you've failed. Why did that happen?

Reasons having to do with your own decision-making: You were an abrasive boss and couldn't retain valuable employees. When you went out to raise seed capital, you had a greedy valuation and refused to compromise, failing to raise money beyond the friends-and-family round. You insisted on cutting your own hair, which looked awful and left a lingering negative impression on potential investors.

Reasons outside of your control: A recession hit just as you went out to raise a seed round, so start-up capital dried up. A leading ride-sharing company branched out into the same space, killing your business.

1 Pick a goal you have or a specific decision you're currently considering.

_____

_____

2 What is a reasonable time period for achieving the goal or having the decision play out?

_____

Imagine it's just after that period of time and things haven't worked out. Why?

3 List up to five reasons why this happened because of your decisions and execution.

1. _____

_____

2. _____

_____

3. _____

_____

4. _____

_____

5. _____

_____

4 List up to five reasons why this happened because of things outside of your control.

1. _____
   _____

2. _____
   _____

3. _____
   _____

4. _____
   _____

5. _____
   _____

5 Did the premortem identify any obstacles
you hadn't identified before? (Circle one.)   *YES   NO*

IF YOU'RE LIKE MOST PEOPLE, doing the premortem helped you identify some reasons for failure that you wouldn't have thought of otherwise.

Research suggests that when you combine mental time travel and mental contrasting, you can produce 30% more reasons for why something might fail. That's an obvious upgrade for your crystal ball. A premortem boosts the clarity with which you can glimpse into the future. And the more complete your view of the future, the better your decision-making will be.

The added benefit of premortems for groups: Turning more heads into more brains

Intuitively, we think that more heads are better than one when it comes to making decisions. Because you can get higher-quality decisions by accessing the outside view, and part of the outside view lives in the heads of other people, a group—that is, more heads—should reveal more of the outside view.

It's simple math.

Unfortunately, the dynamics of teams often stymie that potential advantage. Teams naturally bend toward groupthink. Members confirm one another's beliefs. Once there is a sense that consensus is being reached, team members will (usually unintentionally) often refrain from sharing what's in their head if it diverges from what the group thinks. Sometimes this is because team members change their opinion without realizing it, forgetting that they ever disagreed. Other times, they don't want to be a "squeaky wheel" or a "naysayer." They want to be viewed as a "team player"—agreeable and supportive in building consensus.

Even though each member of a group has the potential to gain more access to the outside view by tapping into the differing opinions that live in multiple heads, in practice teams usually end up with multiple heads expressing the same inside view.

Premortems help teams solve the groupthink problem by exposing and encouraging different points of view. When you do a premortem as a group, being a good team player means coming up the most creative ways the decision might fail, coming up with reasons that the consensus opinion is wrong.

Premortems reveal and reward the squeak.

If you want to peer into the universe of stuff you don't know to see the stuff that disagrees with your beliefs, premortems are a way to do that.

Backcasting: Sharing the secret of your success . . . with yourself

Of course, a complete view of the future depends on exploring more than just the negative possibilities. Preparing for a rainy day is helpful, but it doesn't rain all the time. You need to imagine why you might succeed as well as why you might fail. Exploring both futures will give you the most accurate forecast.

The companion technique to a premortem is known as a *backcast*. When you do a backcast, you imagine and work backward from a positive future. Chip Heath and Dan Heath refer to this process as a *preparade*, imagining in advance why someone is throwing a parade for you.

In a backcast, you imagine your decision has worked out or you've

> **BACKCASTING**
> Imagining yourself at some time in the future, having succeeded at achieving a goal, and *looking back* at how you arrived at that destination.

reached your goal and ask, "Why did that happen?" The steps for backcasting are similar to those for a premortem.

STEPS FOR A BACKCAST

(1) Identify the goal you're trying to achieve or a specific decision you're considering.

(2) Figure out a reasonable time period for achieving the goal or for the decision to play out.

(3) Imagine it's the day after that period of time and you achieved the goal, or the decision worked out well. Looking back from that imagined point in the future, list up to five reasons why you succeeded due to your own decisions and actions or those of your team.

(4) List up to five reasons why you succeeded due to things outside of your control.

(5) If you're doing this as a team exercise, have each member do steps (3) and (4) independently, prior to a group discussion of reasons.

Using the same goal or decision that you used for the premortem, imagine you have succeeded and ask yourself why that happened.

I List up to five reasons why you succeeded because of your decisions and execution.

1. _____

_____

2. _____

_____

3. _____

_____

4. _____

_____

5. _____

_____

2 List up to five reasons why you succeeded because of things outside of your control.

1. _____

_____

2. _____

_____

3. _____

_____

4. _____

_____

5. _____

_____

WHILE YOU NEED BOTH premortems and backcasts to get a clear view of the future, the reason for the emphasis on negative thinking in this chapter is to encourage you to go beyond imagining success. Visualizing a positive future is not difficult for most people. You're probably *already* backcasting all the time.

The relationship between premortems and backcasting is similar to the relationship between the outside view and the inside view. A good decision process starts by considering the outside view and anchors there, because you naturally live in the inside view. The outside view acts to discipline the cognitive biases that reside in the inside view. Likewise, a good decision process starts with a premortem and anchors there because you naturally live in a backcast.

Together, they show you an integrated picture of the future. The premortem reduces the natural tendency toward overconfidence, the illusion of control, and other cognitive biases that cause you to overestimate the chances that things will work out. The backcast evens out the view if you are pessimistic in nature or underconfident.

> Just as accuracy lies in the intersection between the outside view and the inside view, the more accurate view of the future lies in the intersection between a premortem and a backcast.

Most important, you're doing more than just *imagining* success and failure. You're identifying the paths that lead to both results, and multiple ways to access the path to success, as well as the obstacles you have to avoid or manage.

Turning premortems and backcasts into a Decision Exploration Table

It's helpful to see the output of both a premortem and a backcast in one place. You can do this by using a ***Decision Exploration Table***.

You'll see that the Decision Exploration Table on the next page also includes a column for estimating the likelihood that any of the reasons for failure or success will occur. Because all these things (whether within or outside your control) are not equally likely, it's useful to include probabilities as part of the forecast. Combined with an estimate of the impact of these unfavorable or favorable events, you will be better able to prioritize your attention to each.

1 Use the Decision Exploration Table below to record the output of the premortem and the backcast you just performed. Add an estimate of likelihood of each item occurring.

DECISION EXPLORATION TABLE

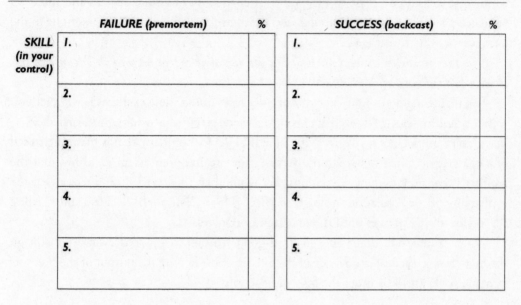

	FAILURE (premortem)	%	SUCCESS (backcast)	%
SKILL (in your control)	1.		1.	
	2.		2.	
	3.		3.	
	4.		4.	
	5.		5.	

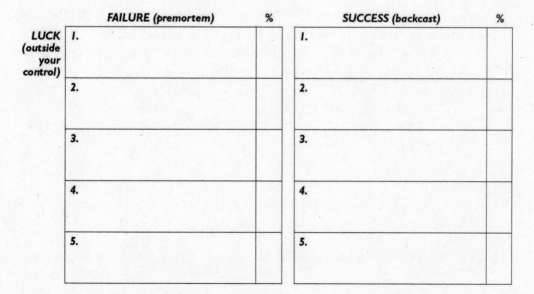

	FAILURE (premortem)	%	SUCCESS (backcast)	%
LUCK (outside your control)	1.		1.	
	2.		2.	
	3.		3.	
	4.		4.	
	5.		5.	

IF YOU HAD A navigation app for your goals and decisions, it would work like a premortem and a backcast and its output would look like the Decision Exploration Table. You've identified two broad categories of future events (those within and outside your control) that could decrease or increase your chances of failure or success and made an educated guess about their likelihood. You now have a good map of what might lie in the path on the way to your goal.

Now that you have the output, how can you use what you've learned in advance to improve your likelihood of succeeding?

The first thing you should always consider after doing these exercises is whether you want to modify your goal or change your decision, given what you've just learned.

As an example, let's say you're with a medical device company that is planning to sell one of its devices in a new market overseas. Your team's premortem identifies that the country is considering new regulations that would ban the device. You forecast that the probability of the regulations going into effect is high. You might decide against selling the device in that market until the uncertainty resolves.

When you decide that you still have good reasons to proceed even after you go through these exercises, in advance of the decision you can use the output of the premortem and backcast to consider the following actions:

1. Modifying your decision to increase the chances of the good stuff happening and decrease the chances of the bad stuff happening.
2. Planning how you'll react to future outcomes, so they don't take you by surprise.
3. Looking for ways to mitigate the impact of bad outcomes if they occur.

[3]

Precommitting to Your Good Intentions:
Making a U-turn on the "road to hell"

The Decision Exploration Table allows you to identify decisions and actions that will help you gain ground toward your goal, as well as decisions and actions that will hinder your progess. Having completed that exercise, you are now in a position to figure out how you can raise barriers to impede behavior that might interfere with your success or lower barriers to encourage behavior that can promote your success.

This decision tool is known as a ***precommitment contract***.

Precommitments of this type are also called *Ulysses contracts*, after an innovative precommitment by Ulysses, the Roman name of the Greek hero of Homer's *Odyssey*. To return home, Ulysses knew his ship had to pass the island of the Sirens. He had been warned that if he or his crew heard the Sirens' song, they would have an irresistible desire to steer their ship to their deaths on the island's rocky shore.

In other words, he had done some quality mental contrasting.

Having identified how he might fail,

> **PRECOMMITMENT CONTRACT**
> An agreement that commits you in advance to take or refrain from certain actions, or raising or lowering barriers to those actions. Such agreements can be with others (for group decisions or to create accountability to another person) or with yourself.

Ulysses took action to make sure he couldn't act on the impulse to steer to his death. Before sailing past the island, he filled his crew's ears with beeswax so they couldn't hear the song. He also ordered his crew to tie him to the mast so that there was no way for him to steer toward the beautiful but deadly song when he heard it.

Ulysses contracts can involve three types of advance commitments:

- Like Ulysses, you can *physically prevent yourself* from making poor decisions.
- You can *raise barriers*, making it harder to execute on actions that will defeat your goals. When you raise barriers, you're not physically preventing yourself from acting, like when you tether yourself to a mast. But you are increasing friction to make it more difficult to tamper with your plans. Raised barriers also provide you with a moment to stop and think before acting.
- You can *lower barriers*, reducing the friction to execute on actions that advance you toward success.

Ulysses contracts that raise barriers can range from putting a lock on the refrigerator and keeping the key in a time-release safe to simply declaring your intentions to a friend. The lock physically keeps you from getting into the refrigerator. Telling a friend about your intentions makes you accountable to another person, a barrier that compels you to stay true to your word.

You are probably already using some Ulysses contracts to help you stick to your decisions.

You avoid driving under the influence by using a ride-sharing service when going out on New Year's Eve, which physically prevents you from getting behind the wheel at the end of the night.

You want to get to work on time so you keep your alarm across the room, which raises a barrier to hitting the snooze button and falling back to sleep.

You decide to eat healthier and you know that late-night snacking is where you'll go wrong. You can throw out all the junk food in your house. You could still have food delivered or go to the nearest drive-through, but getting rid of the junk food increases friction and raises the barrier to giving in to that impulse. You can also stock your house with healthy food or pack a lunch to bring to work with you. That reduces friction and makes it easier to stick to good choices.

Your goal is to save for retirement and you've identified that impulse purchases cause you to overspend. You can set up automatic transfers from your paycheck into a retirement account. That makes it harder for you to bust your budget.

I   Using the Decision Exploration Table you just created, list up to three precommitments you can make to physically prevent yourself from acting contrary to your plans, or precommitments that will raise or lower barriers to decisions you want to discourage or encourage for yourself (or your team).

1. _____

   _____

2. _____

   _____

3. _____

   _____

PRECOMMITMENT CONTRACTS ARE NOT a guarantee that you will never veer from the ideal path to your destination. Unlike Ulysses, you will rarely have a mast handy that you can lash yourself to and thereby guarantee you behave in a certain way. Although precommitment contracts can't ensure that your future decisions will be perfect, they will reduce the chances you'll stray. And even small increases in the quality of your decisions will accumulate over time, making it much more likely you'll reach your destination.

[4]

The Dr. Evil Game: Outthinking the evil genius making sure you fail (P.S. The evil genius is you)

When you conduct a premortem, you are considering an unintentional future failure. Your goal was to succeed but you failed.

But what if you imagined the ways in which you could *intentionally make yourself fail*? That would be the ultimate exercise in negative thinking, building on what you learned from prospective hindsight.

The decision tool for doing this is the **Dr. Evil game**.

In the Dr. Evil game (adapted from Dan Egan), you imagine that Dr. Evil has a mind-control device that he's using to get you to make decisions that guarantee failure. Dr. Evil, being an evil genius, knows he can't make you fail unless he avoids detection. If you make obviously bad decisions, he'll get caught. You and the people around you will notice that you're making bad decisions and his evil plans will be thwarted.

Dr. Evil's diabolical plan has to make you fail *and* avoid detection. His solution is to have you make losing decisions that are easy to explain away for any given instance of that type of decision, but that guarantee failure if you repeat them over time.

You already encountered some of Dr. Evil's work when you were cautioned against treating a free donut as a freeroll. It's a *free* donut—how big could the downside be? Eating a single sweet treat doesn't feel like it will cause you to lose much ground in your goal to eat healthier, and it is a pretty easy exception to justify. It is only over time that you can see how those small losses accumulate.

That's how Dr. Evil gets you. If he wants to make you fail at your nutritional goal, he's not going to deliver you a truckload of cheesecake, popcorn, pizza, and ice cream and have you shovel it all in an hour after you resolve to eat healthier.

Instead, you eat a slice of cheesecake because you are unhappy about a turn in a relationship. A day or so later, you split a bucket of popcorn, but that's because you patched up the relationship and are having such a good time at the movies. Then you eat a slice of pizza at work because you were working late, you were hungry, and the boss ordered pizza for the crew. The next weekend, everyone is eating ice cream at your nephew's birthday party and you join in because you don't want to appear rude.

That's how Dr. Evil makes you fail. He gets you to make small, poor choices that hide in the shadows, keeping you from seeing how repeatedly making those decisions guarantees failure. You see each instance as unique and justifiable and don't see how they fit into a larger scheme.

When you hit the snooze button, you see the upside of another five minutes of sleep. What you don't see is the downside of an accumulating series of decisions that make you unreliable or habitually late. The Dr. Evil game helps you wake up to those categories of decisions before you are beset by them.

STEPS TO PLAY THE DR. EVIL GAME

(1) Imagine a positive goal.
(2) Imagine that Dr. Evil has control of your brain, causing you to make decisions that will guarantee failure.
(3) Any given instance of that type of decision must have a good enough rationale that it won't be noticed by you or others examining that decision.
(4) Write down those decisions.

The output of the Dr. Evil game spots whole categories of decisions that will cause you to fail.

There are two ways to address these categories once you've identified them. First, you should appreciate that these types of decisions require special attention. They need to be elevated in your decision process so that they are less reflexive (where you fail to consider them in the context of their detrimental cumulative impact) and more deliberative.

It is important to pay more attention to the context when making these types of decisions. Ask yourself questions such as "How often have I been making exceptions recently?" or "Will I feel these exceptions were worth it in a week or a month?" This added deliberation provides you with a moment to stop and think, as well as a chance to do a bit of time travel to get in touch with your future self.

This demand for context is especially relevant for team decisions. Team members should be encouraged to question decisions that have easily accepted rationales, looking for situations where exceptions have the potential to become the rule (and that rule undermines achieving the original goal).

Second, you can make a pre-commitment to take those choices out of your hands by making a *category decision*.

CATEGORY DECISION

When you identify a category of poor decisions that will be hard to spot except in the aggregate, you can decide in advance what options you can and cannot choose that fall within that category.

You already make category decisions all the time with dietary choices. If you've decided you're a vegan, that's a category decision—animal products are no longer an option when deciding what to eat. If you follow a Keto diet, simple carbs aren't an option.

There is a big difference between saying "I'm a vegan" and saying "I want to eat less meat." If you say the latter, you are faced with a new decision about whether to eat meat at every meal. And every time you make a new decision, you are within Dr. Evil's grasp.

A common practice of successful professional investors is to make category decisions to avoid investments outside their circle of competence. In facing an opportunity outside of their realm of expertise, particularly one that promises juicy returns, investors run the risk of fooling themselves into thinking that they can make a winning decision. The temptation to wander outside the circle of competence is especially strong if those boundaries are not in place. On the other hand, if they say, "I'm a seed investor" or "I invest only in assets of REITs that are in restructuring or bankruptcy," they are less likely to consider anything else that comes along.

When you make a category decision, you are making a onetime, advance choice about what options you can and cannot choose. This shields you from a series of decisions that are all vulnerable to your worst impulses in the moment.

I For the goal you considered in your Decision Exploration Table, list up to three ways Dr. Evil can make you fail. The justification for each decision must be sufficiently reasonable that someone from the outside looking in would be unlikely to question it if they didn't see the decision in the context of other, similar decisions.

1. _____

_____

2. _____

_____

3. _____

_____

2 Describe at least one category decision you can make as a precommitment to keep yourself out of these repeated "onetime" situations.

_____

_____

_____

_____

_____

ONE THING YOU SHOULD recognize from the Dr. Evil game is that the evil genius is _you_. The reasons that "Dr. Evil" comes up with are precisely the ways that you subtly sabotage yourself.

Dr. Evil doesn't get you with a guillotine blade chopping off your head. Instead, it's a death by a thousand cuts. In any particular instance, your decision is easy to justify. He gives you a good reason to make a choice that causes you to lose a little bit on the path to reaching your goal. Then he piles up a lot of those decisions, killing your plans slowly, without allowing you to be aware that you are taking yourself down.

When you make category decisions, as with other kinds of precommitments, you're not always going to make a decision that falls on the right side of the category. But adopting category decisions will significantly reduce the probability that you will stray, and those gains will add up over time.

[5]

The Surprise Party No One Wants:
When your reaction to a bad outcome can make things worse

Another likely obstacle to achieving a goal is the way you react to a bad outcome. Your decision-making is frequently impaired in the immediate wake of a bad outcome. By planning how you'll handle the slings and arrows of the future, you can better manage those setbacks and avoid making bad outcomes worse.

Right after a bad outcome, especially one due to something outside your control, you can become emotionally compromised. The emotional centers of your brain get aroused, increasing the likelihood that you'll make poor decisions. When activated, the emotional parts of your brain inhibit the parts of your brain responsible for rational thinking. Shutting down those parts of your brain compromises the quality of any decision you make in that state.

This hot emotional state is called *tilt*. When on tilt, you're more likely to make decisions that make a bad situation worse.

You create a diversified portfolio for your investments. The stock market drops 5% in a month, so you reallocate your money out of cash and bonds and into stocks in order to buy the dip. Within a week the market drops another 5%, causing you to panic and sell all your stocks immediately.

That's tilt.

There are quite a few ways that your decision-making can be compromised when you're on tilt.

As an example, let's say you commit to making healthy eating choices. A week later, you eat a couple of donuts in the breakroom. A lot of people respond to that bad decision by saying, "Yeah, I guess today is shot." Then they load up on junk food, thinking they'll start again the next day . . . or next week . . . or maybe *next year's* New Year's resolution. That's the *what-the-hell effect.*

> ### TILT
> When a bad outcome causes you to be in an emotionally hot state that compromises the quality of your decision-making.

Or let's say things aren't going your way on some project in which you've already invested a bunch of resources. You're unlikely to quit in those situations, even when an objective observer would see that quitting is appropriate. In the wake of a bad outcome, it's difficult to see the situation rationally. If you could get to the outside view you would quit, but you don't because you're stuck in the inside view. That's the *sunk cost fallacy*, another example of tilt.

Ways to prepare for setbacks

When you consider how you might respond to negative outcomes *in advance of those things happening*, you're likely to think more rationally. It's easier to come up with the appropriate course of action to take when things don't go your way before those things go wrong than it is after they go wrong.

Identifying how things can go wrong helps reduce tilt in three ways.

First, identifying bad outcomes in advance can reduce the emotional impact those outcomes will have on your decision-making when they do occur. It changes your frame from "I can't believe this happened to me" to "This happened but I knew it was a possibility." When you can reach the latter state in the wake of a bad outcome, you're less likely to go on tilt. This may be one of the reasons why mental contrasting improves outcomes just as Gabriele Oettingen found, because you come to terms in advance with the fact that things may not work out.

Second, you can learn to recognize the signs that you're on tilt so you can identify and address it more quickly. This involves taking a *tilt inventory* of conditions you recognize from past instances when you've been emotionally impaired: Is your face flushed? Do you have trouble keeping your thoughts straight? Do you engage in self-talk about how bad things always happen to you or (like hindsight bias) you should have seen it coming? Do you take things personally, or become confrontational, or use particular language, or engage in some other thought patterns when you're being guided by emotion?

We all have different signs, but you can learn to spot them when they happen to you.

When you've done a tilt inventory and you start checking off those conditions, commit to doing some mental time travel to help you see your situation from the outside view. Essentially, recruit your future self to help calm your present self down.

When you recognize the signs of tilt, ask yourself, "In a week (or a month, or a year), am I going to be happy with any decisions I make right now?" You can also apply the Happiness Test. This time traveling helps you get a better perspective, creating a moment to stop and think that will reduce the chances of making a compromised decision. Additionally, this type of time travel recruits the parts of your brain where rational thought lives, inhibiting your emotional response.

Third, you can precommit to certain actions that you'll take (or refrain from taking) in the wake of bad outcomes. This is tantamount to tying your hands to the mast to prevent emotional decisions. For example, if you've identified that you make bad decisions following sudden drops in the stock market, get someone else to execute trades for you in order to prevent making impulsive trades yourself.

Like other precommitments, you can set advance criteria for how you'll react. If you think you could fall for the sunk cost fallacy, refusing to quit when quitting is the appropriate response, come up in advance with the conditions under which you would quit. Write those down and commit to changing course when those conditions arise. That's particularly effective in a team setting.

Or you might plan how you'll deal with the what-the-hell effect. If you're committing to eat healthier, it's easy to recognize that you won't always make perfect decisions. When you imagine faltering and succumbing to the breakroom donut, you can commit in advance that you won't let one bad decision derail or postpone your goal. This works especially well if you create accountability by declaring your intentions to other people.

| Go back to your Decision Exploration Table and pick one of the ways bad luck might intervene. Use the space below to create a precommitment to how you'll react to that bad luck.

_____

_____

_____

_____

_____

_____

_____

TILT ENCOMPASSES SEVERAL KINDS of emotional reactions to *bad* outcomes. You should recognize that unexpectedly *good* outcomes also have the potential for compromising your decision-making.

You wait until the last minute before writing a paper or studying for an exam. You get an A, and now you think you can wait till the last minute to study for the next exam.

Your business is in a bind, so you're forced to hire someone in a pinch without considering multiple candidates or learning much about your emergency hire. They become an outstanding employee, so you decide you're a quick judge of character who can pick future employees without a process for attracting applicants or conducting interviews.

> **Consider using the same tools for preparing in advance for your reaction to unexpectedly positive outcomes as you do for unexpectedly bad ones.**

In the wake of positive investing results, you overrate your ability to choose stocks or believe that you no longer need the safety net of diversification.

[6]

Deflecting the Slings and Arrows of Outrageous Fortune: "If you can't beat 'em . . . mitigate 'em"

You might think that because luck is, by definition, something you can't control, the only thing you can do when you identify where bad luck might intervene is to plan your reaction and keep your emotions under wraps.

But that's not true.

When you identify the possibility of bad luck, there are things you can do in advance to soften the impact of that bad luck. These things are called **hedges**.

There are three key features of a hedge.

1. A hedge reduces the impact of bad luck when it occurs.
2. A hedge has a cost.
3. You hope you never use it.

This might sound a lot like an insurance policy. Insurance is a classic example of a hedge. When you buy homeowner's insurance, there's obviously a cost to that insurance. But if a fire destroys your house, the insurance will pay most of the financial cost. As anyone who has homeowner's insurance recognizes, you're paying for something you hope you'll never have to use.

One of the things that comes out of a premortem is that you identify places where bad luck might intervene. You should actively evaluate opportunities to hedge against that bad luck.

There are lots of hedges available in everyday situations.

If your heart's desire is an outdoor wedding, a premortem will remind you that a rainstorm can ruin the day. Since your dream wedding is outdoors, you can hedge by renting and setting up a tent in case it rains. The rental costs money and you are hoping you don't have to use the tent, but your day will be saved if the bad luck happens.

> ### HEDGING
> Paying for something that you hope you'll never use to mitigate the impact of a downside event.

Leaving early for the airport to give yourself extra time to make a flight is a hedge. The cost is time you might have to spend hanging out in the airport, but if there is heavy traffic, an accident, or a lengthy delay getting through security, you won't miss your flight.

When Ivan Boesky was supposedly ordering every item on the menu at Tavern on the Green, he was hedging against the chance that the one dish he might order would be bad. It obviously costs a lot of money to order the whole menu just to offset the risk of ordering one item you don't like. For most people, the cost of such a hedge would be unreasonable.

You can execute a less extravagant version of the Boesky hedge if you and a friend each order a different entrée and agree to share. But notice that there is still a cost: If you like your dish, you have to give half of it away.

Anytime you exercise options in parallel, you're hedging. Each additional option has a cost, but it mitigates the effect of the other things you're doing not working out.

1 Using your premortem from the Decision Exploration Table, pick one of the ways you identified that luck can interfere with your plans.

_____

2 Explain how you might mitigate the effect of that bad luck with a hedge.

_____

_____

_____

WHEN YOU'RE CONSIDERING A HEDGE, you're naturally focused on weighing the cost of the hedge against the benefit of reducing the impact of a bad outcome. *But you should also think in advance about how you'll feel if you don't use the hedge.* When you pay for a hedge that you don't end up using, because it doesn't rain or your house never burns down, you might experience regret about having paid for the hedge in the first place. You might feel like you should have known that you wouldn't need it.

But that's just hindsight bias.

Consider that irrational regret in advance so that you can remind yourself why you paid for the hedge in the first place and can avoid the hindsight trap.

[7]

The Power of Negative Thinking Wrap-Up

These exercises were designed to get you to think about the following concepts:

- We are pretty good at setting positive goals for ourselves. Where we fall flat is at executing the things we need to do to achieve them. The gap between the things we know we should do and the decisions we later make is known as the **behavior gap**.
- The message of the **power of positive thinking** is that you'll succeed if you imagine yourself succeeding. Whether explicitly or by reasonable inference, the message is also that failure is the result of thinking about failure.
- Despite the importance of setting positive goals, positive visualization alone won't give you the best route to success. **Negative thinking** helps you identify things that might get in your way so you can identify ways to reach your destination more efficiently.
- Thinking about how things can go wrong is known as **mental contrasting**. You imagine what you want to accomplish and confront the barriers in the way of accomplishing it.
- You can identify more potential obstacles by combining mental contrasting with **mental time travel**, picturing yourself in the future having failed to achieve a goal, and then *looking back* at what got you to that outcome.
- Looking back from an imagined future at the route that got you there is called **prospective hindsight**.
- A **premortem** combines prospective hindsight with mental contrasting. To do a premortem, you place yourself in the future and imagine that you have failed to achieve your goal. You then consider the potential reasons things worked out poorly.
- In addition to helping individuals, premortems can help teams minimize groupthink and maximize access to the outside view by eliciting more diversity of opinions. This is especially true if team members do the premortem independently before discussing it as a group.
- A companion technique to a premortem is **backcasting**, where you work backward from a positive future to figure out why you succeeded.

- You can turn the output of premortems and backcasts, for easy reference, into a **Decision Exploration Table**, which also includes an estimate of the chances of the reasons for failure and success occurring.
- Given what you've learned from creating a Decision Exploration Table, the first thing to ask is whether you should modify your goal or change your decision.
- Once you've established that you're sticking with your goal or decision, you can create **precommitment contracts**, which raise barriers to behavior that interfere with your success or lower barriers to encourage behavior that promotes your success.
- You can also prepare for your reaction to setbacks along the way to your goal. People compound negative outcomes by making poor decisions after a bad result. **Tilt** is a common reaction that occurs in the wake of a bad result. The **what-the-hell effect** and the **sunk cost fallacy** are examples of tilt. Planning for your reaction allows you to create precommitments, establish criteria for changing course, and dampen your emotional reaction in the wake of a setback.
- **The Dr. Evil game** helps identify and address additional ways your behavior in the future might undermine your success. In the game, you note the ways that Dr. Evil would control your mind to *make* you fail through decisions that are justifiable as one-offs but unjustifiable over time.
- The Dr. Evil game can encourage you to adopt a precommitment called a **category decision**, where you decide in advance what options you can and cannot choose when you face a decision that falls within that category.
- You can also address potential bad luck by **hedging**, paying for something that mitigates the impact of a downside event occurring.

THE POWER OF
NEGATIVE THINKING CHECKLIST

Attempt to improve your likelihood of success for a goal you set or a decision that involves future execution by doing the following:

- ☐ Conduct a **premortem** by (a) figuring out a reasonable period for achieving the goal or for the decision playing out; (b) imagining it's the day after that period and you didn't achieve the goal or the decision worked out poorly; (c) looking back from that point in the future and coming up with reasons why you failed, divided into "skill" (within your control) and "luck" (outside your control).

- ☐ Conduct a **backcast** by going through the same exercise but imagining you achieved the goal or succeeded with the decision.

- ☐ Combine the output of the premortem and backcast in a **Decision Exploration Table**, including an estimate of the probability that each item in the table will happen.

- ☐ Ask whether you should modify your goal or change your decision based on the output of the premortem and backcast.

- ☐ Determine whether there are any **precommitment contracts** you can create to reduce the chances of making bad decisions and increase the chances of making good ones.

- ☐ Plan ahead for how you'll proceed if any of the reasons for failure you identified through a premortem happen.

- ☐ Play the **Dr. Evil game** to determine how you might fall short of your goal by making future decisions that are individually justifiable but in aggregate will cause you to fail.

- ☐ Consider adopting **category decisions** that will reduce the chances you make Dr. Evil decisions.

- ☐ Assess what you can do to **hedge** against the impact of bad luck.

Darth Vader, Team Leader: Dark side of the Force incarnate, or unsung hero for negative thinking?

Anyone familiar with the *Star Wars* movies would agree that Darth Vader isn't someone you'd want as a boss. His go-to leadership move is to end discussions by using the Force to choke disgruntled employees.

Given that, you'd think he wouldn't be particularly interested in hearing dissenting views. But, surprisingly, Darth Vader is an advocate of negative thinking.

In the original *Star Wars* film (later subtitled *A New Hope*), the Rebels succeed in part by stealing the plans for the Death Star and identifying a weakness: A torpedo hitting a small external exhaust port can trigger a fatal chain reaction. Luke Skywalker, as part of a Rebel attack on the Death Star, uses the Force to pick the exact right moment to fire a torpedo, hitting the exhaust port and destroying the Death Star.

What if the Galactic Empire had performed a premortem? The Rebels scoured those plans to find a vulnerability, while the Empire believed the Death Star was invulnerable.

The commander of the Death Star tells Darth Vader, "Any attack made by the Rebels against this station would be a useless gesture, no matter what technical data they've obtained. This station is now the ultimate power in the universe."

Darth Vader, facing a classic case of overconfidence bias, is the voice of mental contrasting: "Don't be too proud of this technological terror you've constructed. The ability to destroy a planet is insignificant next to the power of the Force."

When the commander persists in his refusal to consider premortem-style thinking, Vader uses the Force to choke him until he turns blue. It's not a management style any workplace should condone, but at least he did understand the problem of overconfidence and the importance of conducting a premortem. Unfortunately for the Galactic Empire, his message fell on deaf ears (and choked throats).

Dr. Evil on Fourth Down

Dr. Evil's mind-control devices are everywhere, reaching as far as the National Football League. Most teams have excellent analytics estimating the effect on win probability if they go for it on fourth down or kick (punting or attempting a field goal, depending on field position). The data show that going for it often makes sense, but we know that NFL coaches don't always follow the analysis. When they override the analytics, it's almost always by playing too conservatively, kicking rather than going for it.

Coaches are responsible for staying on top of their team's situation in the moment, which allows them to have justifications that sound reasonable as to why going for it is more likely to fail than the stats might suggest: momentum wasn't going their way, the running back wasn't finding a hole, the offensive line was faltering.

Notice that it rarely goes the other way, where the coach goes for it when the analytics favor kicking. That's how you can tell it's a Dr. Evil decision. On any given fourth-down decision, it's hard to argue when the coach tells you he overruled the analytics because of an in-game factor. But if you see that the coach leans to the conservative choice every single time there is a close call, you know it's the work of Dr. Evil.

9

Decision Hygiene

IF YOU WANT TO KNOW WHAT SOMEONE THINKS, STOP INFECTING THEM WITH WHAT YOU THINK

VIENNA GENERAL HOSPITAL—OBSTETRICS WARD, 1847

Dr. Ignaz Semmelweis, in his first medical posting, was trying to figure out why so many mothers of newborns were dying from puerperal sepsis, known as childbed fever.

Hospital conditions bore little resemblance to those of today. Doctors wore surgical gowns crusted with the gory remains of past patients, and they did it with pride. A surgeon's garment was a grisly résumé, a graphic display of experience. Nobody thought there was anything wrong with med students handling corpses and then attending deliveries in an adjoining room, all without washing their hands.

When one of Semmelweis's colleagues accidentally cut himself during an autopsy and died within days of childbed fever, Semmelweis hypothesized that the filthy hands of doctors and students handling dead bodies before attending childbirth caused the deaths of so many new mothers. He instituted a policy of handwashing and the mortality rate from childbed fever dropped from 16% to 2%.

In a striking case of motivated reasoning, his superiors denied the evidence, insulted by the implication that their dirty hands could be responsible for patient deaths. "Doctors are gentlemen," he was told, "and gentlemen's hands are clean."

He lost that job, as he lost two later appointments where he introduced similar policies and got similar results. He died in a public insane asylum in 1865, at the age of forty-seven. As a final indignity, his likely cause of death was an untreated infection.

We know today that Ignaz Semmelweis was right about the danger of infections and their spread through contagion. Just as germs from a corpse can contaminate a healthy patient, your beliefs and opinions can infect other people, contaminating the feedback you're trying to get.

Doctors wash their hands between procedures to reduce mortality. By practicing good decision hygiene, you can stem the spread of infection caused by broadcasting your beliefs.

Over the next several days, conduct the following experiment: Think about something happening in the world that most people will be pretty well aware of and ask for their opinions. It should be something on which people are likely to have a range of views. It might concern a news development, a political issue or candidate, or even something in popular culture like a recent movie or TV show.

1 Pick the topic you're going to ask about. Use the space below to write down your opinion on the matter prior to asking anybody else for theirs.

_____

_____

_____

_____

2 For half the people, when you ask for their opinion, tell them your opinion before they give you theirs. This is likely what you naturally do. For example, if you were asking somebody what they thought of *Forrest Gump*, you might say, "I don't think it should have won the Best Picture Academy Award or received its level of lasting critical acclaim and importance. What do you think?"

Ask at least three people and make a note of their opinions.

Among the people in this group (including you), how much agreement was there on the matter?

Very little agreement   0   1   2   3   4   5   *Lots of agreement*

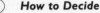

3 For the other half of the people, ask for their opinion without giving your opinion first. If you were asking about *Forrest Gump*, you might say, "What do you think about *Forrest Gump*?"

Ask at least three people and make a note of their opinions.

Among this group (including you), how much agreement was there on the matter?

Very little agreement   0   1   2   3   4   5   *Lots of agreement*

4 Compare the amount of agreement in the first group with the amount of agreement in the second group. Was there a difference? (Circle one.)

| *There was more agreement in the first group* | *There was more agreement in the second group* | *There was the same amount of agreement within the groups* |

5 Did anybody in the second group ask for your opinion before they were willing to give their answer? In other words, did anyone ask, "What do you think?" before they gave their answer. (Circle one.)   *YES   NO*

IF YOU'RE LIKE MOST PEOPLE, you found that there was more agreement in the first group (where you gave your opinion first) than the second. Also, if you're like most people, at least one person in the second group asked you what you thought before they were willing to give you their thoughts.

What this shows is that beliefs are contagious.

You already know that when we peer into the universe of stuff we don't know (including stuff that lives in other people's heads), we like to peer into the part that agrees with us. The problem with offering your opinion first when soliciting someone's advice is that it significantly increases the likelihood that they will express the same belief back to you. That's also why it's likely that someone in the second group asked for your view before giving their answer, so they could avoid accidentally disagreeing with you, which wouldn't feel good.

Agreement feels good. Disagreement feels bad.

This desire for people to agree with what other people are saying is so strong that you can even get people to express agreement with a belief that's objectively, clearly incorrect.

Solomon Asch, one of the most influential psychologists of the twentieth century, performed a classic series of experiments that started by asking people to identify which of the lines on the right is the same length as the line on the left.

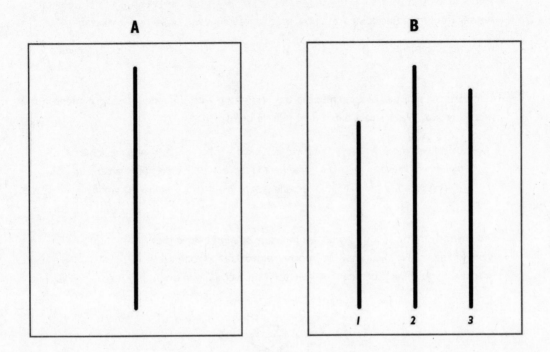

This is an unambiguous test of perception in which you're asking people to tell you what they can see with their own eyes. When you ask them independently, in a nongroup setting, over 99% of people say that the middle line on the right is the same length as the line on the left.

But what happens when somebody asks for your opinion in a group setting and a bunch of people give the same wrong answer before it's your turn to reply? (For example, several people answering that the line on the far right is the same length as the line on the left before you get to give your answer.)

This is exactly what Solomon Asch wanted to find out. The first people to give their answers in his experiment were "plants," told in advance to give and repeat the same incorrect answer. After hearing these confederates give the same, obviously incorrect answer, 36.8% of the actual experimental subjects went along with it and agreed with the group.

If that's happening for something as objectively clear as the different lengths of two lines, imagine how great the influence is for matters that are more subjective, such as the likelihood a job candidate will be a good cultural fit.

This shows how careful you have to be about the contagion of your own beliefs when eliciting feedback from other people. What they tell you may not be true to what lives in their head. One of the best tools for improving your decision-making is to get other people's perspectives. *But you can only do that if you get their actual perspective instead of your perspective parroted back to you.*

[I]

"Two Roads Diverged": The beauty of discovering where somebody else's beliefs differ from your own

Imagine if you could create a map of the facts and opinions that live in somebody else's head and compare that with a map of your own. You would find places that overlap and places that diverge. If there's one thing you've learned from this book, it's that the way you naturally interact with the world makes it much more likely you're going to see the places where the maps overlap, both noticing the stuff that agrees with you and actively seeking it out as well.

You've probably also figured out that *the exciting stuff happens where those maps diverge.* That's where you find corrective information and the stuff you don't know. Exploring that divergence allows you to get closer to what's objectively true.

Where the maps diverge and your opinion and somebody else's are far apart, three things might be true, and they are all good for improving the quality of your decisions:

1. *The objective truth lies somewhere between the two beliefs.*
   When two people are equally well informed and they hold opposite opinions, the truth most likely lies between the two. When that's the case, it's obvious why both people benefit from having discovered the divergence. Both people get the opportunity to moderate their beliefs and get closer to the objective truth.

2. *You could be wrong, and the other person could be right.*
   If you hold an inaccurate belief, the quality of any decision informed by that belief will suffer. A rational person would welcome the chance to change an inaccurate belief, but we know people like learning they're wrong about as much as those doctors liked Semmelweis telling them they were killing patients by not washing their hands. As painful as it might be to find out something you believe is incorrect, the opportunity to change that belief will improve the quality of every single subsequent decision informed in any way by that belief. That seems like a fair trade: a little bit of pain in exchange for higher-quality decisions for the rest of your life.

3. *You could be right, and the other person could be wrong.*
   When this is the case, you might think that only the person who is wrong benefits by getting the chance to reverse an inaccurate belief, because your belief was right

and will remain unchanged. But actually, you benefit from the exchange as well because the act of explaining your belief and conveying it to someone else will improve how well *you* understand it. The better you understand why you believe the things you do, the higher in quality those beliefs become.

While making small talk at a cocktail party, you run into someone who believes the earth is flat. Obviously, you say, "That's not true. The earth is round."

"No," they say, "I used to assume like everybody else that the earth was round. But I've studied this scientifically." They proceed to give you what they consider their best arguments about why the earth is flat (or why there isn't sufficient proof otherwise).

1 Without looking up anything on the internet, use the space below to write down the scientific arguments for why the earth is round off the top of your head. Remember, the parental fallback ("Because I said so") or the equivalent ("Because all scientists say so") isn't an option. "Because I've seen the pictures" is also not an option unless you can explain how you can tell if a picture is doctored or not.

_____

_____

_____

_____

_____

_____

_____

_____

_____

_____

2 On a scale of 0 to 5, how would a neutral third party rate the quality of your counterarguments?

Awful   0   1   2   3   4   5   Terrific

3 If you're like most people, your arguments off the top of your head weren't that strong. Now, take the opportunity to look up the top three scientific reasons for why the earth is round and summarize them here.

_____

_____

_____

_____

_____

_____

4 After doing that research, do you feel that you better understand
why it is that you know the earth is round? (Circle one.)   *YES   NO*

UNLESS YOU STARTED WITH an unusual amount of knowledge about why the earth is round, being challenged to explain it to somebody who believes otherwise improved the quality of that belief. It took it out of the realm of "This is just something that everybody knows" into the realm of "This is something that I understand."

Therein lies the opportunity afforded to you when you hold a belief that is objectively true and you find out somebody believes something different. It gives you the opportunity to understand your own belief better. As John Stuart Mill said, "He who knows only his own side of the case, knows little of that."

Of course, the opportunity to moderate, change, or better understand your belief depends on your ability to access the map of someone else's knowledge and see where their map diverges from your own. Because you're not a mind reader, the primary way to do that is for them to tell you what they believe. But if you infect them with your beliefs before you allow them to give you their own, you're not going to get a representative sample of their knowledge.

You'll get a sample that you think overlaps with your map much more than it actually does.

That's the cautionary tale of the Solomon Asch experiment.

[2]

How to Elicit Uninfected Feedback:
Quarantining your opinion to stop the contagion

You have to rely on other people to tell you what they believe, and if you tell them your opinion first, they will become an unreliable narrator. This can happen for two reasons.

First, when you tell someone what you think before hearing what they think, you can cause their opinion to bend toward yours, oftentimes without them knowing it. *In other words, their opinion can change.* What they believe to be true may start in one place, but upon hearing what you believe, their belief will move toward yours. If they don't know what you think, then the opinion you hear is more likely to be the opinion they start with.

Second, even if their belief doesn't change at all upon hearing yours, *they still may not tell you their true opinion.* This could be because they think *you're wrong* and don't want to embarrass you. Or they might think *they're wrong* and don't want to be embarrassed. Or they just may not want to be a squeaky wheel. That's what happened in the Solomon Asch experiment. It's unlikely anyone actually changed their mind about the lengths of the lines. They were just unwilling to express their dissent out loud.

Have you ever been with a bunch of people when somebody says something that startles you with how wrong it is, but you don't speak up? Whether it's because you don't want to cause friction or be impolite or argue or embarrass them or embarrass yourself, you don't tell them what you think. Isn't that everyone's worst nightmare—occasionally realized—at an extended-family Thanksgiving dinner?

The solution to this is the same as for the first problem: Don't let them know what you think before you find out what they think.

In a situation where you're soliciting feedback one-on-one, it's that simple. Otherwise, you're like a doctor showing up for surgery wearing a germ-encrusted smock.

When I was playing poker for a living, I often sought advice from other players about how I played a difficult hand. When I was soliciting their feedback, I'd tell them the facts that they needed to know to give me good feedback—things like the order of betting in the hand, how many chips each player had in front of them, and whether the other players played a lot of hands or very few.

> The only way somebody can know that they're disagreeing with you is if they know what you think first. Keeping that to yourself when you elicit feedback makes it more likely that what they say is actually what they believe.

What I would avoid telling them was what I actually chose to do in the hand, which was a matter of my opinion—exactly the opinion I wanted in soliciting the feedback. I knew that if I told them what I did, it would lower the quality of the feedback I got.

In describing the hand, I might say, "The player before me raised and I had ace-queen." Instead of saying, "I raised them back. What do you think?" I would say, "What do you think I should have done?" so as not to infect them with what I had actually chosen to do.

Outcomes are also contagious

You go through an extensive hiring process, offering the job to one of three finalists, but within a year you've let the employee go. You're trying to get advice about whether you made a good-quality hiring decision.

No matter what advice you're seeking, you certainly don't want to tell the person who you're asking how it turned out (that you fired the employee) and you may not want to tell them which of the finalists you decided to hire.

Just as you can infect somebody's feedback by letting them know your opinion, you can also infect their feedback if you tell them how it turned out.

It's impossible to be a resulter if you don't know the outcome. It's impossible to succumb to hindsight bias if you don't know the outcome.

You'll likely find that keeping the outcome of a decision to yourself is harder to execute than you might think because, intuitively, we all feel that how the decision turned out is relevant information for the other person to know. That's true if you have a large enough sample size, but not if you're asking about one decision that has one particular result.

Knowing the outcome can ruin the feedback you get because, as you know, the outcome casts a shadow over anyone's ability to see the quality of the decision preceding it. That's why you should keep the result to yourself as much as possible.

A lot of times when you're asking for advice about something that's happened in the past, more than one outcome is sitting in the way. In that case, it's good to *iterate* the feedback, asking for the person's opinion in sequence, stopping the narrative before each result.

In the hiring example, you might start by telling them the position you were trying to fill and ask what they think the key components of the job description should be and the appropriate salary range. Once you've gotten that feedback, you could show them the actual job description and salary range and move on to whether you should have conducted the hiring process in-house or should have hired an outside contractor. Get their opinion prior to telling them the method you chose. After that, you can give them the information about the final candidates and ask which they would have hired, and so on.

Quarantining outcomes and beliefs from the person giving you feedback helps put them in a state of knowledge closer to the one you were in when you made any of your decisions. This is one way that keeping a record, using the decision tools developed in this book, helps you later when you're seeking feedback about your decisions. Tools such as a decision tree, a Knowledge Tracker, or a Decision Exploration Table create a record of your state of knowledge at the time of the decision, which makes it easier to convey that information to get someone's feedback later.

> **To get high-quality feedback, it's important to put the other person as closely as possible into the same state of knowledge that you were in at the time that you made your decision.**

Kevin has been framed!—How you ask for feedback can signal your opinion

Sometimes, when you solicit feedback from other people, you don't realize that the way you're asking the question signals your belief.

One of my children came home one day complaining about a friend of theirs named Kevin. My child declared to me, "Kevin is a total jerk and all my friends agree with me."

When I heard about this unanimous consent about Kevin's jerkiness, I immediately said, "When you asked them what they thought about Kevin, did you say, 'What do you think about Kevin?' or did you say, 'Don't you think Kevin's a total jerk?'" Of course, it was the latter.

You want to be careful about the way that you frame the question, because the frame you choose can signal whether you have a positive or negative view about what you're trying to get feedback on. Try to stay in a neutral frame as much as possible.

> **FRAMING EFFECT**
> **A cognitive bias in which the way that information is presented influences the way that the listener makes decisions about the information.**

THE WORD "DISAGREE" HAS very negative connotations. If you call someone "disagree-able," you're not saying something nice about them. You might have noticed that I've been using the term "diverge" rather than "disagree," and that's on purpose. It has a more neutral connotation. Using the terms "divergence" or "dispersion" of opinion instead of "disagreement" is a more neutral way of talking about places where people's opinions differ, allowing you to better wrap your arms around disagreement.

[3]

How to Quarantine Opinions in a Group Setting

When you're talking to somebody one-on-one, you have a simple solution to the contagion problem. Whatever the feedback is that you're eliciting, don't broadcast your opinion first. But this solution doesn't scale well in a group setting. When you're in a group discussion, you can keep *your* opinion from everyone, but once the first person offers their opinion, the rest of the group is infected.

Our gut tells us that when it comes to decision-making, more heads are better than one. If you elicit more opinions, you get more of the outside view, a wider variety of perspectives, a broader range of beliefs, and that will improve decision quality.

Yet we know that when people are in group settings, the decision quality often isn't better, but because more people are involved in the process, the confidence in the decision goes up. *That's a bad combination: having a lot more confidence in the quality of a decision that isn't necessarily any better.*

That's why belief contagion is particularly problematic in groups.

Research shows that in a group setting, even when individual members of the group have information in their possession that goes against the consensus opinion of the group, they often won't share it.

In an ingenious experiment conducted by Garold Stasser of Miami University and William Titus of Briar Cliff College, four-person groups had to decide which of three candidates was best suited to be student body president. The researchers created dossiers containing positive and negative attributes of each candidate. Based on all the information, Candidate A was designed to be the most favorable. Each member of the groups reviewed the dossiers in advance, indicated their private preference, and then caucused to choose their preference as a group.

For one set of groups (let's call them the "complete-information groups"), each individual member of the group got complete dossiers, including all information available about each candidate. As expected, Candidate A was the private preference of most members and the preferred candidate of these groups.

For the other groups (let's call them the "partial-information groups"), each member's dossier was incomplete. All contained some common information about each candidate, but the remaining information from the profiles was scattered among the members. Based on how the positive and negative information was spread among the dossiers, most of the members of the partial-information groups did not make Candidate A their premeeting preference. (Note: Everyone in the experiment was alerted to the possibility that their dossiers might not be complete and fellow group members might have information of which they were unaware.)

Now here's the trick: If every member of the partial-information groups were to share what they knew in group discussion, they would have the exact same information as the complete-information groups and presumably settle on Candidate A. The question is, did they actually share that information?

The partial-information groups quickly formed a consensus based on their premeeting preferences. Once they saw a consensus forming, members with divergent information (negative on the consensus candidate or positive on the nonpreferred candidates) were unlikely to share it. Unlike in the complete-information groups, where Candidate A was the strong preference, the partial-information groups almost always chose one of the other candidates.

In other words, even though the partial-information groups had in their possession all the information to determine that Candidate A was the best, they didn't share that information and usually landed on a less favorable choice.

This shows that the information that lives in people's heads doesn't necessarily get shared with the group, particularly as a consensus starts to form. The problem, of course, is that if you want to access the potential of the different perspectives team members have to offer, you actually have to hear about those perspectives.

Soliciting feedback independently

The question is how do you scale the solution of quarantining beliefs and outcomes if, after the first person in a group speaks, the quarantine is ruined? You can accomplish this in a group setting by eliciting initial opinions and rationales from each member independently, which you then share with the team members *before the group meets*. This helps alleviate the incomplete-dossier problem, because each member of the group gets exposed to unshared information and the views of others.

The members of a hiring committee have interviewed the finalists. Prior to any of those people having a group discussion, ask each to email their opinion about which candidate they prefer, along with their rationale. Put that feedback together and share it with the group prior to any discussion in a team setting.

An investment committee is deciding whether to make a particular investment. Elicit feedback independently and share it with the group prior to meeting.

A legal team has been asked by the client for a recommendation about the settlement of the case. Ask each person on the team, before discussing it with the others, to give their opinion on the amount of a reasonable settlement as well as an upper and lower bound, and the likelihood the opposing party would settle in that range, along with their rationale. Have them email it to be compiled and shared with the group before a team meeting to discuss the matter.

Research has found that people give feedback that more accurately represents their knowledge and preferences when they do it independently and privately, compared with doing it in a group. Dan Levy, Joshua Yardley, and Richard Zeckhauser of the Harvard Kennedy School found that asking students to raise their hands (the time-honored *group* feedback system in classrooms) caused a herding effect, where, as soon as students saw a consensus developing, they raised their hands to join with the consensus opinion, creating super-majorities.

In contrast, when students answered with electronic clickers so they couldn't see what anybody else was answering, the super-majorities that formed with public hand raising got broken up. Soliciting feedback from students independently provided instructors with a better representation of the students' true knowledge and preferences.

This is what eliciting initial feedback and ideas independently (by email or some other means) does. It reduces the artificial appearance of overlap in opinions, better exposing where beliefs diverge.

Part of the feedback-elicitation process should include specifying the form in which people provide it. This book has described many decision tools that you can ask team members to use for offering feedback: forecasts of specific events or outcomes, outcomes on a decision tree, options to be considered, payoffs, counterfactuals, a Perspective Tracker, the output of a Decision Exploration Table (a premortem and/or a backcast) or the Dr. Evil game, or Ulysses contracts or hedges. You could also ask for feedback in the form of answers to yes or no questions or on a rating scale.

Specifying the type of feedback you're looking for allows the group to make an apples-to-apples comparison of feedback and ideas and identify where there is divergence.

An added layer of protection: Anonymizing feedback

Some opinions are more contagious than others. Some people are more likely to cause other people's opinions to bend toward theirs and cause others to suppress divergent viewpoints. The most contagious beliefs on a team come from higher-status individuals.

Status can derive from a leadership position, experience, expertise, persuasive ability, charisma, extroversion, or even just how articulate a person is.

Ideally, when you're eliciting feedback from members of a group, an idea that's objectively valid doesn't become any more or less valid depending on whether it comes from the CEO or an intern. But in reality, ideas that come from people of lower status don't get equal consideration on the merits.

The way you get around this status-contagion problem is to **anonymize** the initial round of feedback, which quarantines the source from the other members of the group, ensuring that the feedback of lower-status individuals gets more consideration than it generally otherwise would.

But doesn't expertise and experience matter?

You may be thinking right now, "But isn't it rational to give more weight to some feedback based on the source? If the group is getting opinions about the theory of relativity and Einstein's in the room, isn't what he has to say more important than the person just hired out of the intern program?"

Yes, if Einstein is part of the group, there will be times when his opinions should carry far more weight than anyone else's. Those times are when the group is talking about physics. Because of that, opinions can't and shouldn't stay anonymized *forever*.

That said, there are a lot of benefits to having the *first pass* be anonymous.

First, it's hard for people to publicly disagree with team members who have more expertise or are of higher status, whether it's Einstein or the CEO. But it's worse than that because of the **halo effect**, which is the tendency to give the opinions of highly successful people much more weight across the board, even in areas in which they have no expertise.

> **HALO EFFECT**
> A cognitive bias in which a positive impression of a person in one area causes you to have a positive view of that person in other, unrelated, areas.

No one wants to step up and contradict Einstein's feedback, whether it's about the theory of relativity or whether to sue the landlord.

Second, for all the value that expertise provides, subject-matter experts aren't impervious to bias. As Philip Tetlock has shown, when you're a subject-matter expert, you have a tendency to get entrenched in your worldview and that makes it harder to climb out from that trench and see things from a perspective that differs from your own robust model of the world.

This is a big advantage of anonymizing the initial round of feedback. Members will naturally see things from different perspectives. Because each member of the group doesn't know the source of any of the perspectives, those viewpoints are more likely to get real consideration. Team members won't know whose opinion to disregard or elevate.

Group members with lower status may have different, valuable perspectives. Sometimes, they see innovative solutions others don't see because they aren't as anchored to the status quo. In a macro sense, when you look at the history of the world, each subsequent generation, by offering its different view, becomes responsible for innovative leaps and paradigm shifts. By initially anonymizing feedback, those outside-the-box perspectives get a chance to breathe.

But-Why'd

Of course, the least experienced members of the group aren't always geniuses-in-waiting and their next contribution won't always be the groundbreaking idea that propels the group to heights of success. Frequently, their perspective simply reflects a lack of understanding.

A good group process encourages feedback that includes giving people the space to express a lack of understanding. The group as a whole benefits from that because it affords the experts the opportunity to better understand *why* they believe what they do, and also affords them the opportunity to transfer their knowledge to the other members of the group. And sometimes it gives them an opportunity to repair inaccuracies in the things that they believe.

It's like the experience of every parent when their child asks them to explain something, and their child says, "But why?"

"Mommy, why is the sky blue?"

Pleased with yourself, you show off your knowledge of light refraction to your five-year-old and answer, "The sky is actually all the different colors of the rainbow. But the air around the earth only lets our eyes see the blue color."

But then your five-year-old follows with, "*But why?* Why does the air around the earth only let us see the blue color?"

And then you have to answer that question. It goes on until you butt up against the limits of your own knowledge, at which point the exchange usually ends with you saying, "Because I said so!" or "Isn't it time to watch *Dora the Explorer*?" or "Wanna get some ice cream?"

In the same way that a child exposes what you know and what you don't know, all groups benefit from getting *but-why'd*.

Quick-and-dirty: An alternative for lower-impact, easier-to-reverse decisions

You might be thinking at this point, "If we did this for every decision we had to make as a team, we probably couldn't make more than a handful of decisions a month."

Obviously, this type of decision process (soliciting feedback independently and distributing it in anonymized form for review before group discussion) takes additional time. But the time-accuracy trade-off still applies. For lower-impact, easier-to-reverse decisions, the group can still contain the contagion in a way that doesn't take quite as much time, through a quick-and-dirty version of this feedback elicitation process.

When you're in a group setting considering a decision, each member can write down their opinions and rationales on a piece of paper, passing the papers to one person, who reads them aloud or writes them on a whiteboard before discussion. That doesn't take much extra time and gives everyone a chance to express an initial position before hearing what others think.

If you want to save even more time, you can have people write their opinions and rationales down and each member can then read theirs out loud, but it's imperative that you start with the most junior member of the group, whose opinion is least contagious (and who is most likely to get infected by the higher-status members, depriving the group of hearing their authentic perspective).

[4]

Spin Doctrine: Checklisting the relevant details and being accountable to provide them

If people don't have the relevant information to provide high-quality feedback, all the quarantining in the world won't help your decisions. Their feedback will only be as good as the input you give them. In other words, junk in, junk out—quarantines or otherwise.

If you're asking for somebody's feedback on a job candidate without mentioning that the candidate was convicted of embezzling from their previous employer, are you likely to get good-quality feedback?

If you represent the plaintiff in a lawsuit and are deciding whether to settle a case on the eve of the trial, what's the point of getting the advice of a seasoned trial attorney if you don't tell them that the case was recently reassigned to a judge with a prodefendant reputation?

Of course, it's unlikely someone would leave out details as obviously relevant as these. But in all sorts of ways, some bigger and some smaller, when we're left to our own devices, the narratives that we spin when we're asking others for advice naturally tend to highlight, lowlight, and omit pieces of information in a way that helps lead the person to agree with the conclusion we've already reached.

This generally is not done to fool other people. It's mostly to fool yourself. The way you spin these narratives makes it more likely that you'll hear about the parts of their map that overlap with yours, rather than the parts that diverge, lowering the quality of the feedback you get.

Using the outside view to stop the narrative from spinning

We've identified a key bottleneck in the decision process, that the quality of the feedback that you get is limited by the quality of the information that you input into that process. Our narratives naturally live in the inside view, biased to support our own perspective of the world. It logically follows that one way to address this problem is to get to the outside view, putting yourself in the shoes of the person giving the feedback instead of the feedback seeker.

You can get to the outside view by asking yourself, "If somebody were seeking my opinion about this type of decision, what are the things that I would need to know to feel like I could give them high-quality feedback?" Make a checklist of those details and then provide them to anyone you are seeking advice from.

You can do this for any decision, but it's especially useful for decisions that repeat because you can think about it before you're facing any particular instance of that decision. When you're in the midst of a decision, you've probably already formed an opinion about your preferred option. Once that happens, your preference will distort what information you think you would need to know. By building this checklist in advance, you won't be as influenced by the specifics of a decision on which you've already formed an opinion, making it easier to be objective and get to the outside view.

What should make it onto the checklist?

For any decision that you have under consideration, that checklist of relevant information will differ, but it will commonly focus on the applicable goals, values, and resources, along with the details of the situation. You want to provide what the person needs to know to give worthwhile feedback—and nothing more.

First and foremost, you need to communicate what it is that you want to accomplish. People have different goals and values and those things matter. The right option for one person might differ from the right option for another.

If you're asking for advice on a vacation destination, the person you're asking should know your goals, preferences, and limitations. If you tell them you want to go to someplace that's sunny in February and has a lot of history, but you don't tell them that you only have three days for your vacation, they might recommend Australia, perhaps because they had a wonderful time when they spent two weeks there.

In poker I asked other players for feedback about hands all the time. Because I knew I was going to be doing that repeatedly and I wanted a good checklist of information to provide, I asked myself, "If someone came to me asking for feedback about a hand, what are the things I'd need to know to give them good advice?" That included things such as the order of betting, how many chips the other players had in front of them, etc. I made a checklist for myself of those details and tried to make sure, whenever I asked for someone's advice, that I included everything on that checklist.

Partial information doesn't get you "partially good" feedback.

If you're making a hiring decision, it's important to include your goals, values, and resources. Is your aim to hire someone with experience who, in turn, will help train future new hires? Do you value a sunny disposition? The relevant facts about the candidates include their CVs, what their references said, and what their interviews consisted of.

Once you've made such a checklist, you need to hold yourself accountable to providing those details to people you're asking for feedback. This will reduce the chance that you'll spin the narrative to fit an opinion you've already formed and will increase the quality of the feedback you receive.

Developing a checklist for a team can be done using the same process as eliciting any other feedback in a group setting. Ask group members independently to answer the question: "If someone came to me asking for feedback on this category of decision, what would I need to know?" Bring the answers together, anonymize them for distribution to group members, and discuss it as a team. The product of this will be a master checklist for information that has to be provided to any team members being asked for feedback.

Members of the group should hold one another accountable to that checklist. Anybody eliciting feedback has the responsibility to provide the information on the checklist, and anybody being asked for feedback must request that all the information on the checklist be provided.

Develop a checklist of information that needs to be shared for a decision you repeatedly make in your work or personal life. You can do this individually or as a team exercise.

I Write down a personal or professional decision that comes up repeatedly.

_____

_____

_____

_____

_____

2 If someone came to you and asked for feedback on a decision of that type, what are the things that you would need to know to be able to give high-quality feedback?

Use the space below to provide a comprehensive list of the information you would need to give high-quality feedback about the best course of action. Start the list with your goals, what you value, and your resources.

_____

_____

_____

_____

_____

_____

_____

_____

_____

_____

_____

_____

_____

WHETHER IT'S WITHIN A group or just two people asking each other for advice, it's important to *agree* that everyone participating in the feedback process is accountable to the checklist.

Without an agreement to hold one another accountable, the person on the other end of that narrative often assumes that if details are emphasized, they must be especially relevant. And if details are deemphasized or omitted, it's because they aren't important to the decision.

Generally, when details are left out, people will offer their advice anyway. Maybe this is because people think it would be rude when somebody's asking for advice to say "I can't help you." Or maybe it's because we all have so much confidence in the value of our opinions that we think we can give them high-quality advice despite not having all the facts.

Real accountability to a checklist means that if somebody can't provide the information necessary for you to give high-quality feedback, you should refuse to give it—not to be mean but to be *kind*.

When I was teaching poker, students of mine would sometimes come to me and describe hands where they couldn't remember some of the facts on the checklist. As an example, a student might ask me if they should have called a bet on the last card of a hand, but they couldn't remember how much money was in the pot. In that case, I would refuse to tell them whether they should have called the bet, because if I didn't know the size of the pot, my opinion would have no value and anything I told them would be gibberish.

My unwillingness to give them what was essentially worthless—and potentially misleading—feedback created many future benefits for such students. For one thing, they would start paying attention to the size of the pot. You could make a solid bet that the next time they asked me about a hand, they'd know that information, because they knew that if they wanted my feedback, they would have to tell me the pot size. This is a detail they obviously weren't paying attention to (or they'd have known it initially) and something they'd continue to ignore if I let them gloss over it without putting on the brakes.

More important, my refusal created the opportunity for them to understand *why* knowing the size of the pot is crucial. In future hands, regardless of whether they asked for feedback or not, they were going to pay attention to this key detail and incorporate it in their on-the-spot poker decision-making.

These benefits of adhering to a checklist accrue whether it has to do with the size of the pot in poker or how many time-outs you have left when you're calling a football play late in the fourth quarter.

Or how important cultural fit is when you're hiring a new employee.

Or how important the judge's potential prodefendant reputation is to the value of your lawsuit.

Or how important the depth of management is when you're considering buying stock in a new electric-car company.

Having a good checklist in place helps you combat biasing narratives and provides a framework within which to process information as you make future decisions.

[5]

Final Thoughts

You're going to make thousands and thousands of decisions across your lifetime, some of which will work out and some of which won't. The goal of good decision-making can't be that every single decision will work out well. Because of the intervention of luck and incomplete information, that's an impossible goal.

The decisions you make are like a portfolio of investments. Your goal is to make sure that the portfolio as a whole advances you toward your goals, even though any individual decision in that portfolio might win or lose.

Think about it like someone who's flipping houses. Their goal is to make money across all the houses that they flip, but they might make or lose money on any individual house they renovate. They can't know in advance which particular houses in their portfolio will end up underwater. If they could, they would obviously only invest in properties that would make money.

The same is true for your decisions. Your goal is, across the portfolio of all the decisions that you make in your life, to advance toward your goals rather than retreat away from them. But like the house flipper, any individual decision might work out poorly. Embracing that fact is necessary for becoming a better decision-maker.

If you go into your decisions thinking that you can somehow guarantee that things work out, it's going to be very hard for you to take an open-minded walk through the universe of stuff that you don't know. Instead, you're going to take that walk in a permanent defensive crouch, constantly fending off the possibility that you made a bad decision or had an incorrect belief.

That defensive crouch is eventually going to get very uncomfortable.

When you approach bad results by swatting away the possibility that you made a bad decision or had an incorrect belief, it might feel like you're being self-compassionate. Processing outcomes in this way might make you feel better in the moment, as will reflexively taking credit for when things work out.

But if all you do is seek confirmation that the quality of your decisions is good and the things you believe are true, you can't expect to be an effective learner. Your ability to improve your decision quality will be hamstrung.

Your future self is depending on you to make quality decisions and keep improving them. *Real self-compassion* is about not letting that person—all the future versions of yourself—down.

[6]

Decision Hygiene Wrap-up

These exercises were designed to get you thinking about the following concepts:

- One of the best ways to improve the quality of your beliefs is to get other people's perspectives. When their beliefs diverge from yours, it improves your decision-making by exposing you to corrective information and the stuff you don't know.
- **Beliefs are contagious**. Informing somebody of your belief before they give their feedback significantly increases the likelihood that they will express the same belief back to you.
- Exercise **decision hygiene** to stem the infection of beliefs.
- The only way somebody can know that they're disagreeing with you is if they know your opinion first. **Keep your opinions to yourself when you elicit feedback.**
- The **frame** you choose can signal whether you have a positive or negative view about what you're trying to get feedback on. Stay in neutral as much as possible.
- The word "disagree" has very negative connotations. Using "**divergence**" or "**dispersion**" of opinion instead of "disagreement" is a more neutral way of talking about places where people's opinions differ.
- **Outcomes can also infect the quality of feedback**. Quarantine others from the way things turned out while eliciting their feedback.
- When you're asking for feedback about something that's happened in the past and several outcomes are sitting in the way, **iterate feedback**.
- For feedback of any kind, put the person, as closely as possible, into the state of knowledge you were in when you made the decision.
- **Group settings** offer the potential of improving decision quality if you can access the different perspectives of the group. Often, this potential is undermined by the tendency of groups to coalesce around consensus quickly, discouraging members with information or opinions that disagree with the consensus from sharing them.
- Groups can better fulfill their decision-making potential by exercising **group decision hygiene**, soliciting initial opinions and rationales independently before sharing with the group.
- Due to the **halo effect**, opinions from high-status members of the group are especially contagious.

- **Anonymizing feedback on the first pass** allows ideas to be better considered on their merits rather than according to the status of the individual who holds the belief.

- For lower-impact, easier-to-reverse decisions, the group can still contain the contagion through a **quick-and-dirty** version of this process, where group members write down their opinions and someone reads them aloud or writes them on a whiteboard before discussion, or where members read their own opinions aloud in reverse order of seniority.

- **The quality of feedback is limited by the quality of the input into the feedback elicitation process.** We tend to spin narratives that highlight, lowlight, or even omit information that isn't helpful to the conclusion that we would like others to reach.

- Give the other person what they need to know to give you a quality opinion and no more.

- Access the outside view by asking yourself, "If someone came to me asking my opinion about this kind of decision, what would I need to know to give good advice?"

- Build a **checklist** of relevant details for repeating decisions and make that checklist *before* you're in the midst of a decision. Such a list should focus on the applicable goals, values, and resources, along with the details of the situation.

- Members of a group should hold one another **accountable to the checklist**. If someone is eliciting feedback and they can't provide details on the checklist, there should be an agreement not to give feedback.

DECISION HYGIENE CHECKLIST

When you're seeking feedback from others, exercise good decision hygiene in the following ways:

☐ Quarantine others from your opinions and beliefs when asking for feedback.

☐ Frame your request for feedback in a neutral fashion, to keep from signaling your conclusions.

☐ Quarantine others from outcomes when asking about past decisions.

☐ If you're asking for feedback involving multiple outcomes, iterate the feedback.

☐ Explain the form of the output you're seeking.

☐ Prior to being in the midst of a decision, make a checklist of the facts and relevant information you would need to provide feedback for such a decision.

☐ Have the people seeking and giving feedback agree to be accountable to provide all the relevant information, asking for anything that has not been provided, and refusing to give feedback if the person seeking feedback can't provide relevant information.

When you're involved in a group setting, exercise the following *additional* forms of decision hygiene:

☐ Solicit feedback independently, before a group discussion or before members express their views to one another.

☐ Anonymize the sources of the views and distribute a compilation to group members for review, in advance of group meetings or discussion.

Acknowledgments

THIS BOOK WOULD NOT EXIST without the many incredible people who have offered thought partnership, who have given me insightful critiques of my past and present work, who have been my cheerleaders, and who have supported me in those moments where I felt I couldn't find my way to finishing this book.

Thank you to Jim Levine, my literary agent, for being my head cheerleader, for believing in me before I ever wrote a book in this space, and for sticking with me through this second one. He offered sage advice, handholding, and amazing advocacy. Thank you, Jim, and everyone at Levine Greenberg Rostan Literary Agency.

Niki Papadopoulos, the world's best editor and, more important, an amazing friend, deserves so much credit for what is in these pages. In particular, she saw the path to this book to not merely be a workbook for *Thinking in Bets* (as it was originally conceived) but as a book that would stand on its own merits. That gave me the space to explore a lot of new ground and go deeply into topics I otherwise wouldn't have. In addition, her frank and blunt critique of the very first pages massively changed the trajectory of this book. She also gave me the space to find my way through writing a book that took twice the time and ended up twice the length as planned. I will always remember her saying, with great compassion as I fretted over the timeline, "I believe books take as long as they need to take to be written." Thank you, Niki.

Thank you to everyone at Portfolio and in the Penguin Random House family, with special mention to Kimberly Meilum, Niki's editorial assistant, who coordinated the layout and had the task of making sure I met deadlines; Jamie Lescht, who coordinated marketing; and Adrian Zackheim, for believing in my work and for his leadership at such an amazing company as Portfolio.

I am deeply indebted to Michael Craig, who has been essential to producing this book. In addition to being a great friend, he has been incredibly generous with his talents as editor, researcher, test-audience member, contributor of ideas and examples, compiler, and organizer of this material. I am confident that this book would not exist without him.

I am so grateful for the help of the many brilliant, accomplished behavioral scientists who encouraged me, unselfishly shared their time and ideas and input, taught me, treated me as a colleague, and constantly inspired me to earn their respect and friendship.

Michael Mauboussin acted as a thought partner on this journey, reading each chapter as I produced it and offering insightful critique as I went along. His hands are deep in this work. I am unbelievably lucky to have had a person of his caliber willing to read every word and offer me such in-depth guidance.

Phil Tetlock and Barb Mellers are both inspirations to me and mentors. Their body of work on forecasting and expert judgment is woven throughout this book, touching nearly every page. I have never had a conversation with them that did not make me smarter.

Cass Sunstein let me bounce ideas off him and was also willing to read the manuscript as I produced it, giving me not just excellent feedback but also comfort that what I was producing might be worthwhile.

Daniel Kahneman led the way in creating the space now known as behavioral economics and his work has inspired much of what appears in this book. He has also been generous with his time, allowing me to bounce ideas off him. (Danny, I'm sorry I didn't change the title to something more to your liking. That was Niki's fault.)

Ted Seides gets a special thank-you for introducing me to Frank Brosens, who then introduced me to Cass Sunstein (thank you, Frank!). And Josh Wolfe gets a special thank-you for introducing me to Daniel Kahneman.

Abraham Wyner was always available for long lunches, where we meandered through the concepts in this book. Much of the way that the ideas are framed within these pages are a direct result of those conversations and this book is much better for his thought partnership.

Adam Grant let me present an early version of some of the ideas in this book to his class at UPenn and gave me access to his students, several of whom read the manuscript and provided valuable feedback. Thanks go not only to Adam but to those students as well: Rachel Abbe, Zachary Drapkin, and Matthew Weiss.

Through Adam's class, I also met Meghna Sreenivas, who became my amazing research assistant. She is also a top-notch human.

Dan Levy and Richard Zeckhauser both influenced my thinking about decision hygiene. They each were kind enough to spend the time to discuss their ideas with me and alert me to helpful reference materials.

Special thanks to all the readers of early versions of the manuscript for their time and feedback, including Michael Burns, Sonal Chokshi, Seth Godin, Rick Jones, Greg Kaplan, Carl Rosin, Vidushi Sharma, Jordan Thibodeau, Douglas Vigliotti, and Paul Wright. I enjoyed (and obviously benefited greatly) from swapping ideas with so many smart, accomplished thinkers. Thank you for helping to set the manuscript on its course when I was trying to figure out what this book would be and for putting up with reading some very rough versions.

Peter Attia inspired me with his passion for archery. Dan Egan told me about the Damien game, which became the inspiration for the Dr. Evil game. You are truly an evil genius. Timothy Houlihan and Kurt Nelson have become great friends of mine during this process and were instrumental in helping me find the voice of this book, course correcting after a bumpy early start. Shane Parrish has been so generous to offer me a platform for my ideas, not just through his podcast but also by letting me road test some of these ideas at one of his workshops.

I have benefited greatly from the perspectives of Daniel Crosby, Morgan Housel, Brian Portnoy, Hal Stern, Jim and Patrick O'Shaugnessy, Wes Grey, and David Foulke, who offered their insights into many of the ideas in this book and inspired me to do better.

Many of the examples and ideas in this book were made better by my many long and winding conversations with Joe Sweeney, my friend and the executive director of the Alliance for Decision Education, the nonprofit I cofounded dedicated to building the field of decision education in K-12 education. Thank you, Joe, and a huge thank-you to the staff of the Alliance and everyone who helps support the organization.

Thank you to Jenifer Sarver, Maralyn Beck, Luz Stable, Alicia McClung, and Jim Doughan for keeping my life in order.

Lila Gleitman continues to be my mentor and an inspiration to me. At ninety years old, she is still my most valuable thought partner. I aspire to be able to attain some fraction of the precision and creativity of her thought. She is also one of the funniest people I know. There is no way for me to express my gratitude for her friendship or adequately express my love for her.

Most important of all, thank you to my family for supporting me—my husband, my kids, my brother and sister, my dad, and all the members of our extended family. They have been unbelievably supportive and understanding through this process. I am lucky to have all of you in my life. I love you infinity.

Writing, speaking, and consulting on decision strategy has given me the opportunity to meet with, share ideas with, and become friends with many brilliant thinkers in business, management, innovation, financial markets, and other professions. This includes people who also use their skills to communicate and educate about decision strategy as authors, writers, speakers, consultants, and podcast hosts.

I don't have the space to include all the opportunities I've received to develop the ideas that formed this book in podcasts, interviews, and discussions with others working in this area. I've also developed a lot of the material in this book with the help of workshops, keynotes, and consulting work I've done with numerous business and professional groups. Thank you to everyone who gave me a platform to express my ideas, roadtest them, and benefit from the responses and feedback.

I am the most anxious about the acknowledgments section of this book. I fear I cannot sufficiently express my gratitude to this community I am so lucky to be a part of. And I imagine that after this book is in print, I will remember more than one person I left out of this section and be mortified. I hope whoever that is, you know that I am no less grateful to you than to anyone who made it onto these pages.

Chapter Notes

CHAPTER 1: RESULTING

Charting the relationship between decision quality and outcome quality [p. 10]

See also Mitch Morse, "Thinking in Bets: Book Review and Thoughts on the Interaction of Uncertainty and Politics," Medium.com, December 9, 2018, and J. Edward Russo and Paul Schoemaker, *Winning Decisions: Getting It Right the First Time* (New York: Doubleday, 2002).

Star Wars and Resulting [p. 23–24]

The cost of the original *Star Wars* film and the box office for the film and for the franchise, as of January 17, 2020, came from "Box Office History for Star Wars Movies," www.the-numbers.com/movies/franchise /Star-Wars#tab=summary. The details of Disney's 2012 acquisition of the franchise came from the press release announcing the transaction, reported by Steve Kovach, "Disney Buys Lucasfilm for $4 Billion," October 30, 2012, *Business Insider*, www.businessinsider.com/disney-buys-lucasfilm-for-4-billion-2012-10.

Innumerable retellings of the history of *Star Wars* include its initial rejection by United Artists, along with other studios passing on the project, including Universal and Disney. The Syfy Wire version is from Evan Hoovler, "Back to the Future Day: 6 Films That Were Initially Rejected by Studios," Syfy Wire, July 3, 2017, www.syfy.com/syfywire/back-to-the-future-day-6-hit-films-that-were-initially-rejected -by-studios. The quote from George Lucas about the film's history appeared in Kirsten Acuna, "George Lucas Recounts How Studios Turned Down 'Star Wars' in Classic Interview," *Business Insider*, February 6, 2014, www.businessinsider.com/george-lucas-interview-recalls-studios-that-turned-down-movie-star -wars-2014-2.

"Nobody knows anything" is from William Goldman, *Adventures in the Screen Trade: A Personal View of Hollywood and Screenwriting* (New York: Warner Books, 1983).

CHAPTER 2: AS THE OLD SAYING GOES, HINDSIGHT IS NOT 20/20

Aliases for hindsight bias [p. 29]

See Neal Roese and Kathleen Vohs, "Hindsight Bias," *Perspectives on Psychological Science* 7, no. 5 (2012): 411–26.

Clinton vs. Trump: polling error in foresight and hindsight [pp. 44–45]

The voting and electoral college numbers from the 2016 presidential election came from Wikipedia, en.wikipedia.org/wiki/2016_United_States_presidential_election.

The sources of the postelection headlines attributing Clinton's loss to her campaign's mistaken priorities (deploying more resources in Florida, North Carolina, and New Hampshire, and fewer resources in Pennsylvania, Michigan, and Wisconsin) were Ronald Brownstein, "How the Rustbelt Paved Trump's Road to Victory," *The Atlantic*, November 10, 2016, www.theatlantic.com/politics/archive/2016/11 /trumps-road-to-victory/507203/; Sam Stein, "The Clinton Campaign Was Undone by Its Own Neglect and a Touch of Arrogance, Staffers Say," *Huffington Post*, November 16, 2016, www.huffpost.com /entry/clinton-campaign-neglect_n_582cacb0e4b058ce7aa8b861; Jeremy Stahl, "Report: Neglect and Poor Strategy Cost Clinton Three Critical States," *Slate*, November 17, 2016, slate.com/news-and -politics/2016/11/report-neglect-and-poor-strategy-helped-cost-clinton-three-critical-states.html.

The sources of the preelection headlines that, in contrast, questioned Trump's—not Clinton's—campaign priorities were Philip Bump, "Why Was Donald Trump Campaigning in Johnstown, Pennsylvania?," *Washington Post*, October 22, 2016, www.washingtonpost.com/news/the-fix/wp/2016/10/22/why-was -donald-trump-campaigning-in-johnstown-pennsylvania/?utm_term=.90a4eb293e1f; John Cassidy, "Why Is Donald Trump in Michigan and Wisconsin?," *New Yorker*, October 31, 2016, www.newyorker .com/news/john-cassidy/why-is-donald-trump-in-michigan-and-wisconsin.

The information about the polling numbers in individual states came from FiveThirtyEight.com.

CHAPTER 3: THE DECISION MULTIVERSE

The Man in the High Castle [p. 67]

Information about the Amazon Studios series *The Man in the High Castle* came from plot summaries on Wikipedia, IMDB.com, and Amazon.com. See also Philip K. Dick, *The Man in the High Castle* (New York: Putnam, 1962).

CHAPTER 4: THE THREE PS

Predictions in decision-making: Tetlock and Mellers

Chapters 4–6, with their focus on estimating probability and improving forecasts, are informed throughout by the research of Philip Tetlock and Barbara Mellers. Their work should be essential reading for any deeper dive into subjects related to predictions in decision-making.

Don't taunt the bison [p. 70]

The incident in which the man taunted a bison on a road at Yellowstone National Park occurred on the evening of July 31, 2018, and was widely reported. This particular picture of the bison appeared in *USA Today*. David Strege, "Yellowstone Tourist Foolishly Taunts Bison, Avoids Serious Injury," USAToday .com, August 2, 2018, ftw.usatoday.com/2018/08/yellowstone-tourist-foolishly-taunts-bison-avoids -serious-injury. A video of the bison on the road appears on CNN.com, "Man Taunts Charging Bison," August 3, 2018, www.cnn.com/videos/us/2018/08/03/man-taunts-bison-yellowstone-national-park-hln -vpx.hln.

Archer's mindset [p. 80]

The metaphor of the archer's mindset was inspired by Dr. Peter Attia's passion for archery during a podcast episode I did on *The Drive*, which he hosts, peterattiamd.com/podcast/.

Probability terms and their equivalents [p. 86]

For the article on the Mauboussins' survey, see Andrew Mauboussin and Michael Mauboussin, "If You Say Something Is 'Likely,' How Likely Do People Think It Is?," *Harvard Business Review*, HBR.org, July 3, 2018, hbr.org/2018/07/if-you-say-something-is-likely-how-likely-do-people-think-it-is, as well as https://probabilitysurvey.com.

Bovine guessing [p. 99]

An account of Francis Galton's experiment in estimating the weight of an ox appeared in the introduction to James Suroweicki's *The Wisdom of Crowds: Why the Many Are Smarter than the Few and How Collective Wisdom Shapes Business, Economies, Societies and Nations* (New York: Random House, 2004). NPR's *Planet Money Podcast* conducted an online version of this experiment. Jacob Goldstein, "How Much Does This Cow Weigh?," NPR.org, July 17, 2015, www.npr.org/sections/money/2015/07/17/422881071/how-much-does-this-cow-weigh; Quoctrung Bui, "17,205 People Guessed the Weight of a Cow. This Is How They Did," NPR.org, August 7, 2015, www.npr.org/sections/money/2015/08/07/429720443/17-205-people-guessed-the-weight-of-a-cow-heres-how-they-did. The picture of Penelope and the graph appeared in the August 7 article.

CHAPTER 5: TAKING DEAD AIM AT THE FUTURE

The shock test [p. 112]

I'm indebted to Abraham Wyner for suggesting this idea over lunch one day, as I am also indebted to him for many of the ideas woven through this book.

Taxed by imprecision [p. 121]

An explanation of the standards involved appears in Damon Fleming and Gerald Whittenburg, "Accounting for Uncertainty," *Journal of Accountancy*, September 30, 2007, www.journalofaccountancy.com/issues/2007/oct/accountingforuncertainty.html. The ranges for the different terms comes from a summary in "Tax Opinion Practice—Confidence Levels for Written Tax Advice," June 12, 2014, taxassociate.wordpress.com/2014/06/12/tax-opinion-practice/. I'm indebted to Ed Lewis for bringing this practice among tax attorneys to my attention.

CHAPTER 6: TURNING DECISIONS OUTSIDE IN

Pros and cons lists as a servant to the inside view [p. 129]

Chip Heath and Dan Heath, in *Decisive: How to Make Better Choices in Life and Work* (New York: Crown, 2013), describe the history of the pros and cons list in detail and analyze its flaws, including its inability to combat the challenge of bias in decision-making.

Examples of the better-than-average effect [p. 133]

Better-than-average teachers: K. Patricia Cross, "Not Can, But *Will* College Teaching Be Improved?," *New Directions for Higher Education* 17 (1977): 1–15.

Better-than-average drivers: Ola Svenson, "Are We All Less Risky and More Skillful than Our Fellow Drivers?," *Acta Psychologica* 47, (1981): 143–48.

Better-than-average in social skills: College Board, Student Descriptive Questionnaire, 1976–1977, Princeton, NJ: Educational Testing Service.

Better-than-average in responsibility and judgment: Emily Stark and Daniel Sachau, "Lake Wobegon's Guns: Overestimating Our Gun-Related Competences," *Journal of Social and Political Psychology* 4, no. 1 (2016): 8–23. Stark and Sachau cited all these examples and sources, along with numerous additional findings of the better-than-average effect.

Where accuracy lives illustration [p. 134]

Michael Mauboussin shared this illustration with me, which he uses in some presentations. It has appeared in Michael Mauboussin, Dan Callahan, and Darius Majd, "The Base Rate Book: Integrating the Past to Better Anticipate the Future," Credit Suisse Global Financial Strategies, September 26, 2016.

How being smart makes motivated reasoning worse [p. 135]

Daniel Kahan and colleagues have done substantial research on this aspect of motivated reasoning. See Daniel Kahan, David Hoffman, Donald Braman, Danieli Evans, and Jeffrey Rachlinski, "They Saw a Protest: Cognitive Illiberalism and the Speech-Conduct Distinction," *Stanford Law Review* 64 (2012): 851–906; and Daniel Kahan, Ellen Peters, Erica Dawson, and Paul Slovic, "Motivated Numeracy and Enlightened Self-Government," *Behavioural Public Policy* 1, no. 1 (May 2017)), 54–86.

In addition, some of the influential work on "myside bias" (or "blind spot bias") includes Richard West, Russell Meserve, and Keith Stanovich, "Cognitive Sophistication Does Not Attenuate the Bias Blind Spot," *Journal of Personality and Social Psychology* 103, no. 3 (September 2002), 506–19; Keith Stanovich and Richard West, "On the Failure of Cognitive Ability to Predict Myside and One-Sided Thinking Biases," *Thinking & Reasoning* 14, no. 2 (2008): 129–67; and Vladimira Cavojova, Jakub Srol, and Magalena Adamus, "My Point Is Valid, Yours Is Not: Myside Bias in Reasoning About Abortion," *Journal of Cognitive Psychology* 30, no. 7 (2018): 656–69. An instructive article on myside bias, which brought the work of Cavojova and colleagues (along with other recent research) to my attention is from Christian Jarrett, "'My-side Bias' Makes It Difficult for Us to See the Logic in Arguments We Disagree With," *BPS Research Digest*, October 9, 2018, digest.bps.org.uk/2018/10/09/my-side-bias-makes-it-difficult-for-us-to-see-the-logic-in-arguments-we-disagree-with/.

Examples of base rates [pp. 136]

Divorce rates: Centers for Disease Control, National Center for Health Statistics, National Health Statistics Reports, Number 49, March 22, 2012, www.cdc.gov/nchs/data/nhsr/nhsr049.pdf.

Death from heart disease: Centers for Disease Control, Heart Disease Facts, www.cdc.gov/heartdisease/facts.htm.

Population in big cities: U.S. Census, census.gov/popclock.

High school grads immediately going to college: NCHEMS Information Center for Higher Education Policymaking and Analysis, 2016, www.higheredinfo.org/dbrowser/?year=2016&level=nation&mode=graph&state=0&submeasure=63.

Restaurant failures: Rory Crawford, "Restaurant Profitability and Failure Rates: What You Need to Know," FoodNewsFeed.com, April 2019, www.foodnewsfeed.com/fsr/expert-insights/restaurant-profitability-and-failure-rates-what-you-need-know.

Marriage and divorce: Casey Copen, Kimberly Daniels, Jonathan Vespa, and William Mosher, "First Marriages in the United States: Data from the 2006–2010 National Survey of Family Growth," National Health Statistics Reports, March 22, 2012.

Base rates for gym membership [p. 138]

Zachary Crockett, "Are Gym Memberships Worth the Money?," TheHustle.co, January 5, 2019, thehustle.co/gym-membership-cost.

Kyle Hoffman, "41 New Fitness & Gym Membership Statistics for 2020 (Infographic)," NoobGains.com, August 28, 2019, htnoobgains.com/gym-membership-statistics/.

A sunnier disposition? [p. 147]

David Schkade and Daniel Kahneman, "Does Living in California Make People Happy? A Focusing Illusion in Judgments of Life Satisfaction," *Psychological Science* 9, no. 5 (September 1998): 340–46.

CHAPTER 7: BREAKING FREE FROM ANALYSIS PARALYSIS

How much time we spend deciding what to eat, watch, and wear [p. 149]

Eat: The average American couple spends 132 hours a year deciding what to eat. SWNS, "American Couples Spend 5.5 Days a Year Deciding What to Eat," NewYorkPost.com, November 17, 2017, nypost.com /2017/11/17/american-couples-spend-5-5-days-a-year-deciding-what-to-eat/.

Watch on Netflix: Netflix users spend an average of eighteen minutes on a given day deciding what to watch. Russell Goldman and Corey Gilmore, "New Study Reveals We Spend 18 Minutes Every Day Deciding What to Stream on Netflix," Indiewire.com, July 21, 2016, www.indiewire.com/2016/07 /netflix-decide-watch-studies-1201708634/.

Wear: A poll of 2,491 women found that they spend an average of sixteen minutes deciding what to wear on weekday mornings and fourteen minutes on weekend mornings. Tracey Lomrantz Lester, "How Much Time Do You Spend Deciding What to Wear? (You'll Never Believe What's Average!)," Glamour .com, July 13, 2009, www.glamour.com/story/how-much-time-do-you-spend-dec.

Poking at the world [pp. 150–51]

I came across this great critique by Tim Harford in the *Financial Times*, "Why Living Experimentally Beats Taking Big Bets," www.ft.com/content/c60866c6-3039-11e9-ba00-0251022932c8, that pointed out that *Thinking in Bets* hadn't emphasized well enough that not all bets are big. Many decisions are tiny, low-impact bets for information gathering. (They've been referred to in poker as probe bets.) As Harford explained, you need to do lots of experimentation in decisions to gather intel. In part thanks to that critique, the emphasis on this point appears here.

Freerolling [p. 156]

According to Wikipedia, "freeroll" became a gambling expression from the practice, in the early 1950s, of Las Vegas hotel-casinos offering guests a "free roll" of nickels upon check-in to play the slot machines.

When a decision's hard, that means it's easy [p. 162]

I was discussing this concept over that same lunch with Abraham Wyner and he suggested this beautiful way to sum up how to think about two very close, high-impact options, a clear reminder of the power of Adi's observations, and lunch's place as one of the most important meals of the day.

The only-option test [p. 164]

Koen Smets explained this concept in "More Indifference: Why Strong Preferences and Opinions Are Not (Always) for Us," Medium.com, May 3, 2019, medium.com/@koenfucius/more-indifference -cdb2b1f9d953?sk=f9cb494adfb86451696b3742f140e901.

College students transferring schools [p. 169]

National Student Clearinghouse Research Center, "Transfer & Mobility—2015," July 6, 2015, nscresearchcenter .org/signaturereport9/; Valerie Strauss, "Why So Many College Students Decide to Transfer," *Washington Post*, January 29, 2017, www.washingtonpost.com/news/answer-sheet/wp/2017/01/29/why-so-many -college-students-decide-to-transfer/.

Two-way-door decisions [p. 170]

Jeff Bezos, "Letter to Shareholders," Amazon.com 2016 Annual Report," www.sec.gov/Archives/edgar/data/1018724/000119312516530910/d168744dex991.htm; Richard Branson, "Two-Way Door Decisions," Virgin.com, February 26, 2018, www.virgin.com/richard-branson/two-way-door-decisions.

The legend of Ivan Boesky [p. 171]

This apocryphal story of Ivan Boesky ordering every item on the menu at Tavern on the Green is included because it illustrates, albeit in an extreme fashion, the concept of choosing multiple options in parallel. Public versions of the tale refer to it as a "legend," something that "reportedly" happened. Myles Meserve, "Meet Ivan Boesky, the Infamous Wall Streeter Who Inspired Gordon Gekko," *Business Insider*, July 26, 2012, www.businessinsider.com/meet-ivan-boesky-the-infamous-wall-streeter-who-inspired-gordon-gecko-2012-7; Nicholas Spangler and Esther Davidowitz, "Seema Boesky's Rich Afterlife," *Westchester Magazine*, November 2010, www.westchestermagazine.com/Westchester-Magazine/November-2010/Seema-Boesky-rsquos-Rich-Afterlife/.

Leave It to Beaver [p. 175]

Leave It to Beaver, "The Haircut," October 25, 1957 (original U.S. air date), written by Bill Manhoff, IMDb.com, www.imdb.com/title/tt0630303/.

The Terminator [p. 180]

The Terminator, directed by James Cameron (Los Angeles: Orion Pictures,1984), written by James Cameron and Gale Anne Hurd.

Satisficing vs. maximizing [p. 181]

Some helpful articles describing the research and practical importance of satisficing versus maximizing include Kate Horowitz, "Why Making Decisions Stresses Some People Out," MentalFloss.com, February 27, 2018 (which described recent research by Jeffrey Hughes and Abigail Scholer, "When Wanting the Best Goes Right or Wrong: Distinguishing Between Adaptive and Maladaptive Maximization," *Personality and Social Psychology Bulletin* 4, no. 43 (February 8, 2017): 570–83), http://mentalfloss.com/article/92651/why-making-decisions-stresses-some-people-out; Olga Khazan, "The Power of 'Good Enough,'" TheAtlantic.com, March 10, 2015, www.theatlantic.com/health/archive/2015/03/the-power-of-good-enough/387388/; Mike Sturm, "Satisficing: A Way Out of the Miserable Mindset of Maximizing," Medium.com, March 28, 2018, medium.com/@MikeSturm/satisficing-how-to-avoid-the-pitfalls-of-the-maximizer-mindset-b092fe4497af; and Clare Thorpe, "A Guide to Overcoming FOBO, the Fear of Better Options," Medium.com, November 19, 2018, medium.com/s/story/a-guide-to-overcoming-fobo-the-fear-of-better-options-9a3f4655bfae.

CHAPTER 8: THE POWER OF NEGATIVE THINKING

Sticking to New Year's Resolutions [p. 184]

Ashley, Moor, "This Is How Many People Actually Stick to Their New Year's Resolutions," December 4, 2018, www.msn.com/en-us/health/wellness/this-is-how-many-people-actually-stick-to-their-new-year-e2-80-99s-resolutions/ar-BBQv644.

The behavior gap and *The Behavior Gap* [p. 184]

Carl Richards, *The Behavior Gap*: *Simple Ways to Stop Doing Dumb Things with Money* (New York: Portfolio, 2012).

Norman Vincent Peale [p. 184]

Peale's relationships with Eisenhower, Nixon, and Trump are widely documented, including on Wikipedia, en.wikipedia.org/wiki/Norman_Vincent_Peale. Peale officiated at Trump's first wedding, as well as the wedding of David Eisenhower (President Eisenhower's only grandson) and Julie Nixon (one of President Nixon's daughters). Charlotte Curtis, "When It's Mr. and Mrs. Eisenhower, the First Dance Will be 'Edelweiss,'" *New York Times*, December 14, 1968, timesmachine.nytimes.com/timesmachine/1968/12/14/76917375.html?pageNumber=58; Andrew Glass, "Julie Nixon Weds David Eisenhower, Dec. 22, 1968," Politico.com, December 22, 2016, www.politico.com/story/2016/12/julie-nixon-weds-david-eisenhower-dec-22-1968-232824; Paul Schwartzman, "How Trump Got Religion—and Why His Legendary Minister's Son Now Rejects Him," *Washington Post*, January 21, 2016, www.washingtonpost.com/lifestyle/how-trump-got-religion—and-why-his-legendary-ministers-son-now-rejects-him/2016/01/21/37bae16e-bb02-11e5-829c-26ffb874a18d_story.html; Curtis Sitomer, "Preacher's Preacher Most Enjoys Helping People One-on-One," *Christian Science Monitor*, May 25, 1984, www.csmonitor.com/1984/0525/052516.html.

Mental contrasting [p. 186]

See Gabriele Oettingen, *Rethinking Positive Thinking: Inside the New Science of Motivation* (New York: Current, 2014); Gabriele Oettingen and Peter Gollwitzer, "Strategies of Setting and Implementing Goals," in *Social Psychological Foundations of Clinical Psychology*, edited by J. Maddox and J. Tangney (New York: Guilford Press, 2010).

Premortems [pp. 189–93]

Gary Klein's ideas are an influential starting point to my approach on premortems. See Gary Klein, "Performing a Project Premortem," *Harvard Business Review* 85, no 9 (September 2007): 18–19; and Gary Klein, Paul Sonkin, and Paul Johnson, "Rendering a Powerful Tool Flaccid: The Misuse of Premortems on Wall Street," February 2019 draft, capitalallocatorspodcast.com/wp-content/uploads/Klein-Sonkin-and-Johnson-2019-The-Misuse-of-Premortems-on-Wall-Street.pdf.

Effectiveness of combining mental time travel and mental contrasting [p. 192]

The research about the 30% increase in reasons for failure is from Deborah Mitchell, J. Edward Russo, and Nancy Pennington, "Back to the Future: Temporal Perspective in the Explanation of Events," *Journal of Behavioral Decision Making* 2, no. 1 (January 1989): 25–38.

Backcasting: a "preparade" [p. 193]

See Chip Heath and Dan Heath, *Decisive: How to Make Better Choices in Life and Work* (New York: Crown, 2013).

The Dr. Evil game [p. 202]

This game was originally suggested to me by Dan Egan; he called it the "Damien" game. I adapted the game to include the constraint that people from the outside would not be able to spot that any individual decision was poor.

Darth Vader's management style [p. 215]

The quotes from the movie came from George Lucas's Revised Fourth Draft Script of *Star Wars, Episode IV, A New Hope*, January 15, 1976, www.imsdb.com/scripts/Star-Wars-A-New-Hope.html.

Dr. Evil on fourth down in the NFL [p. 216]

Andrew Beaton and Ben Cohen, "Football Coaches Are Still Flunking on Fourth Down," *Wall Street Journal*, September 16, 2019, www.wsj.com/articles/football-coaches-are-still-flunking-their-tests-on-fourth-down-11568642372; Dan Bernstein, "Revolution or Convention—Analyzing NFL Coaches' Fourth-Down Decisions in 2018," *Sporting News*, January 17, 2019, www.sportingnews.com/us/nfl/news/revolution-or-convention-analyzing-nfl-coaches-fourth-down-decisions-in-2018/1kyyi026urad31 qwvitnbz2rnc; Adam Kilgore, "On Fourth Down, NFL Coaches Aren't Getting Bolder. They're Getting Smarter," *Washington Post*, October 8, 2018, www.washingtonpost.com/sports/2018/10/09/fourth-down-nfl-coaches-arent-getting-bolder-theyre-getting-smarter/; NYT 4th Down Bot, "Fourth Down: When to Go for It and Why," *New York Times*, September 5, 2014, www.nytimes.com/2014/09/05/upshot/4th-down-when-to-go-for-it-and-why.html; Ty Schalter, "NFL Coaches Are Finally Getting More Aggressive on Fourth Down," FiveThirtyEight.com, November 14, 2019, fivethirtyeight.com/features/nfl-coaches-are-finally-getting-more-aggressive-on-fourth-down/.

CHAPTER 9: DECISION HYGIENE

Dr. Semmelweis and Victorian medicine [p. 217]

Lindsey Fitzharris, *The Butchering Art: Joseph Lister's Quest to Transform the Grisly World of Victorian Medicine* (New York: Scientific American/Farrar, Straus and Giroux, 2017), 46. The quote about the trusty, crusty apron was from an account by Berkeley Moynihan, a pioneering surgeon who was one of the first to use rubber gloves—*approximately forty years after Semmelweis's death*. Additional details on the life and death of Dr. Ignaz Semmelweis came from Codell Carter and Barbara Carter, *Childbed Fever: A Scientific Biography of Ignaz Semmelweis* (Livingston, NJ: Transaction Publishers, 2005), 78; Duane Funk, Joseph Parrillo, and Anand Kumar, "Sepsis and Septic Shock: A History," *Critical Care Clinics* 25 (2009): 83–101.

The Asch experiment [pp. 220–21]

Solomon Asch, "Opinions and Social Pressure," *Scientific American* 193, no. 5 (November 1955): 31–35.

John Stuart Mill [p. 224]

John Stuart Mill's *On Liberty*, apart from being one of the most influential books ever written on individual rights and the relationship between authority and liberty, expresses powerful, enduring concepts about decision-making. See specifically chapter 2, "Of the Liberty of Thought and Discussion." Jonathan Haidt and Richard Reeves collaborated on a short, edited version of the best of chapter 2, illustrated by Dave Cicirelli, *All Minus One: John Stuart Mill's Ideas on Free Speech Illustrated* (New York: Heterodox Academy, 2018). (It's available as a free downloadable PDF at heterodoxacademy.org/mill/.)

The Stasser and Titus experiment [pp. 229–30]

Garold Stasser and William Titus, "Pooling of Unshared Information in Group Decision Making: Biased Information Sampling During Discussion," *Journal of Personality and Social Psychology* 48, no. 6 (1985): 1467–78.

The Levy, Yardley, and Zeckhauser experiment [p. 231]

Dan Levy, Joshua Yardley, and Richard Zeckhauser, "Getting an Honest Answer: Clickers in the Classroom," *Journal of the Scholarship of Teaching and Learning* 17, no. 4 (October 2017): 104–25.

Limitations and checks on subject-matter experts [pp. 231–34]

Philip Tetlock has studied and written extensively about the role of expertise in decision-making, including specifically the role of experts in group decisions. See Philip Tetlock and Dan Gardner, *Superforecasting: The Art and Science of Prediction* (New York: Crown, 2015), and Philip Tetlock, *Expert Political Judgment: How Good Is It? How Much Can We Know?* (Princeton, NJ: Princeton University Press, 2005).

Quick-and-dirty [p. 234]

Harvard Professor Richard Zeckhauser is a big fan of having members of decision groups write down their opinions and read them aloud, starting with the most junior person.

General References and Suggested Further Reading

Ariely, Dan. *Predictably Irrational: The Hidden Forces That Shape Our Decisions*. Revised and expanded edition. New York: HarperCollins, 2009.

Brockman, John, ed. *Thinking: The New Science of Decision-Making, Problem-Solving, and Prediction*. New York: HarperPerennial, 2013.

Cialdini, Robert. *Influence: The Psychology of Persuasion*. Revised edition. New York: HarperCollins, 2009.

Dalio, Ray. *Principles: Life and Work*. New York: Simon & Schuster, 2017.

Duhigg, Charles. *The Power of Habit: Why We Do What We Do in Life and Business*. New York: Random House, 2012.

———. *Smarter Better Faster: The Secrets of Being Productive in Life and Business*. New York: Random House, 2016.

Ellenberg, Jordan. *How Not to Be Wrong: The Power of Mathematical Thinking*. New York: Penguin, 2014.

Epstein, David. *Range: Why Generalists Triumph in a Specialized World*. New York: Riverhead, 2019.

Feynman, Richard. "Cargo Cult Science." *Engineering and Science* 37, no. 7 (June 1974): 10–13.

———. *The Pleasure of Finding Things Out: The Best Short Works of Richard P. Feynman*. New York: Perseus Publishing, 1999.

Firestein, Stuart. *Ignorance: How It Drives Science*. New York: Oxford University Press, 2012.

Gilbert, Daniel. *Stumbling on Happiness*. New York: Alfred A. Knopf, 2006.

Haidt, Jonathan. *The Righteous Mind: Why Good People Are Divided by Politics and Religion*. New York: Pantheon Books, 2012.

Holmes, Jamie. *Nonsense: The Power of Not Knowing*. New York: Crown, 2015.

Kahneman, Daniel. *Thinking, Fast and Slow*. New York: Farrar, Straus & Giroux, 2011.

Kahneman, Daniel, and Amos Tversky. "On the Psychology of Prediction." *Psychological Review* 80, no. 4 (July 1973): 237–51.

Levitt, Steven, and Stephen Dubner. *Freakonomics: A Rogue Economist Explores the Hidden Side of Everything*. New York: HarperCollins, 2005.

Loewenstein, George, Daniel Read, and Roy Baumeister, eds. *Time and Decision: Economic and Psychological Perspectives on Intertemporal Choice.* New York: Russell Sage Foundation, 2003.

Marcus, Gary. *Kluge: The Haphazard Evolution of the Human Mind.* New York: Houghton Mifflin, 2008.

Marcus, Gary, and Ernest Davis. *Rebooting AI: Building Artificial Intelligence We Can Trust.* New York: Pantheon, 2019.

Mauboussin, Michael. *The Success Equation: Untangling Skill and Luck in Business, Sports, and Investing.* Boston: Harvard Business Review Press, 2012.

———. *Think Twice: Harnessing the Power of Counterintuition.* Boston: Harvard Business School Publishing, 2009.

Mauboussin, Michael, Dan Callahan, and Darius Majd. "The Base Rate Book: Integrating the Past to Better Anticipate the Future," Credit Suisse Global Financial Strategies, September 26, 2016.

Merton, Robert K., "The Normative Structure of Science," 1942. In *The Sociology of Science: Theoretical and Empirical Investigations*, edited by Norman Storer. Chicago and London: University of Chicago Press, 1973.

Mill, John Stuart. *On Liberty.* London: John W. Parker and Son, 1859.

Moore, Don. *Perfectly Confident: How to Calibrate Your Decisions Wisely.* New York: HarperBusiness, 2020.

Page, Scott. *The Model Thinker: What You Need to Know to Make Data Work for You.* New York: Hachette, 2018.

Parrish, Shane. *The Great Mental Models: General Thinking Concepts.* Ottawa, Canada: Latticework, 2020.

Pink, Daniel. *When: The Scientific Secrets of Perfect Timing.* New York: Riverhead, 2018.

Pinker, Steven. *Enlightenment How: The Case for Reason, Science, Humanism, and Progress.* New York: Viking, 2018.

Rescher, Nicholas. *Luck: The Brilliant Randomness of Everyday Life.* New York: Farrar Straus & Giroux, 1995.

Shermer, Michael. *The Believing Brain: From Ghosts and Gods to Politics and Conspiracies: How We Construct Beliefs and Reinforce Them as Truths.* New York: Times Books, 2011.

Silver, Nate. *The Signal and the Noise: Why So Many Predictions Fail—but Some Don't.* New York: Penguin, 2012.

Suroweicki, James. *The Wisdom of Crowds: Why the Many Are Smarter than the Few and How Collective Wisdom Shapes Business, Economies, Societies and Nations.* New York: Random House, 2004.

Taleb, Nassim. *Fooled by Randomness: The Hidden Role of Chance in Life and in the Markets.* New York: Random House, 2004.

Tetlock, Philip. *Expert Political Judgment: How Good Is It? How Much Can We Know?* Princeton, NJ: Princeton University Press, 2005.

Tetlock, Philip, and Dan Gardner. *Superforecasting: The Art and Science of Prediction.* New York: Crown, 2015.

Thaler, Richard. *Misbehaving: The Making of Behavioral Economics.* New York: W. W. Norton & Co., 2015.

Thaler, Richard, and Cass Sunstein. *Nudge: Improving Decisions About Health, Wealth, and Happiness.* New York: Penguin, 2008.

Tversky, Amos, and Daniel Kahneman. "Judgment Under Uncertainty: Heuristics and Biases." *ONR Technical Report* (August 1973).

Von Neumann, John, and Oskar Morgenstern. *Theory of Games and Economic Behavior.* Princeton, NJ: Princeton University Press, 2004.

Weinberg, Gabriel, and Lauren McCann. *Super Thinking: The Big Book of Mental Models.* New York: Penguin/Portfolio, 2019.

Selected References

Arbesman, Samuel. *The Half-Life of Facts: Why Everything We Know Has an Expiration Date*. New York: Current, 2012.

Ariely, Dan, and Jeff Kreisler. *Dollars and Sense: How We Misthink Money and How to Spend Smarter*. New York: Harper, 2017.

Ariely, Dan, and Klaus Wertenbroch. "Procrastination, Deadlines, and Performance: Self-Control by Precommitment." *Psychological Science* 13, no. 3 (2002): 219–24.

Arkes, Hal, and Catherine Blumer. "The Psychology of Sunk Cost." *Organizational Behavior and Human Decision Processes* 35, no. 1 (1985): 124–40.

Arvai, Joseph, and Ann Froschauer. "Good Decisions, Bad Decisions: The Interaction of Process and Outcome in Evaluations of Decision Quality." *Journal of Risk Research* 13, no. 7 (October 2010): 845–59.

Asch, Solomon. "Opinions and Social Pressure." *Scientific American* 193, no. 5 (1955): 31–35.

Bar-Eli, Michael, Azar Ofer, Ilana Ritov, Yael Keidar-Levin, and Galin Schein. "Action Bias Among Elite Soccer Goalkeepers: The Case of Penalty Kicks." *Journal of Economic Psychology* 28, no. 5 (October 2007): 606–21.

Baron, Jonathan, and John Hershey. "Outcome Bias in Decision Evaluation." *Journal of Personality and Social Psychology* 54, no. 4 (1988): 569–79.

Browne, Basil. "Going on Tilt: Frequent Poker Players and Control." *Journal of Gambling Behavior* 5, no 1 (March 1989): 3–21.

Burch, E. Earl, and William Henry. "Opportunity Costs: An Experimental Approach." *Accounting Review* 45, no. 2 (1970): 315–21.

Cavojova, Vladimira, Jakub Srol, and Magalena Adamus. "My Point Is Valid, Yours Is Not: Myside Bias in Reasoning About Abortion." *Journal of Cognitive Psychology* 30, no. 7 (2018): 656–69.

Chapman, Gretchen, and Eric Johnson. "Anchoring, Activation, and the Construction of Values." *Organizational Behavior and Human Decision Processes* 79, no. 2 (August 1999): 115–53.

Clear, James. *Atomic Habits: An Easy & Proven Way to Build Good Habits & Break Bad Ones.* New York: Avery, 2018.

Cochran, Winona, and Abraham Tesser. "The 'What the Hell' Effect: Some Effects of Goal Proximity and Goal Framing on Performance." In *Striving and Feeling: Interactions Among Goals, Affect, and Self-Regulation*, edited by L. Martin and Abraham Tesser. New York: Lawrence Erlbaum Associates, 1996.

Coyle, Daniel. *The Culture Code: The Secrets of Highly Successful Groups.* New York: Bantam, 2018.

Cross, K. Patricia. "Not Can, But Will College Teaching Be Improved?" *New Directions for Higher Education* 17 (1977): 1–15.

De Wit, Frank, Lindred Greer, and Karen Jehn. "The Paradox of Intragroup Conflict: A Meta-Analysis." *Journal of Applied Psychology* 92, no. 2 (2012): 360–90.

Dekking, F. M., C. Kraaikamp, H. P. Lopuhaä, and L. E. Meester. *A Modern Introduction to Probability and Statistics: Understanding Why and How.* London: Springer Science & Business Media, 2005.

Dion, Karen, Ellen Berscheid, and Elaine Walster. "What Is Beautiful Is Good." *Journal of Personality and Social Psychology* 24, no. 3 (1972): 285–90.

Duarte, Jose, Jarret Crawford, Charlotta Stern, Jonathan Haidt, Lee Jussim, and Philip Tetlock. "Political Diversity Will Improve Social Psychological Science. *Behavioral and Brain Sciences* 38 (January 2015): 1–58.

Dunning, David. "The Dunning–Kruger Effect: On Being Ignorant of One's Own Ignorance." In *Advances in Experimental Social Psychology*, volume 44. San Diego: Academic Press, 2011.

Edwards, Kari, and Edward Smith. "A Disconfirmation Bias in the Evaluation of Arguments." *Journal of Personality and Social Psychology* 71, no. 1 (1996): 5–24.

Eskreis-Winkler, Lauren, Katherine Milkman, Dena Gromet, and Angela Duckworth. "A Large-Scale Field Experiment Shows Giving Advice Improves Academic Outcomes for the Advisor." *PNAS* 116, no. 30 (July 23, 2019): 14808–810.

Festinger, Leon. *A Theory of Cognitive Dissonance.* Stanford, CA: Stanford University Press, 1957.

Fischhoff, Baruch. "Hindsight Is Not Equal to Foresight: The Effect of Outcome Knowledge on Judgment Under Uncertainty." *Journal of Experimental Psychology: Human Perception and Performance* 1, no. 3 (August 1975): 288–99.

Franz, Timothy, and James Larson. "The Impact of Experts on Information Sharing During Group Discussion." *Small Group Research* 33, no. 4 (August 2002): 383–411.

Frederick, Shane, George Loewenstein, and Ted O'Donoghue. "Time Discounting and Time Preference: A Critical Review." *Journal of Economic Literature* 40, no. 2 (June 2002): 351–401.

Friedman, Jeffrey. *War and Chance: Assessing Uncertainty in International Politics.* New York: Oxford University Press, 2019.

Friedman, Jeffrey, and Richard Zeckhauser. "Handling and Mishandling Estimative Probability: Likelihood, Confidence, and the Search for Bin Laden." *Intelligence and National Security* 30 (2015): 77–99.

Gigerenzer, Gerd, Ulrich Hoffrage, and Heinz Kleinbölting. "Probabilistic Mental Models: A Brunswikian Theory of Confidence." *Psychological Review* 98, no. 4 (1991): 506–28.

Gigone, Daniel, and Reid Hastie. "The Common Knowledge Effect: Information Sharing and Group Judgment." *Journal of Personality and Social Psychology* 65, no. 5 (1993): 959–74.

Gilbert, Daniel. "How Mental Systems Believe." *American Psychologist* 46, no. 2 (February 1991): 107–19.

Gilbert, Daniel, Roman Tafarodi, and Patrick Malone. "You Can't Not Believe Everything You Read." *Journal of Personality and Social Psychology* 65, no. 2 (August 1993): 221–33.

Gino, Francesca, Don Moore, and Max Bazerman. "No Harm, No Foul: The Outcome Bias in Ethical Judgments." Harvard Business School NOM Working Paper 08-080, 2009.

Gino, Francesca, and Gary Pisano. "Why Leaders Don't Learn from Success." *Harvard Business Review* 89, no. 4 (April 2011): 68–74.

Godker, Katrin, Peiran Jiao, and Paul Smeets. "Investor Memory." July 2019 draft. www.uibk.ac.at/credence
-goods/events/sfb-seminar/documents/sfb_seminar_19_smeets_paper.pdf.

Gollwitzer, Peter, and Paschal Sheeran. "Implementation Intentions and Goal Achievement: A Meta-
Analysis of Effects and Processes." *Advances in Experimental Social Psychology* 38 (2006): 69–119.

Guwande, Atul. *The Checklist Manifesto: How to Get Things Right.* New York: Metropolitan Books, 2009.

Haidt, Jonathan, and Richard Reeves, eds. *All Minus One: John Stuart Mill's Ideas on Free Speech Illustrated.*
New York: Heterodox Academy, 2018.

Hammond, John, Ralph Keeney, and Howard Raiffa. "The Hidden Traps in Decision Making." *Harvard
Business Review* 76, no. 5 (September–October 1998): 47–58.

Harford, Tim. "Why Living Experimentally Beats Taking Big Bets." *Financial Times*, February 14, 2019.

Hastorf, Albert, and Hadley Cantril. "They Saw a Game: A Case Study." *Journal of Abnormal and Social
Psychology* 49, no. 1 (January 1954): 129–34.

Heath, Chip, and Dan Heath. *Decisive: How to Make Better Choices in Life and Work.* New York: Crown,
2013.

Heck, Patrick, Daniel Simons, and Christopher Chabris. "65% of Americans Believe They Are Above Average in Intelligence: Results of Two Nationally Representative Surveys." *PLoS ONE* 13, no. 7 (2018):
e0200103.

Horowitz, Kate. "Why Making Decisions Stresses Some People Out." MentalFloss.com, February 27, 2018.

Hughes, Jeffrey, and Abigail Scholer. "When Wanting the Best Goes Right or Wrong: Distinguishing Between Adaptive and Maladaptive Maximization." *Personality and Social Psychology Bulletin* 43, no. 4
(2017): 570–83.

Jarrett, Christian. "'My-Side Bias' Makes It Difficult for Us to See the Logic in Arguments We Disagree
With." *BPS Research Digest* (October 9, 2018).

Johnson, Hollyn, and Colleen Seifert. "Sources of the Continued Influence Effect: When Misinformation
in Memory Affects Later Inferences." *Journal of Experimental Psychology: Learning, Memory, and Cognition* 20, no. 6 (November 1994): 1420–36.

Johnson-Laird, Philip. "Mental Models and Probabilistic Thinking." *Cognition* 50, no. 1 (June
1994):189–209.

Kahan, Daniel, David Hoffman, Donald Braman, Danieli Evans, and Jeffrey Rachlinski. "They Saw a
Protest: Cognitive Illiberalism and the Speech-Conduct Distinction." *Stanford Law Review* 64 (2012):
851–906.

Kahan, Daniel, and Ellen Peters. "Rumors of the 'Nonreplication' of the 'Motivated Numeracy Effect' Are
Greatly Exaggerated." Cultural Cognition Project, Working Paper No. 324, 2017.

Kahan, Daniel, Ellen Peters, Erica Dawson, and Paul Slovic. "Motivated Numeracy and Enlightened Self-
Government." *Behavioural Public Policy* 1, no. 1 (May 2017): 54–86.

Kahneman, Daniel. "Maps of Bounded Rationality: A Perspective of Intuitive Judgment and Choice."
American Economic Review 93, no. 5 (December 2003): 1444–75.

Kahneman, Daniel, and Gary Klein. "Conditions for Intuitive Expertise: A Failure to Disagree." *American
Psychologist* 64, no. 6 (September 2009): 515–26.

Kahneman, Daniel, Jack Knetsch, and Richard Thaler. "The Endowment Effect, Loss Aversion, and Status
Quo Bias." *Journal of Economic Perspectives* 5, no. 1 (Winter 1991): 193–206.

Kahneman, Daniel, Paul Slovic, and Amos Tversky, eds. *Judgment Under Uncertainty: Heuristics and Biases.*
New York: Cambridge University Press, 1982.

Kahneman, Daniel, and Amos Tversky. "Choices, Values, and Frames." *American Psychologist* 39, no. 4
(April 1984): 341–50.

———. "Intuitive Prediction: Biases and Corrective Procedures." Defense Advanced Research Project
Agency, Technical Report PTR-1042-77-6, June 1977.

———, "Prospect Theory: An Analysis of Decision Under Risk." *Econometrica: Journal of the Econometric Society* 47, no. 2 (March 1979), 263–91.

Khazan, Olga. "The Power of 'Good Enough.'" TheAtlantic.com, March 10, 2015.

Klein, Gary. "Performing a Project Premortem." *Harvard Business Review* 85, no. 9 (September 2007), 18–19.

Klein, Gary, Paul Sonkin, and Paul Johnson. "Rendering a Powerful Tool Flaccid: The Misuse of Premortems on Wall Street." February 2019 draft. capitalallocatorspodcast.com/wp-content/uploads/Klein -Sonkin-and-Johnson-2019-The-Misuse-of-Premortems-on-Wall-Street.pdf.

Laakasuo, Michael, Jussi Palomäki, and Mikko Salmela. "Emotional and Social Factors Influence Poker Decision Making Accuracy. *Journal of Gambling Studies* 31, no. 3 (2015): 933–47.

Langer, Ellen. "The Illusion of Control." *Journal of Personality and Social Psychology* 32, no. 2 (1975): 311–28.

Larson, James, Pennie Foster-Fishman, and Christopher Keys. "Discussion of Shared and Unshared Information in Decision-Making Groups," *Journal of Personality and Social Psychology* 67, no. 3 (1994): 446–61.

Lerner, Jennifer, and Philip Tetlock. "Accounting for the Effects of Accountability." *Psychological Bulletin* 125, no. 2 (March 1999): 255–75.

———. "Bridging Individual, Interpersonal, and Institutional Approaches to Judgment and Decision Making: The Impact of Accountability on Cognitive Bias." In *Emerging Perspectives on Judgment and Decision Research*, edited by S. Schneider and J. Shanteau. Cambridge, UK: Cambridge University Press, 2003.

Levitt, Steven, and Stephen Dubner. *Think Like a Freak*. New York: HarperCollins, 2014.

Levy, Dan, Joshua Yardley, and Richard Zeckhauser. "Getting an Honest Answer: Clickers in the Classroom." *Journal of the Scholarship of Teaching and Learning* 17, no. 4 (October 2017): 104–25.

Lyon, Don, and Paul Slovic. "Dominance of Accuracy Information and Neglect of Base Rates in Probability Estimation." *Acta Psychologica* 40, no. 4 (August 1976): 287–98.

MacCoun, Robert, and Saul Perlmutter. "Blind Analysis as a Correction for Confirmatory Bias in Physics and in Psychology." In *Psychological Science Under Scrutiny: Recent Challenges and Proposed Solutions*, edited by Scott Lilienfeld and Irwin Waldman. Oxford, UK: Wiley Blackwell, 2017.

———. "Hide Results to Seek the Truth: More Fields Should, Like Particle Physics, Adopt Blind Analysis to Thwart Bias." *Nature* 526, no. 7572 (October 8, 2015): 187–90.

Mauboussin, Andrew, and Michael Mauboussin. "If You Say Something Is 'Likely,' How Likely Do People Think It Is?" HBR.org, July 3, 2018.

Mauboussin, Michael, Dan Callahan, and Darius Majd. "The Base Rate Book: Integrating the Past to Better Anticipate the Future," Credit Suisse Global Financial Strategies, September 26, 2016.

Mitchell, Deborah, J. Edward Russo, and Nancy Pennington. "Back to the Future: Temporal Perspective in the Explanation of Events." *Journal of Behavioral Decision Making* 2, no. 1 (January 1989): 25–38.

Mitchell, Terence, and Laura Kalb. "Effects of Outcome Knowledge and Outcome Valence on Supervisors' Evaluations." *Journal of Applied Psychology* 66, no. 5 (1981): 604–12.

Moore, Don, and Derek Schatz. "The Three Faces of Overconfidence." *Social & Personality Psychology Focus* 11, no 8 (August 2017): e12331.

Morse, Mitch. "Thinking in Bets: Book Review and Thoughts on the Interaction of Uncertainty and Politics." Medium.com, December 9, 2018.

Murdock, Bennett. "The Serial Position Effect of Free Recall." *Journal of Experimental Psychology* 64, no. 5 (1962): 482–88.

Nickerson, Raymond. "Confirmation Bias: A Ubiquitous Phenomenon in Many Guises." *Review of General Psychology* 2, no. 2 (1998): 175–220.

O'Brien, Michael, R. Alexander Bentley, and William Brock. *The Importance of Small Decisions*. Cambridge, MA: MIT Press, 2019.

Oettingen, Gabriele. *Rethinking Positive Thinking: Inside the New Science of Motivation*. New York: Current, 2014.

Oettingen, Gabriele, and Peter Gollwitzer. "Strategies of Setting and Implementing Goals." In *Social Psychological Foundations of Clinical Psychology*, edited by J. Maddox and Tangney. New York: Guilford Press, 2010.

Pachur, Thorsten, Ralph Hertwig, and Florian Steinmann. "How Do People Judge Risks: Availability Heuristic, Affect Heuristic, or Both?" *Journal of Experimental Psychology: Applied* 18, no. 3 (2012): 314–330.

Phillips, Katherine, Katie Liljenquist, and Margaret Neale. "Is the Pain Worth the Gain? The Advantages and Liabilities of Agreeing with Socially Distinct Newcomers." *Personality and Social Psychology Bulletin* 35, no. 3 (2009): 336–50.

Price, Vincent, Joseph Cappella, and Lilach Nir. "Does Disagreement Contribute to More Deliberative Opinion?" *Political Communication* 19, no. 1 (January 2002): 95–112.

Rapp, David. "The Consequences of Reading Inaccurate Information." *Current Directions in Psychological Science* 25, no. 4 (2016): 281–85.

Richards, Carl. *The Behavior Gap: Simple Ways to Stop Doing Dumb Things with Money*. New York: Penguin/Portfolio, 2012.

Robinson, John. "Unlearning and Backcasting: Rethinking Some of the Questions We Ask About the Future." *Technological Forecasting and Social Change* 33, no. 4 (July 1998): 325–38.

Roese, Neal, and Kathleen Vohs. "Hindsight Bias." *Perspectives on Psychological Science* 7, no. 5 (2012): 411–26.

Ross, Michael, and Fiore Sicoly. "Egocentric Biases in Availability and Attribution." *Journal of Personality and Social Psychology* 37, no. 3 (March 1979): 322–36.

Russo, J. Edward, and Paul Schoemaker. *Winning Decisions: Getting It Right the First Time*. New York: Doubleday, 2002.

Samuelson, William, and Richard Zeckhauser. "Status Quo Bias in Decision Making." *Journal of Risk and Uncertainty* 1 (1988): 7–59.

Schkade, David, and Daniel Kahneman. "Does Living in California Make People Happy? A Focusing Illusion in Judgments of Life Satisfaction." *Psychological Science* 9, no. 5 (September 1998): 340–46.

Schoemaker, Paul, and Philip Tetlock. "Superforecasting: How to Upgrade Your Company's Judgment." *Harvard Business Review* 94 (May 2016): 72–78.

Schwardmann, Peter, and Joel van der Weele, "Deception and Self-Deception." *Nature Human Behaviour* 3, no. 10 (2019), 1055–61.

Schwartz, Barry. *The Paradox of Choice: Why More Is Less*. New York: HarperCollins, 2003.

Schwartz, Barry, Andrew Ward, John Monterosso, Sonya Lyubomirsky, Katherine White, and Darrin Lehman. "Maximizing Versus Satisficing: Happiness Is a Matter of Choice." *Journal of Personality and Social Psychology* 83, no. 5 (2002): 1178–97.

Schwartz, Janet, Daniel Mochon, Lauren Wyper, Josiase Maroba, Deepak Patel, and Dan Ariely. "Healthier by Precommitment." *Psychological Science* 25, no. 2 (2014): 538–46.

Sheikh, Hasan, and Cass Sunstein. "To Persuade As an Expert, Order Matters: 'Information First, Then Opinion' for Effective Communication." October 24, 2019 draft. ssrn.com/abstract=3474998.

Simonson, Itamar. "The Influence of Anticipating Regret and Responsibility on Purchase Decisions." *Journal of Consumer Research* 19, no. 1 (June 1992): 105–18.

Slovic, Paul, Melissa Finucane, Ellen Peters, Donald MacGregor. "The Affect Heuristic." *European Journal of Operational Research* 177, no. 3 (2007): 1333–52.

Smets, Koen. "More Indifference: Why Strong Preferences and Opinions Are Not (Always) for Us." Medium.com, May 3, 2019.

Stanovich, Keith, and Richard West. "On the Failure of Cognitive Ability to Predict Myside and One-Sided Thinking Biases." *Thinking & Reasoning* 14, no. 2 (2008): 129–67.

Stark, Emily, and Daniel Sachau. "Lake Wobegon's Guns: Overestimating Our Gun-Related Competences." *Journal of Social and Political Psychology* 4, no. 1 (2016): 8–23.

Stasser, Garold, and William Titus. "Pooling of Unshared Information in Group Decision Making: Biased Information Sampling During Discussion," *Journal of Personality and Social Psychology* 48, no. 6 (1985): 1467–78.

Staw, Barry. "The Escalation of Commitment to a Course of Action." *Academy of Management Review* 6, no. 4 (1981): 577–87.

Stone, Peter. *The Luck of the Draw: The Role of Lotteries in Decision Making.* New York: Oxford University Press, 2011.

Sturm, Mike. "Satisficing: A Way Out of the Miserable Mindset of Maximizing." Medium.com, March 28, 2018.

Sunstein, Cass. "Historical Explanations Always Involve Counterfactual History." *Journal of Philosophy of History* (November 2016), 433–40.

Sunstein, Cass, and Reid Hastie. *Wiser: Getting Beyond Groupthink to Make Groups Smarter.* Boston: Harvard Business Press, 2014.

Svenson, Ola. "Are We All Less Risky and More Skillful than Our Fellow Drivers?" *Acta Psychologica* 47 (1981): 143–48.

Sweeney, Joseph. "Beyond Pros and Cons—Start Teaching the Weight and Rate Method." Medium.com, October 22, 2018.

Thaler, Richard. "Mental Accounting and Consumer Choice." *Marketing Science* 4, no. 3 (1985): 199–214.

———. "Mental Accounting Matters." *Journal of Behavioral Decision Making* 12, no. 3 (1999): 183–206.

Thorpe, Clare. "A Guide to Overcoming FOBO, the Fear of Better Options." Medium.com, November 19, 2018.

Trope, Yaacov, and Ayelet Fishbach. "Counteractive Self-Control in Overcoming Temptation." *Journal of Personality and Social Psychology* 79, no. 4 (2000): 493–506.

Trouche, Emmanuel, Petter Johansson, Lars Hall, and Hugo Mercier. "The Selective Laziness of Reasoning." *Cognitive Science* (2015): 1–15.

Tversky, Amos, and Daniel Kahneman. "Advances in Prospect Theory: Cumulative Representation of Uncertainty." *Journal of Risk and Uncertainty* 5, no. 4 (1992): 297–323.

———. "Availability: A Heuristic for Judging Frequency and Probability." *Cognitive Psychology* 5, no. 2 (1973): 207–32.

———. "Evidential Impact of Base Rates." *ONR Technical Report* (May 1981).

———. "Extensional Versus Intuitive Reasoning: The Conjunction Fallacy in Probability Judgment." *Psychological Review* 90, no. 4 (October 1983): 293–315.

———. "The Framing of Decisions and the Psychology of Choice." *Science* 211, January 30, 1981, 453–58.

———. "Loss Aversion in Riskless Choice: A Reference-Dependent Model." *Quarterly Journal of Economics* 106, no. 4 (November 1999); 1039–61.

———. "Rational Choice and the Framing of Decisions." *Journal of Business* 59 (1986): 251–278.

Ullmann-Margalit, Edna, and Sidney Morganbesser. "Picking and Choosing." *Social Research* 44, no. 4 (Winter 1977): 757–85.

Weller, Chris. "A Neuroscientist Explains Why He Always Picks the 2nd Menu Item on a List of Specials." *Business Insider*, July 28, 2017.

West, Richard, Russell Meserve, and Keith Stanovich. "Cognitive Sophistication Does Not Attenuate the Bias Blind Spot." *Journal of Personality and Social Psychology* 103, no. 3 (September 2002): 506–19.

Wheeler, Michael. "The Luck Factor in Great Decisions." HBR.org, November 18, 2013.

———. "The Need for Prospective Hindsight." *Negotiation Journal* 3, no. 7 (January 1987): 7–10.

Zeckhauser, Richard. "Investing in the Unknown and Unknowable." *Capitalism and Society* 1, no. 2 (2006): 1–39.

Zweig, Jason, and Phil Tetlock. "The Perilous Task of Forecasting." *Wall Street Journal*, June 17, 2016.

About the Author

Annie Duke is an author, corporate speaker, and consultant in the decision-making space. Annie's book, *Thinking in Bets: Making Smarter Decisions When You Don't Have All the Facts*, is a national bestseller. As a former professional poker player, Annie won more than $4 million in tournament poker before retiring from the game in 2012. Prior to becoming a professional player, Annie was awarded a National Science Foundation Fellowship to study cognitive psychology at the University of Pennsylvania.

Annie is the cofounder of the Alliance for Decision Education, a nonprofit whose mission is to improve lives by empowering students through decision skills education. She is also a member of the National Board of After-School All-Stars and the board of directors of the Franklin Institute. In 2020, she joined the board of the Renew Democracy Initiative.